Culture and Customs of Ukraine

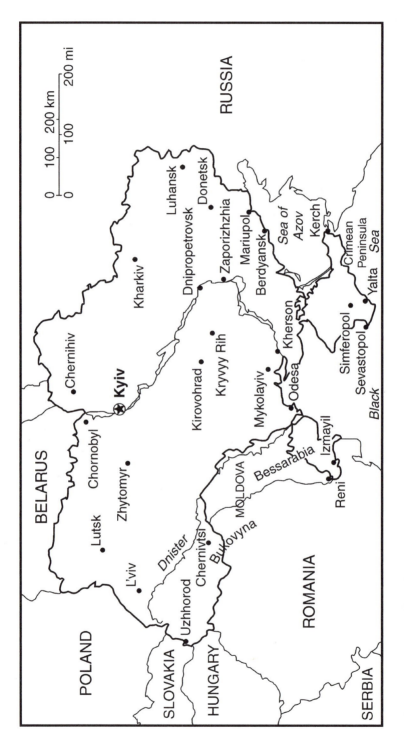

Ukraine. Courtesy of Bookcomp, Inc.

Culture and Customs
of Ukraine

ADRIANA HELBIG, OKSANA BURANBAEVA, AND VANJA MLADINEO

Culture and Customs of Europe

GREENWOOD PRESS
Westport, Connecticut • London

Library of Congress Cataloging-in-Publication Data

Helbig, Adriana.
　　Culture and customs of Ukraine / Adriana Helbig, Oksana Buranbaeva and Vanja Mladineo.
　　　　p. cm. — (Culture and customs of Europe)
　　Includes bibliographical references and index.
　　ISBN 978–0–313–34363–6 (alk. paper)
　　1. Ukraine—Civilization. 2. Ukraine—Social life and customs. I. Buranbaeva, Oksana.
II. Mladineo, Vanja. III. Title. IV. Series.
　　DK508.4.H45　2009
　　947.7—dc22　　　　　　　　　　　2008027463

British Library Cataloguing in Publication Data is available.

Library of Congress Catalog Card Number: 2008027463
ISBN: 978–0–313–34363–6

First published in 2009

Greenwood Press, 88 Post Road West, Westport, CT 06881
An imprint of Greenwood Publishing Group, Inc.
www.greenwood.com

Printed in the United States of America

The paper used in this book complies with the
Permanent Paper Standard issued by the National
Information Standards Organization (Z39.48–1984).

10 9 8 7 6 5 4 3 2 1

The authors dedicate this book to Marijka Stadnycka Helbig and to the memory
of Omelan Helbig;
to Rimma Buranbaeva, Christoph Merdes, and Ural Buranbaev;
to Marko Pećarević.

Contents

Series Foreword

THE OLD WORLD and the New World have maintained a fluid exchange of people, ideas, innovations, and styles. Even though the United States became the de facto world leader and economic superpower in the wake of a devastated Europe in World War II, Europe has remained for many the standard bearer of Western culture.

Millions of Americans can trace their ancestors to Europe. The United States as we know it was built on waves of European immigration, starting with the English who braved the seas to found the Jamestown Colony in 1607. Bosnian and Albanian immigrants are some of the latest new Americans.

In the Gilded Age of one of our great expatriates, the novelist Henry James, the Grand Tour of Europe was de rigueur for young American men of means, to prepare them for a life of refinement and taste. In a more recent democratic age, scores of American college students have Eurailed their way across Great Britain and the Continent, sampling the fabled capitals and bergs in a mad, great adventure, or have benefited from a semester abroad. For other American vacationers and culture vultures, Europe is the prime destination.

What is the New Europe post–Cold War, post Berlin Wall in a new millennium? Even with the different languages, rhythms, and rituals, Europeans have much in common: they are largely well educated, prosperous, and worldly. They also have similar goals and face common threats and form alliances. With the advent of the European Union, the open borders, and the Euro and considering globalization and the prospect of a homogenized Europe, an updated survey of the region is warranted.

Culture and Customs of Europe features individual volumes on the countries most studied and for which fresh information is in demand from students and other readers. The Series casts a wide net, inclusive of not only the expected countries, such as Spain, France, England, and Germany, but also countries such as Poland and Greece that lie outside Western Europe proper. Each volume is written by a country specialist, with intimate knowledge of the contemporary dynamics of a people and culture. Sustained narrative chapters cover the land, people, and brief history; religion; social customs; gender roles, family, and marriage; literature and media; performing arts and cinema; and art and architecture. The national character and ongoing popular traditions of each country are framed in an historical context and celebrated along with the latest trends and major cultural figures. A country map, chronology, glossary, and evocative photos enhance the text.

The historied and enlightened Europeans will continue to fascinate Americans. Our futures are strongly linked politically, economically, and culturally.

Preface

WHEN OKSANA BAIUL won the gold medal in ice skating at the 1994 Winter Olympics, the medal ceremony was delayed as skating officials searched frantically for a tape of the Ukrainian anthem. More than a decade and a half has passed since that international event, when the world first watched the Ukrainian flag rise to honor an athlete who embodied the Ukrainian spirit of struggle and perseverance. Having shed the cloak of imperial domination and the yoke of communism, Ukraine has become a society in which citizens grapple with the fast-paced changes introduced by democratic and market reforms. A nation-state defined by a multitude of ethnic groups, religions, languages, and worldviews, Ukraine is a kaleidoscope of old and new ideas and practices. This book examines Ukraine's cultural framework through the lenses of history, politics, family, social networks, artistic expression, religion, custom, and tradition. From the dark experiences of war to the warmth of the kitchen table, this volume charts a journey through a country that has built fast trains in the post-Soviet era but whose people are constantly reminded that they still travel on Soviet-era tracks.

Acknowledgments

WE ARE DEEPLY grateful to Mark Andryczyk, Gennadi Poberezny, and Maria Rewak for their expert reading of this manuscript and to Maxim Tarnawsky for his expert advice on certain topics.

We wish to thank Rafis Abazov, who helped make this project happen.

This project would not have been possible without the guidance of Kaitlin Ciarmiello of Greenwood Publishing Group.

We also wish to thank the following colleagues and friends for their support throughout the project and for their feedback on individual chapters: Rimma Buranbaeva, Marijka Stadnycka Helbig, Damir Huremović, Olya Kolomyyets, Samantha Lach, Ingrid Lee, Erica Marcus, Christoph Merdes, Petro Mishchenko, Anna Nadezhina, Natalia Nakhapetian, Maxim Novichenko, Natalia Palidwor Sonevytska, Kudrat Virk, and Catherine Wanner. Special thanks to Natasha Kipp for her editorial assistance.

Chronology

PREHISTORY

ca. 4000–2000 B.C.	Trypillian culture flourishes.
ca. 1150–950 B.C.	The Cimmerians dominate Ukrainian lands.
ca. 750 B.C.	The Scythians chase the Cimmerians out of Ukrainian territory.
513 B.C.	The Scythians defend their territory by defeating Persian king Darius I.
339 B.C.	The Macedonians defeat the Scythians.
ca. 100 B.C.–A.D. 100	The Sarmatians populate Ukrainian lands.
ca. A.D. 500	Slavs begin arriving in Ukrainian lands.

KYIVAN RUS'

878–912	Prince Oleh reigns.
882	The state of Kyivan Rus' is established.
911	Prince Oleh invades Constantinople.
945–962	Princess Olha reigns.

957	Princess Olha embarks on a diplomatic mission to Constantinople.
962–972	Prince Sviatoslav reigns.
965–969	Prince Sviatoslav defeats the Khazars and the Volga Bulgarians.
980–1015	Prince Volodymyr the Great reigns.
988	The Kyivan Rus' realm is Christianized.
1036–1054	Prince Yaroslav the Wise reigns.
cc. 1113	Monk Nestor compiles *The Primary Chronicle* (Chronicle of the Bygone Years).
1113–1125	Grand Prince Volodymyr Monomakh reigns.
1240	Invading Mongol armies overrun Kyiv.

GALICIA-VOLHYNIA

1253	A papal representative crowns Danylo king of Galicia-Volhynia.
1264	King Danylo dies.

POLISH AND LITHUANIAN RULE

1340	King Casimir of Poland conquers Galicia.
1366	A war between Poland and Lithuania ends with the Poles occupying Galicia and a part of Volhynia.
1368	Lithuanian Prince Algirdas occupies Kyiv and controls approximately half of Kyivan Rus' territory.
1385	The Union of Krevo between Lithuania and Poland transfers Lithuanian and Ukrainian lands to the Polish crown.
1508	Ukrainian nobles rise up against Grand Prince Sigismund, led by Mykhailo Hlynsky.
1568	The Union of Lublin is formed.

COSSACK UPRISING

1648	Hetman Bohdan Khmelnytsky leads the Great Cossack Revolt.
1649	Triumphant Khmelnytsky enters Kyiv.

| 1651 | Khmelnytsky is defeated and signs the Treaty of Bila Tserkva. |
| 1654 | Cossacks accept a Muscovy protectorate in the Pereiaslav Agreement. |

RUSSIAN IMPERIAL AND POLISH RULE

1656	The Muscovy tsar concludes peace with Poland in defiance of the Pereiaslav Agreement.
1657	Hetman Khmelnytsky dies.
1708	Hetman Ivan Mazepa allies the Cossacks with Sweden.
1709	The forces of Catherine the Great destroy the Cossack Zaporozhian Sich.
1765	Sloboda Ukraine becomes part of the Russian Empire.
1775	Zaporozhzhian lands become part of the Russian Empire.
1783	Peasants are officially deprived of the right to leave their landlords, formalizing serfdom. The Ukrainian nobility are granted privileges equal to those of the Russians.
1785	Hetmanate becomes part of the Russian Empire.
1795	Polish rule over the Right Bank ends.
1848	The Supreme Ruthenian Council is established in L'viv.
	Serfdom is abolished in Galicia.
1861	Serfdom is abolished in eastern Ukrainian lands.

WORLD WAR I AND IMMEDIATE POSTWAR YEARS

1917

March	The Ukrainian Central Rada is formed.
November	The Central Rada proclaims an autonomous Ukraine.
December	The Bolsheviks invade Ukraine.

1918

| January | The Central Rada proclaims an independent Ukrainian National Republic. |

February	The Brest-Litovsk Treaty is concluded between Ukraine and the Central Powers.
March	German forces enter Ukraine.
April	The Central Rada is disbanded.
	Hetmanate is established.
November	German forces withdraw from Ukraine.
Late 1918	The West Ukrainian People's Republic is established.
Early 1919	The Ukrainian People's Republic is established.
1919	The Polish military victory in eastern Galicia ends the Western Ukrainian People's Republic.
1920	The Red Army conquers Ukraine.

SOVIET UKRAINE AND WORLD WAR II

1920

December	Soviet Ukraine allies with the Russian Soviet Federated Socialist Republic.
1922	Ukraine becomes one of the four constitutive republics of the Union of Soviet Socialist Republics (USSR).
1924	The Soviet constitution is passed.
1932–1933	Forced famine/genocide, *Holodomor* (extermination by hunger), causes 7–10 million deaths in eastern Ukraine.
1938	Joseph Stalin orchestrates the liquidation of the leadership of the Ukrainian Soviet government and Communist Party.
1941	
June	Germany invades the Soviet Union.
November	Erich Koch becomes the *Reichskommissar* of Ukraine.
December	Most of Ukraine is occupied by Germany.
1942	The Ukrainian Insurgent Army (UPA) is organized in Volhynia and Polissia.
1943	
November	The westward-advancing Red Army captures Kyiv.

1944

October   The German occupation of Ukrainian lands ends.

1953   Stalin dies.

1972   First Secretary of the Ukrainian Communist Party Petro Shelest is removed from his position.

1976   Ukrainian Helsinki Group is formed.

1985   Mikhail Gorbachev becomes the head of the USSR.

1989   Rukh, the People's Movement for Restructuring in Ukraine, is formed.

1990   The first partially free elections for Parliament are held in Ukraine.

MODERN UKRAINE

1991

August   Parliament declares Ukrainian independence.

December   The referendum in support of independence is passed.

1996

June   Parliament adopts the Ukrainian constitution.

2000

September   Opposition journalist Heorhii Gongadze is last seen alive.

November   Oleksandr Moroz implicates President Kuchma in Gongadze's murder after the journalist's decapitated body is found.

2001

February   "Ukraine without Kuchma" protests begin.

April   President Kuchma replaces Prime Minister Yushchenko.

2004

November   Viktor Yushchenko and Viktor Yanukovych engage in a presidential election standoff.

                        The Orange Revolution begins.

December	Presidential elections are repeated.
2005	
January	Yushchenko is sworn in as president.
	Tymoshenko becomes prime minister.
September	President Yushchenko dismisses Tymoshenko.
2007	
April	President Yushchenko dismisses parliament.
September	Parliamentary elections are held.
	Tymoshenko becomes prime minister again.

1

Context

UKRAINE CLAIMED A place on the geopolitical map of Europe in 1991 as an independent state after centuries of being part of foreign empires and unions. Ukraine today plays a pivotal role in the European as well as the global context due to its sheer size, distinct geopolitical location, large population, abundant natural resources, and significant prospects for the future. Ukraine's independence from the Soviet Union and the ensuing politically and economically turbulent years have sparked international interest in this complex region. Recent expansions of the European Union (EU) eastward have made the European political and economic space increasingly more inclusive. This extension of the common European identity toward previously marginalized eastern countries has forced their inhabitants to redefine their sense of regional belonging and their prospects and hopes for the future. Though as of 2008, it is one of the several remaining European countries that are not part of the European Union, Ukraine is a democracy with an industrial market economy that sees much of its future with Europe. Ukraine's historical ties and longstanding relationship with Russia, despite ongoing political, economic, and cultural tensions, situate Ukraine to act as a physical, political, economic, and cultural bridge between the European community, on one hand, and Russia and the countries of the former Soviet Union on the other.

Ukraine's positioning between various powers has contributed to a wealth of ethnic diversity and a rich cultural heritage. Scholars, poets, politicians, artists, religious leaders, and musicians, many of whom are mentioned in this

Flags of Ukraine (left) and the European Union (right) adorn the Ministry of Foreign Affairs in Kyiv, 2008. Photo by Adriana Helbig.

book, have helped shape the country and its peoples. The Ukrainian language has not only survived the pressures of Russification and Polonization, but has, through the works of poets such as Ivan Kotliarevsky, Taras Shevchenko, and Ivan Franko, become a guardian of Ukrainian artistic expression and, by extension, Ukrainian national identity. Most recently, the remarkable events of the Orange Revolution in late 2004 put the country front and center of international events as a positive example of nonviolent political change, turning a new page in Ukraine's history.

THE PLACE

Ukraine, with its land area of more than 230,000 square miles (approximately 6,000,000 square kilometers), is a country the size of France. The Ukrainian landscape consists predominantly of lowlands and plateaus that extend from the northern plains and marshes of Polissia through the Central Plateau of Volhynia and Podilia and the eastern border with Russia to the southern valleys along the shore of the Black Sea and the Sea of Azov. Excluding the Carpathian Mountains in the west and the Crimean Mountains on the Crimean Peninsula on the Black Sea, the elevation of the Ukrainian

Tourist activities in the Carpathian Mountains. Photo by Adriana Helbig.

countryside is quite low, no higher than 1,600 feet (500 meters). Among the five percent of Ukrainian territory that is higher, the highest peak is Hoverla in the Carpathians, rising at 6,760 feet (2,061 meters).[1] The Hoverla summit offers beautiful views of the surrounding mountainous landscape, though it often has stormy and cloudy weather. As part of a recent tradition, many Ukrainians climb this mountain peak every year on August 24 in celebration of the Ukrainian national independence day. In fostering popular appreciation for and awareness of the beautiful nature of the Carpathians, the regional tourist industry is growing rapidly, with hiking and rural tourism prevailing in the summers and skiing in the winters.

Most of Ukraine has a temperate continental climate similar to many European countries along the same geographical latitude, though with somewhat colder winters. The exception is the Crimean Riviera in the south, with its Mediterranean-type climate. The winters in Ukraine are cool in the south (Crimea) and become increasingly colder toward the north. The average temperature in January, the coldest month, is 26°F (–3°C) in the southwest and 18°F (–8°C) in the northeast. Summers are warm in the north and hot in the south, with average temperatures in July, the warmest month, at 73°F (23°C) in the southeast and 64°F (18°C) in the northwest. Average precipitation is highest in the north and west, while significantly lower in the east and south.

Most of the rain falls in June and July. It snows mostly from early November to late February. Ukraine's climate and geography allow people to enjoy sunny beaches in the summer and snow-covered peaks in the winter.

Throughout history, the Ukrainian landscape has held a prominent place in literature, music, and folklore. Often referred to as the breadbasket of Europe, Ukraine's fertile lowlands have been the realm of hardworking sedentary peoples engaged in agriculture and cattle raising. Twenty-five percent of the world's black soil is located in Ukraine. The black earth, *chornozem,* has, time and again, wooed foreign invaders. Through the centuries, from the invasions of the nomadic peoples in the first millennium B.C. to the German invasion during World War II and Soviet rule, Ukrainian lands have been coveted by their more powerful and aggressive neighbors. Ukraine's geography and size made it both more attractive to invaders and more difficult to defend. Furthermore, its geopolitical position on the eastern frontiers of Europe made Ukraine vulnerable to the power struggles and the continuously growing or diminishing spheres of influence among the Western and the Eastern powers.

Ukrainian lands are crisscrossed by a network of rivers. The longest is the Dnipro. It is approximately 620 miles (about 1,000 kilometers) long in Ukraine and divides the country into east and west. Left Bank Ukraine, designating lands to the east of the Dnipro, is known in Ukrainian as *Livoberezhna.* Right Bank Ukraine, west of the Dnipro, is called *Pravoberezhna.* The Dnipro is the third longest river in Europe and has always been more than merely a main waterway in Ukraine. The Dnipro was the economic lifeblood of historic states on Ukrainian lands, such as Kyivan Rus' and the Cossack state, which developed along the banks of the river. At a different time in history, sections of the Dnipro became a natural boundary between the Russian and Polish spheres of influence. Today, the Dnipro is an important route in shipping and passenger transportation and a source of hydroelectric power and commercial fishing. Aside from the Dnipro, the Dniester and the Southern Boh also flow into the Black Sea in the south as part of the Pontic watershed. The Syan and the Buh flow into the Baltic Sea in the north via the Vistula in the Baltic watershed. The direction of the flow of rivers in this landscape has had its effect on Ukrainian history, particularly on the development of cities. The majority of the oldest and most important urban centers in Ukraine developed on or near major rivers. Kyiv, Cherkasy, Dnipropetrovsk, and Zaporizhzhia are on the Dnipro, Odesa is near the mouth of the Dniester, L'viv is on the Poltva and near the Buh, and Chernihiv is on the Desna (a tributary of the Dnipro). The proximity of all these cities to rivers attests to the historical importance of rivers as sources of income and means of communication vital for the survival of city dwellers. In western Ukraine, in

The hydroelectric dam in Zaporizhzhia, built in the late 1920s, is one of the largest in Europe and draws power from the mighty Dnipro River. Photo by Adriana Helbig.

particular, the two watersheds become intertwined, making communication between the Baltic Sea and the Black Sea possible, characterizing this region as an important trading route.

The regional divisions of modern Ukraine are delineated along 24 administrative units, or *oblasts:* Cherkasy, Chernihiv, Chernivtsi, Dnipropetrovsk, Donetsk, Ivano-Frankivsk, Kharkiv, Kherson, Khmelnytsk, Kirovohrad, Kyiv, Luhansk, L'viv, Mykolaiv, Odesa, Poltava, Rivne, Sumy, Ternopil, Vinnitsya, Volhynia, Transcarpathia (Zakarpattia), Zaporizhzhia, and Zhytomyr. There is also one autonomous region (Crimea, or Avtonomna Respublika Krym) and two municipalities (Kyiv and Sevastopol) with *oblast* status. However, these divisions are purely administrative and do not necessarily reflect traditional and historical regional divisions. Looking at Ukraine through a historic and geopolitical lens reveals a division into several, more traditional, regions: Sloboda Ukraine, Zaporizhzhia, Donbas, Siver, Volhynia, Podilia, Galicia (Halychyna), Transcarpathia (Zakarpattia), Bukovyna, Odesa (Black Sea lands), and Crimea. However, the broadest regional division of Ukraine commonly utilized in everyday life and in the media is the division into western and eastern Ukraine. This is commonly used as shorthand for the dichotomous view of the country, where western and central Ukraine represents the less urbanized, more agricultural, more ethnically homogeneous Ukraine and, politically, a pro-European region. In this division, eastern and southern Ukraine represent a more urbanized, industrial, ethnically and linguistically more mixed (with a larger ethnic Russian population), and, politically, a pro-Russian region. Though this division is somewhat simplistic, some of the mentioned characteristics of eastern and western Ukraine are often reflected in parliamentary and presidential elections.[2] At the risk of solidifying this simple east-west division of Ukraine, the selected traditional regions addressed subsequently nevertheless reflect the most prominent and interesting geographic, historical, political, and ethnolinguistic differences within Ukraine. Despite the existing regional differences, however, and a degree of autonomy awarded to Crimea, Ukraine is constitutionally a unitary state, not a federation. The following Ukrainian traditional regions reflect a sampling of the ethnic, linguistic, geographic, historic, and administrative diversity present in Ukraine today.

Galicia, known in Ukrainian as *Halychyna,* is a historical region of western Ukraine that today consists of roughly three administrative units (L'viv, Ternopil, and Ivano-Frankivsk) and encompasses about 10 percent of Ukrainian territory. It is the land of fields and farmlands, very rural and traditional. Throughout its turbulent history, Galicia, together with Volhynia, was one of the independent successor principalities of Kyivan Rus' immediately following its demise. From the mid-fourteenth century until the eighteenth century, it was a province of Poland, and then a part of the Austro-Hungarian Empire from the late eighteenth century until World War I. It was briefly a part of Nazi Germany during World War II. Because of this history, Galicians have tended to organize politically and resist militarily in defense of the Ukrainian nation and language. Furthermore, L'viv, Galicia's charming regional capital, has been the traditional seat of the Ukrainian Greek Catholic (Uniate) Church, one of the main religious denominations in western Ukraine. Its strong sense of national pride, long and complex history with Poland, a Central European cultural feel, and physical proximity to Western Europe make Galicia a distinctly separate region within Ukraine.

Bordering Galicia is another notable region in western Ukraine: Transcarpathia. It is one of the most recently integrated Ukrainian regions, having been incorporated into Ukraine only in 1946. This westernmost region in Ukraine contains its largest mountain chain and its highest peak, forming a natural boundary between the rest of Ukraine. The mountains created a physical border with the east, spurring Transcarpathia's population to turn toward Western neighbors, historical contact that has allowed for a cultivation of closer economic and cultural ties with neighboring countries such as Poland, Slovakia, Hungary, and Romania. This is a region of pristine mountainous landscapes rich in bountiful forests, mineral springs, biodiversity, and mineral deposits.

The economy is based around logging and timber processing, food processing, and a developing tourist industry. Hungarians represent Transcarpathia's largest minority and comprise approximately 12 percent of the region's population.

The Donbas historic region encompasses two easternmost administrative units—Donetsk and Luhansk—with just under 10 percent of the Ukrainian territory and about 15 percent of the population, most of which lives in cities.[3] Coal mining and heavy industry are the mainstays of the economy in this region, given that it accounts for about a fifth of all industrial production in Ukraine and contains nearly half of its coal deposits. The proportion of ethnic Russians in this region is just under 40 percent. Nevertheless, almost two-thirds of the population of this region declares Russian to be its mother tongue.[4] Because of its population composition and due to its proximity to and history with Russia, Donbas is one of the regions in Ukraine with strong economic and cultural ties with Russia. Since Ukraine's independence, there has, on occasion, been political friction in the region, such as the massive strike of its coal miners in 1993. More than 200 coal miners die in Ukraine each year due to hazardous working conditions in old mines.[5] This is among the worst statistics in the world.

Crimea's geography, politics, history, and population distinctly set it apart from other Ukrainian regions. Crimea has had a tumultuous history, having

Coal miners in Donetsk, Ukraine, 1988. Bruno Barbey, Magnum Photos.

been ruled at different times by ancient Greeks, Byzantines, Tatars, Ottomans, and Russians. It was the stage of many important political and military developments such as the Crimean War in the nineteenth century and the historic Yalta Conference of 1945. Following the expulsion of the Crimean Tatar population to Central Asia by Joseph Stalin's government in 1944, the Crimean Autonomous Soviet Socialist Republic (in existence since 1921) was dissolved as an administrative entity in 1945, and Crimea became one of the *oblasts* in the Russian Soviet Federative Socialist Republic. In 1954 it became a part of the Ukrainian Soviet Socialist Republic. After Ukraine's declaration of independence in 1991, Crimean political activities in the first half of the 1990s revolved around a separatist rhetoric that culminated in a passing of the Crimean constitution, declaring the peninsula a sovereign state and the election of a pro-Russian Crimean president. The government in Kyiv responded by institutionally restricting Crimea's autonomy. Crimea today, however, is still the only autonomous region in Ukraine. It is the only region where the majority of the population is ethnic Russian—just under 60 percent. Furthermore, Sevastopol in Crimea is home to a Russian naval base and the Black Sea Fleet, thanks to a 20-year agreement concluded between Russia and Ukraine. Crimea also has a significant Tatar population—just over 12 percent, according to the 2001 census. This number has the potential to grow due to the organized repatriation of the Tatar population from Central Asian countries, mainly Uzbekistan, since the late 1980s. Another unique aspect of Crimea is its location. It is a peninsula surrounded by the Sea of Azov and the Black Sea, with a mild Mediterranean climate. In the north it consists mainly of plains and lowlands, while the south is mountainous. Agriculture, food processing, fishing, and tourism are the backbone of the Crimean economy.

Even a cursory survey of Ukraine's traditional and historic regions needs to include Kyiv. It is the capital city of Ukraine and, according to the 2001 census, has a population of over 2.6 million people. It is a young European capital and, at the same time, is one of the oldest cities in Europe. Kyiv lies on the banks of the Dnipro River and is the historic center of Ukrainian lands. According to legend, the city was founded in the fifth century A.D. by three brothers, Kyi, Shchek, and Khoryv, and their sister Lybyd. The siblings, in search of a new home and fleeing from invaders, arrived at the banks of the Dnipro, where they founded a settlement and named it after the eldest brother. Archeological evidence suggests that the Kyiv region has been inhabited since as early as 3000 B.C. and that the city has existed since the sixth century A.D. By the tenth century, Kyiv had become the center of the large expanses of eastern Slavic lands united under Kyivan Rus' rulers and one of the largest and most powerful cities in Europe. The introduction of Christianity during this period further increased the importance of Kyiv, contributing to its rise as a spiritual as well as an economic and political center. By the twelfth century, Kyiv excelled in architecture, craftsmanship, and art, with over four hundred churches as testimony to its accomplishments. The city's population reflected its prosperity, making it one of the most populous cities in medieval Europe at the time. This period of prosperity ended in the thirteenth century, when Kyiv experienced a devastating Mongol invasion. A century later, it came under Lithuanian rule, reducing even further its already weakened political and economic status. In the fifteenth century, Kyiv survived another invasion, this time by the Tatars.

Foreign rule of Kyiv continued with Polish domination following the Union of Lublin in the late sixteenth century. Approximately a century later, the Cossack leader Bohdan Khmelnytsky drove the Poles out of Kyiv. By the end of the seventeenth century, Kyiv fell under the control of Muscovite rulers and remained under their control for the next two hundred years. The first half of the twentieth century was a turbulent time for Kyiv, marred by wars, revolutions, material destruction, and human losses, which left their mark on this vibrant city. A series of historic events ignited by the Ukrainian proclamation of independence and the Red Army entering Kyiv in 1918 and culminating with the German invasion of 1941 brought devastation to thousands of Kyivans, among them Kyiv's significant Jewish population.

More recent history carries its own tragedies, namely, the 1986 explosion of the reactor at the Chornobyl nuclear power plant, approximately 70 miles north of Kyiv. In the immediate aftermath of the accident, 28 employees, emergency workers, clean-up workers, and area residents died from radiation exposure, while more than 360,000 residents were evacuated from the contaminated areas.[6] Two decades later, the long-term consequences on the health of the population are still not entirely clear, but many resulting illnesses have become a day-to-day reality of those affected by radiation.

Kyiv has historically been a key center of Orthodox Christianity and home to numerous churches and monasteries, among them St. Sophia's Cathedral and the Kyievo-Pecherska Lavra (Kyivan Cave Monastery), both United Nations Educational, Scientific, and Cultural Organization (UNESCO) World Heritage Sites. As a center of academic learning in Ukraine, Kyiv is the seat of the Taras Shevchenko University of Kyiv and the Kyiv Mohyla Academy, one of the oldest and most prominent institutions of higher learning in the country. Since Ukrainian independence, Kyiv's role as an administrative center has increased significantly. As the seat of the national government, it houses the most important government buildings, such as the Mariyinskyi Palace (the official residence of the president of the republic), the Verkhovna Rada (the Ukrainian national parliament), and the National Bank of Ukraine. Kyiv is the cultural heart of Ukraine, home to a significant number of museums

New construction in Kyiv—view from Kyievo-Pecherska Lavra (Kyivan Cave Monastery), 2008. Photo by Adriana Helbig.

that range from the specific, such as that dedicated to the writer Mikhail Bulgakov, to the broad, such as the National Art Museum, which houses a collection of Ukrainian art that spans centuries. Kyiv also hosts a number of annual film, art, and music festivals. Not surprisingly, this city, defined by its many churches, monuments, museums, universities, theatres, shops, cafés, and restaurants, strongly appeals to its inhabitants and visitors alike.

Ukrainians share their national borders with Russia, Belarus, Poland, Slovakia, Hungary, Romania, and Moldova. Ukraine's longest border is with Russia, which spans over 900 miles (1,500 kilometers). To an extent, the length of this border, which runs along the eastern and northeastern edges of the Ukrainian lands, reflects the significant influence Russia has had on Ukrainian history and still exerts on its current affairs. Ukraine's relationship with Russia since the fall of Soviet Union has been influenced by many factors, such as historical colonial legacy, economic dependence, profiles of respective leaderships, and, more recently, energy issues, foreign policy, and internal political developments in both countries. Depending on the region, attitudes of Ukrainians range from feelings of co-patriotism and ancient connection with Russia to historical animosity. Recent Ukrainian leaderships' aspirations toward EU and North Atlantic Treaty Organization (NATO) integration have, on occasion, been interpreted by Russia's leaders as a provocation against historically rooted relationships.

Kyiv's famous folk market, Andriivskyi Uzviv, near St. Andrew's Church. Photo by Adriana Helbig.

While NATO membership as a foreign policy goal of Ukraine has received strong support from the United States, Russia has expressed its vehement opposition. The EU is one of Ukraine's most important trading partners and donates much financial assistance for development. However, the path of Ukraine toward joining the EU is likely to be long, complex, and tenuous, due primarily to greater conceptual questions of EU enlargement. Considering Ukraine's turbulent history with Poland, Polish-Ukrainian relations, on the other hand, have been surprisingly constructive and positive since Ukrainian independence. With Poland in NATO and the EU, and Ukraine declaring the same general intent, the strategic interests and westward leanings of both countries seem to be aligned. Relations with Moldova have, in the past, been burdened by the so-called frozen conflict in Transdniestria, a narrow territory between the Dniester River and the Ukrainian border, which proclaimed independence from Moldova in 1990. Subsequent fighting, lasting insecurity, and political deadlock have made this region a hotbed of crime and poverty, forcing Ukraine to become involved in a decade and a half of partially successful peace brokering.

THE PEOPLE

Ukraine's census of 2001 put the country's total population at approximately 48.5 million. In terms of number of inhabitants, Ukraine is sixth in

Europe, with a population larger than Spain's and smaller than Italy's. For comparison, there are a few million people less in Ukraine than in New York State and California combined. The average population density is approximately 205 people per square mile (80 people per square kilometer), but generally, eastern industrial regions are more densely populated in contrast to western agricultural areas (excluding Galicia). Historically and consistently, the majority of ethnic Ukrainians were peasants who led a rural way of life. From the times of the first settlers in this region, agriculture and a pastoral existence were the cornerstones of life. Since much of the city folk throughout the centuries were either Polonized or Russified, the village and village life came to represent all things Ukrainian in nationalist movements, literature, and folklore. This has changed drastically over the last half-century, with about 67 percent of ethnic Ukrainians today living in cities.

Another important element in the articulation of ethnic Ukrainian identity was the Cossack movement of the sixteenth century. The Cossacks were steppe dwellers and militiamen who stood up to the political, economic, social, and national oppression, first by the Tatars and the Turks and later the Poles and the Russians, and became synonymous with independence and freedom in Ukraine. Many an epic poem, short story, and legend evokes the image of the freedom-fighting and authority-defying Cossack standing in defense of the Ukrainian way of life and identity. Ivan Franko's short story "Khmelnytsky and the Soothsayer" conveys an imagined episode from the life of one of the greatest hetman leaders of the Cossacks, Bohdan Khmelnytsky, and his role in liberating Ukraine from a hostile power—Poland—and establishing a Cossack Hetman state, the Hetmanate. Centuries of unfulfilled Ukrainian yearning for self-determination left their mark on Ukrainian consciousness as much as the Cossack accomplishments. Repeatedly torn between its historically powerful neighbors and conquerors, in particular, Poland and the Russian Empire, Ukrainian national identity was forged in the face of these dominating powers and in defiance of their cultural policies of Russification and Polonization. In light of such struggles, particularly in regard to the period of Bohdan Khmelnytsky, the significant Jewish population living in the territories of Ukraine at that time were among those who suffered the most by being caught in the crossfire.

In the face of such foreign influences, Ukrainians have historically turned to religion. Though almost 40 percent of the Ukrainian population declares itself as having no religion, throughout history, religious identity has been a key part of being ethnically Ukrainian. Major denominations in Ukraine today are the Ukrainian Orthodox Church–Kyiv Patriarchate (UOC-KP), the Ukrainian Orthodox Church–Moscow Patriarchate (UOC-MP), the Ukrainian Autocephalous Orthodox Church (UAOC), and the Ukrainian

Greek Catholic Church, sometimes referred to as the Uniate Church. Both the UOC-KP and the UOC-MP practice Orthodox rites. However, the UOC-MP recognizes the Russian patriarch as the head of the Church, while the UOC-KP recognizes the Ukrainian patriarch. The latter was formed in the early 1990s following Ukrainian independence, with the goal of becoming the national Orthodox Church. Though it has not been recognized by the Ecumenical Patriarchate of Constantinople, the Kyiv Patriarchate has gained significant following in Ukraine since its conception. The UAOC was formed in 1921 with the goal of seeking religious autonomy from Moscow and consequently faced significant persecution. Both the UAOC and the UOC-KP came into existence during periods of awakening of Ukrainian national consciousness. The Ukrainian Greek Catholic Church has been a prominent denomination in western Ukraine, recognizing the pope as head of the Church. In the past, rather than reinforcing ties with Polish rule in western Ukraine, the Greek Catholic Church contributed to the preservation of a separate Catholic Ukrainian identity by setting itself apart from both Orthodox and Catholic churches.

Throughout history, the Ukrainian language has most consistently been the glue that kept Ukrainians, particularly peasants and lower classes, together, preserving their sense of ethnic belonging. The Ukrainian language has survived in the face of overwhelming cultural and linguistic pressures from foreign overlords. In fact, appeals for preservation of the language were frequently used as a code for inspiring Ukrainian national sentiments and raising awareness of a common national identity. In earlier times, peasants were inadvertent guardians of the language, but as times changed and the question of national expression and survival became more immediate, particularly in the nineteenth century, different groups in society, such as the intelligentsia and writers, took on the role of safeguarding the language. Literary notables such as Taras Shevchenko, Ivan Franko, and Lesia Ukrainka, nurtured and enriched the Ukrainian language through their artistic accomplishments and helped awaken and shape Ukrainian ethnic identity.

About 78 percent of the population of Ukraine are ethnic Ukrainians; 17 percent are Russians. Ethnic minorities, including Belarusians, Moldavians, Crimean Tatars, Hungarians, Romanians, Poles, Bulgarians, Jews, Roma, and others, each comprise less than 1 percent of the population. However, due to historical factors, each *oblast* has its own particular ethnic make-up. For instance, in the Odesa region, Russians make up about 20 percent, Bulgarians 6 percent, and Moldavians 5 percent of the population. Unlike some of the other former republics of the Soviet Union and some newly independent Eastern European states, Ukraine has fewer ethnic clashes or other difficulties between its majority population and national minorities. A significant integrating factor was probably the granting of citizenship to all ethnicities residing in Ukraine at the time of independence. The Declaration of Rights of Nationalities protects the status of national minorities and their languages.[7] In fact, Ukraine's official policy toward its ethnic minorities is regarded as one of the more successful ones in comparison to other former Soviet and Eastern European countries. The status of the Russian minority following independence stirred up some political issues in Crimea and, to a much lesser extent, in Donbas. The numbers of ethnic Russians are the largest in these regions, where issues of linguistic rights dominate cultural rights discourse. Some 8 million ethnic Russians living in Ukraine today share a linguistic identity and a general sense of connection and cultural closeness to Russia, though many ethnic Ukrainians also speak Russian as their first language and feel an affinity with Russia. The number of ethnic Russians in Ukraine increased significantly through several waves of Russification and repopulation by Russians, particularly since the beginning of the twentieth century. In the 1930s the ethnic Russian population rose as a result of Stalin's Russification policy, a backlash to the Ukrainianization movement of the 1920s. In the post–World War II years, many Russians migrated to Ukraine as part of Soviet repopulation and industrialization efforts to replace the Ukrainian population devastated by a forced famine, *Holodomor,* in 1932–1933, and war. Most ethnic Russians immigrated to Crimea and southern and eastern cities, but some also moved to western cities such as L'viv.

THE PAST

Much of the current scholarly interpretation of Ukrainian history was shaped by the outlook of nineteenth-century Russian and twentieth-century Soviet historians, who viewed Ukrainians as an inherent part of the greater Russian people, with a common, indivisible Kyivan Rus' ancestry. Early Ukrainian history was understood within a framework of Russian imperial history and the Soviet Union, where manipulated historical facts were used to forge a common Soviet populace. An opposing view has been advocated by Ukrainian historians, who trace the history of the Ukrainian people to the first inhabitants of the region of today's Ukraine. They view Ukrainian history as separate from Russian.

The first recognizable civilization in the territory of Ukraine was the Trypillian culture. Living in the area between the Dniester, Prut, and Boh rivers, north of the Black Sea coast in the period between 4000 and 2000 B.C., this agricultural, sedentary, and patriarchal culture had knowledge of mechanical devices such as the wooden plow.[8] Its existence probably came to an end because of the influx of nomadic peoples into Ukrainian territories from the east and the north, the first of which were the Cimmerians. These nomadic horseman warriors inhabited lands between the Don and the Dniester rivers between 1150 and 950 B.C. The reference to the Cimmerians in the *Odyssey* is probably the first, albeit vague, Western literary mention of Ukrainian lands and their inhabitants.[9] Around 750 B.C., the Cimmerians were chased out of Ukrainian territory by another warrior nomadic civilization: the Scythians. They lived along the Dnipro River and around the northern shores of the Black Sea. The upper classes in Scythian society were royalty and notables, fierce warriors on horseback who lived from war booty and tributes from their sedentary and lower-class Scythian and non-Scythian subjects. Though occasional fortified settlements existed, the majority of the Scythian inhabitants lived as nomads. They engaged in commerce with the Greek colonies on the Black Sea, and most of the information about the Scythians is revealed from Greek sources. In fact, having defeated the Persian king Darius I in 513 B.C., Scythians inspired the Greek historian Herodotus to produce the first significant historical written record of a civilization on Ukrainian territory. The end of the Scythian period came with their defeat at the hands of the Macedonians in the fourth century B.C. The Sarmatians were the next in the progression of nomadic peoples to inhabit Ukraine. They struggled to establish their dominance over this territory with varying degrees of success from the second century B.C. until the second century A.D. Their culture was similar to and overlapped with the Scythians.' Women had a more prominent role among the Sarmatians. These earliest times in Ukrainian lands were marked by coexistence between two distinct yet inter-woven ways of life: agricultural and sedentary versus nomadic and military.

Beginning with the sixth century A.D., the Slavs, predominantly agricul-tural peoples, began to arrive in Ukrainian lands. They organized themselves in tribes and clans without a centralized political hierarchy. During the Slavic migrations, the fragmentation among Eastern, Southern, and Western Slavs resulted in Eastern Slavs settling in Ukrainian, Belarusian, and Russian lands. The Eastern Slavs likely took part in the rise of Kyivan Rus', a political entity based around the city of Kyiv. The exact progression by which Kyivan Rus' came into existence as well as the ethnic groups that drove its formation is a subject of much debate among scholars. The process likely began with the slow integration of the Eastern Slavic tribes into larger fortified protopolitical units ruled by chieftains, whose creation was either prompted by the threat from expanding Scandinavian peoples in the north or was in fact actively guided by them. *The Primary Chronicle,* a history of Kyivan Rus' originally compiled and written by the monk Nestor as one of the first Eastern Slavic chronicles, offers one account of the founding of Kyivan Rus'. According to the *Chronicle,* Rurik, a Varangian (Viking) ruler, founded the Kyivan Rus' state and the dynasty that ruled Kyivan Rus' for centuries.

Though historically the existence of Rurik is questionable, his presumed successor Oleh was the first known historical figure to rule Kyivan Rus'. Oleh conquered the city of Kyiv in 882 and united the surrounding tribes, effectively founding the Kyivan Rus' state. By the end of the ninth century, Oleh had established Kyivan Rus' as a regional power by exerting control over the surrounding Eastern Slavic tribes, invading Constantinople, and forcing the Byzantines into signing a favorable trade treaty with Kyivan Rus'. The next noteworthy ruler of the early Kyivan Rus' period was Olha, wife of Ihor (Oleh's successor) and regent for her underage son, and a distinguished sovereign in her own right. Her reign (945–962) was characterized by her diplomatic efforts, which included a peace mission to Constantinople, where she held negotiations with the Byzantine emperor, revealing the importance and strength of her dominion. She undertook reforms in tribute gathering to pacify her people and was the first sovereign of Kyivan Rus' to embrace Christianity. Princess Olha was later canonized, and in modern Ukraine, July 24 is celebrated as her feast day. In the second half of the tenth century, her son and successor Sviatoslav, a fearless warrior prince, united the remaining independent Eastern Slavic tribes in a series of successful conquests. He fought and defeated the neighboring Khazars and the Volga Bulgarian kingdom, extending the territories of Kyivan Rus' to their broadest expanses, stretching from the Volga to the Danube and from the Black Sea to the Gulf of Finland. The early Kyivan Rus' rulers established rudimentary political order among most Eastern Slavic tribes. They built on their traditional tribal and communal structures and set the foundation for economic development based on agriculture and commerce. Their foreign policy was dominated by relations with the Byzantine Empire, their close and powerful neighbor.

With the death of Sviatoslav, the main challenge facing his successors became obvious: the survival and consolidation of a vast empire. The three Kyivan princes who followed Sviatoslav—Volodymyr the Great, Yaroslav the Wise, and Volodymyr Monomakh—were largely successful in overcoming this challenge. Volodymyr earned his moniker "the Great" as a result of his policies designed to politically unify his realm. He expanded the territories of Kyivan Rus' to an area of just over 300,000 square miles (800,000 square kilometers) by annexing Galicia and Volhynia.[10] Volodymyr accepted Christianity in 988 and orchestrated a policy of Christianization of his subjects in his effort to consolidate the rule of his dynasty. Yaroslav the Wise continued his father Volodymyr's legacy of supporting and building up the church as a unifying element throughout Kyivan Rus'. During Yaroslav's reign (1036–1054), numerous churches and monasteries were established, Kyiv's St. Sophia Cathedral among them. His appreciation for the importance of diplomatic relations was evident in his familial connections to many European kingdoms such as Sweden, Poland, Hungary, Norway, and France. Possibly the greatest feat of Yaroslav the Wise, however, is the creation of the legal code of Kyivan Rus', known as *Rus'ka Pravda*. This document contained the existing customary laws of the land, codified and systematized, and was the first written legal code of Eastern Slavs. Yaroslav's rule is commonly considered as the peak of the Kyivan Rus' state. Volodymyr Monomakh, who became a grand prince in the twelfth century, sought to preserve the unity of Kyivan Rus' and defended the realm against attacking nomadic peoples, the Polovtsians. He codified the expanded version of the *Rus'ka Pravda* and introduced economic reforms. During the reign of these three renowned sovereigns, Kyivan Rus' became a relatively well integrated and functioning society and polity.[11] The end of Volodymyr Monomakh's rule, however, marked the beginning of the end of Kyivan Rus'. The ensuing struggles among subsequent Kyivan princes greatly contributed to the fragmentation of Kyivan Rus' and the demise of the state's influence in the region. This political downfall was coupled with Kyiv's diminishing economic importance as a trade route. Finally, in 1240, the invading Mongol armies destroyed Kyiv, thus sealing the fate of Kyivan Rus'.

After the Mongol invasion, Galicia and Volhynia were two of the three provinces in Kyivan Rus' that united and remained independent for the longest period, thus becoming the hub of Ukrainian political activity. Their precarious geopolitical position was the source of both their importance and their

St. Volodymyr the Great on Ukraine's one Hryvnia banknote. The Hryvnia was the currency in Kyivan Rus'; it was introduced as the currency of Ukraine in 1996. National Bank of Ukraine.

fragility. The independent survival of Galicia-Volhynia was effected greatly by balancing relations between its ruling prince and the invading Mongols to the east, on one hand, and its western and northern neighbors Poland, Hungary, and Lithuania, on the other. This fragile balance lasted from the mid-thirteenth century until the mid-fourteenth century. The internal political strength of Galicia-Volhynia rested among the rich landowners, who made their fortunes from fertile land. Their most important ruler, Danylo, initiated crusades against the Mongols and briefly allied these provinces with the pope and the Catholic Church and was crowned king in 1253. This move, though relatively short-lived, had far-reaching consequences in western Ukrainian lands. The demise of these two provinces made the downfall of Kyivan Rus' complete, but their brief independent existence ultimately helped preserve the Kyivan legacy and helped protect them from complete assimilation with their western neighbors.

Following the downfall of Kyivan Rus', Ukrainian lands became the periphery of neighboring empires and remained so for centuries to come. This process began in the early thirteenth century with the rise of the Grand Duchy of Lithuania, strengthened through the unification of the Lithuanian tribes. The consolidation of Lithuanian power was complete within a century, with their victory over the Mongols in 1362. By then, most of the Ukrainian lands were ruled by Lithuanian princes, and the Duchy of Lithuania became the largest political entity in Europe.[12] Under Lithuanian rule, there were initially no significant changes in the administrative, religious, and cultural structures in the Ukrainian lands. The Grand Duchy comprised smaller semi-independent principalities ruled by Lithuanian grand princes, who allowed Ukrainian nobles to retain a relatively high degree of control over their affairs. In 1340 King Casimir of Poland entered Galicia, provoking a response from the local Ukrainian nobility as well as from the Lithuanian rulers. The subsequent fighting between Lithuanians and Poles lasted for two decades, ending in 1366. Poland gained control of Galicia and part of Volhynia.[13]

In 1385 a formal Union of Krevo linked the royal dynasties of Poland and Lithuania, whereby Jagiello, the Grand Prince of Lithuania, accepted the Polish crown in return for his acceptance of Catholicism. This union began the process of weakening the Ukrainian nobility and strengthening the Catholic Polish and Lithuanian nobility as well as consolidating the majority of Ukrainian lands under the Polish crown. During this period the position of the Orthodox Rus' population and the Orthodox nobility deteriorated, even resulting in the migration of a sizeable number of nobility to lands under the control of Muscovy, a rising independent grand duchy with ideological claims to Kyivan Rus' heritage. With the weakening of the Lithuanian Grand Duchy by the early sixteenth century, Poland began to exert more and more control over Ukrainian lands. In 1569 Lithuanian and Polish nobles formed the Union of Lublin, creating a Polish-Lithuanian Commonwealth and transforming these two formerly autonomous political entities into a single union. Economic activity under Polish and Lithuanian rule became increasingly focused on agriculture and moved away from trade, slowing urbanization and increasing reliance on serfdom. The inferior position of the Orthodox Rus' elite and the counter-reformation efforts of the Catholic Church in lands under Polish control initiated the Polonization of the Rus' elite. As a result, the Ukrainian language and the Orthodox faith became more and more associated with lower classes in society.

During this period a new class in society began to develop on the eastern frontier of the Ukrainian lands in reaction to the rigid and oppressive political rule in the west and the tightening of economic opportunities for commoners. The eastern frontier was a sparsely populated steppe lying between the territory of the Polish-Lithuanian Commonwealth and the Crimean Tatar controlled lands. These peasants and townspeople-turned-frontiersmen became known as Cossacks, derived from the Turkic word *quzzaq* meaning "freeman." At first, Cossacks focused their efforts on fighting the Tatars. With time, they directed their attention to the Polish-Lithuanian-controlled lands. They lived in fortified centers and recognized one of their elders as their ruler, the hetman, while initially still acknowledging the authority of the Polish king. With the strengthening of Cossack military might, however, conflicts with local authorities representing the Polish crown became inevitable and resulted in several uprisings in the late sixteenth and the first half of the seventeenth centuries. Aside from demanding recognition for their own status as a distinct social class, the Cossacks became the most important supporters of the Orthodox Church. These Cossack positions created serious antagonisms with the Polish nobility. The earlier rebellions culminated in the Great Revolt of 1648, led by Bohdan Khmelnytsky, a Cossack hetman, an astute politician, and an accomplished military leader. Anticipating a fight with the Poles, Khmelnytsky allied the Cossacks with the Crimean Tatars. Fast military victories won by the Cossacks against the Poles galvanized much popular support among the peasants. In January 1649 a victorious Khmelnytsky entered Kyiv with his army, though he reached no decisive political agreement with the Poles regarding Cossack demands.

Fighting continued, though, and later that year, betrayed by the Tatar ruler, the defeated Khmelnytsky was forced into a peace treaty with the Poles. The Zboriv Treaty recognized the Cossack elite's and Orthodox nobility's authority over Cossack territory and gave the Orthodox Metropolitan a seat in the Polish senate. Though acknowledging Cossack-ruled lands as a military and political reality, the treaty was never implemented. The second round of fighting began a couple of years later, resulting in a crushing defeat of Khmelnytsky's army and the signing of another, much less favorable treaty. The Bila Tserkva Treaty of 1651 afforded the Cossacks with none of the desired legitimacy or protection. Not willing to accept the conditions of this treaty at a time of shifting alliances, the Cossacks looked for support elsewhere and finally, in the 1654 Pereiaslav Agreement, accepted the protection of the Muscovy tsar over the Cossack lands. As an Orthodox ruler, the tsar's faith and inclinations were considered more acceptable for the likewise Orthodox Cossacks. With the military help of their new ally, the Cossacks took a renewed stand against their Polish adversaries. This new alliance soured for the Cossacks, however, when the tsar signed a peace treaty with Poland two years later, breaking the promise of Pereiaslav. In the years immediately following the uprising, Cossack society was characterized by its remarkable egalitarianism and mobility. A Muscovite census of 1654 revealed that half of the adult male population in the Ukrainian lands under Muscovy rule belonged to the Cossacks.[14] With time, as an elite class within Cossack society developed and grew stronger, a rift emerged between the privileged and the common Cossacks, causing unrest and, ultimately, contributing to the ruin of Cossack rule. This internal disintegration was greatly assisted by external powers, in particular, Poland (on the Right Bank of the Dnipro River), Muscovy (in the Hetmanate and in Sloboda Ukraine), and the Ottoman Empire (in Zaporozhian lands), which, by the end of the seventeenth century, had most of the Ukrainian lands partitioned among them.

Following the demise of the Cossack state, the Hetmanate became the center of political and cultural life in the Ukrainian lands. This was an autonomous region under the Cossack system of government, which contained only a fraction of the territory controlled by Khmelnytsky. It was under the rule of Muscovy but initially had a high degree of control over its internal affairs. The centralized Russian Empire, however, aimed to transform its initially nominal rule over the Ukrainian lands into complete economic and political control. Hetman Ivan Mazepa made an attempt at defying Russian rule by allying the Cossacks with Sweden in 1708 and taking advantage of Russo-Swedish hostilities during the Great Northern War. A year later, the forces of Catherine the Great destroyed the Zaporozhian Sich (a fortified center of the Cossack territory) and executed numerous Cossacks in retaliation. By the eighteenth century, much of the former authority of the hetmans was lost, and the weakened Cossack administration and army was disbanded. In 1783, peasants were officially deprived of the right to leave their landlords, de facto formalizing serfdom, while the Ukrainian nobility was granted privileges equal to those of the Russian. With this move the final opposition to the dismantling of the Hetmanate was eliminated. The Hetmanate became an integral part of the Russian Empire in 1785, following Sloboda Ukraine in 1765 and Zaporozhian lands in 1775. Polish rule over the Right Bank ended in 1795. As a result of the dissolution of Poland-Lithuania and the subsequent partitions of Poland, the majority of the territory of the Ukrainian lands and about half of its population became part of the Russian Empire. In the same partitions, Galicia and Bukovyna became part of the Austrian realm.

The next period in Ukrainian history is marked by the division of its territory between two powerful empires—the Russian and the Austrian—but also by great changes in the Ukrainian lands. Having gained control of about 80 percent of the Ukrainian territory in the mid-nineteenth century, Russian imperial rule proceeded to firm up its control through a wide range of reforms in all aspects of society such as the entrenchment of the empirical bureaucracy, the introduction of military conscription, and the founding of Russian universities in Kharkiv and Kyiv. As one of his most significant reforms, the Russian tsar Alexander II abolished serfdom in Russian-ruled Ukrainian lands in 1861. At this time, the introduction of *zemstva* (sgl. *zemstvo*), local self-rule committees, brought a degree of local self-government to the Ukrainian population. *Zemstva* were allowed to impose local taxes, and their representatives had the right to be popularly elected. Despite these positive changes, there was still no space for the expression of Ukrainian ethnic identity in the Ukrainian lands under Russian imperial rule. The remaining 20 percent of Ukrainian territories (Galicia, Bukovyna, and Transcarpathia) were in the hands of the Habsburgs. Austrian rule in Ukrainian lands resulted in modernizing this part of the empire and, in particular, in relieving the abject poverty of the peasants who made up the vast majority of the population and whose difficult socioeconomic situation characterized this region of Ukraine. The Habsburg monarchs Maria Theresa and her son Joseph II spearheaded reform policies by introducing a centralized bureaucracy, strengthening the rule of law, and instituting educational reforms. In 1848 the Supreme Ruthenian Council was established in L'viv and encompassed secular intelligentsia and the clergy. This was the first modern Ukrainian political organization that publicly advocated for the recognition of a distinct Ukrainian identity. It announced its intention to fight for the political and economic rights of the Ukrainian people. That same year, under Habsburg rule, the peasants were finally freed from serfdom. Their economic position did not, however, significantly improve since this policy in fact restricted their access to land and increased their living costs. The second part of the nineteenth century witnessed an emergence of a Ukrainian national consciousness among members of the intelligentsia in western and eastern Ukraine. Social and economic changes included industrialization, increased mobility of the peasantry, and the concentration of economic activities in growing urban centers. The end of the nineteenth and the beginning of the twentieth centuries witnessed the proliferation of political parties influenced by nationalist and socialist ideologies. However, while the sense of Ukrainian identity and the preservation of the Ukrainian national idea grew and developed in Galicia during this time (and to an extent in the other Habsburg-ruled Ukrainian lands), the Ukrainian national movement in eastern Ukrainian lands was much more adamantly suppressed by Russian rulers.

During World War I, Ukrainians found themselves on opposing sides of the conflict. The Russian army is estimated to have had 3.5 million Ukrainian soldiers in its ranks, while the Austrian army counted 250,000 Ukrainians.[15] As the war progressed, ethnic Ukrainians under the weakening Austro-Hungarian Empire grew louder in their demands for a higher degree of political independence. Galicia and Bukovyna, by virtue of their location, were at the heart of the eastern front. They experienced heavy fighting and suffered significant loss of life. Most of the state-building activity of western Ukrainians during the war, therefore, centered on political activism in Vienna and attempts to gain political advances within a reformed Habsburg Empire. The collapse of the Russian Empire in February 1917, on the other hand, radically changed the position of ethnic Ukrainians in eastern Ukrainian lands. As a counterweight to the new Russian provisional government born out of the revolution, the Ukrainian socialist moderates formed the Central Rada (council) as their governing body. This organization drew support from the intelligentsia, petty bureaucrats, lower clergy, junior officers, and wealthier peasants. Russian conservatives and radicals were mostly opposed to its establishment. Without an established army and bureaucracy as well as with inexperienced politicians and lack of quality leadership, the Central Rada quickly demonstrated its inability to maintain law and order and ensure a properly functioning government. The October Revolution in Petrograd and the Central Rada's November proclamation of an autonomous Ukrainian Republic escalated the conflict between the Central Rada and the Bolsheviks. It culminated in December with the Bolshevik invasion of Ukraine. In January 1918 the Central Rada proclaimed the Ukrainian National Republic to be an independent and free state, turning the fighting into an interstate conflict. In an attempt to stand up to the Bolsheviks, the Central Rada turned to foreign countries for help, ultimately signing the Brest-Litovsk Treaty with the Central Powers. As a result, in March 1918, Germans entered Ukraine and, in April, disbanded the Central Rada. The Hetmanate was quickly established as the next Ukrainian government, proclaiming the Ukrainian state with the support of powerful landowners and industrialists. Though its accomplishments were notable in establishing a central bureaucracy and educational infrastructure, this government provoked resistance from the disadvantaged classes in society and subsequently faced its own defeat after the withdrawal of German troops in November 1918.

The Ukrainian People's Republic (UNR) was reestablished after the fall of the Hetmanate government. It lasted from the beginning of 1919 until the end of 1920 and was mired in conflicts, uprisings, invasions, and outright war. During this time of chaos and total disintegration of societal constructs, massive pogroms in the Dnipro region led to the deaths of 30,000–60,000 Ukrainian Jews.[16] In 1918 the West Ukrainian People's Republic (ZUNR) was established following the dissolution of the Habsburg Empire. This political entity was meant to include eastern Galicia, Bukovyna, and Transcarpathia but managed to hold on to only Galicia. Its proclamation quickly sparked a war with the newly independent Polish state. During its brief eight-month existence, the ZUNR entered into a union with the UNR, unifying the Ukrainian lands in one state for the first time in modern history. The end of the ZUNR, or the western province of a newly united Ukraine, came with a Polish military victory in eastern Galicia in the summer of 1919. The end of World War I ushered in a phase of turbulence and war in eastern and western parts of Ukraine. Western Ukrainian lands were divided between Poland, Romania, and Czechoslovakia. Carpathian Ruthenia (Karpats'ka Ukrayina) declared its autonomy within Czechoslovakia in 1938. It declared independence on March 15, 1939 but was immediately occupied by Hungary. Eastern Ukraine, following several years of intense fighting between Bolsheviks, the Whites, and peasants, was ultimately conquered by the Red Army in late 1920. Despite concerted efforts to secure political control of their territory and gain internationally recognized independence, in the end, the Ukrainian national movements failed to secure lasting freedom.

Following the Bolsheviks' victory, Soviet Ukraine became allied with Soviet Russia in December 1920. Ukraine formally became part of the Union of Soviet Socialist Republics (USSR) as one of the four constituting states in December 1922 by signing the Union Treaty, which was in fact never ratified. According to the 1924 Soviet constitution, responsibility for governing was divided between the Union and the governments of the republics, with republican governments having authority over agriculture, internal affairs, justice, education, health, and social services. Originally, the republics had authority over foreign and defense ministries as well, though not for long. Vladimir Lenin's death in 1924 and the relatively low degree of consolidation and unclear future direction of the Communist Party in the 1920s allowed for a revival of Ukrainian national consciousness and the promotion of the Ukrainian language and culture, particularly in education and media. The 1930s under Stalin brought vast socioeconomic changes such as collectivization of peasant land holdings into large communally owned farms, significant investments in industrialization, expansion of the transportation system, and rapid urbanization. The resulting Famine of 1932–1933 is the greatest tragedy in Ukrainian history. Known in Ukrainian as *Holodomor,* meaning "extermination by hunger," the famine took 7–10 million Ukrainian victims in eastern Ukraine. The horror was intentionally induced by Stalin to weaken Ukrainian nationalism and gain control over Ukrainian agricultural lands. The United States, Australia, and several European countries have recognized the famine of 1932–1933 as an act of genocide. With a significant Ukrainian population resulting from migration in the late nineteenth and twentieth centuries, Canada commemorates the fourth Saturday in November as the Ukrainian Famine and Genocide *Holodomor* Memorial Day.

The 1930s were also the time of purges aimed against Stalin's real and perceived political opponents within the Communist Party and other public institutions. In Ukraine the purges culminated in the extermination of cultural activists, intellectuals, and in the liquidation of the entire leadership of the

Memorial in Kyiv to victims of the Soviet-era famine/genocide *Holodomor* (Extermination by Hunger), 1932–1933. Photo by Adriana Helbig.

Ukrainian Soviet government and Communist Party by 1938. Cultural centralization mirrored political centralization and led to the Russification of education and public life, bringing to an end the Ukrainianization movement of the 1920s.

While the German invasion of Poland sparked the outbreak of World War II, the existence of the German-Soviet nonaggression pact enabled the Soviet Red Army to move into Poland, occupy eastern Galicia, western Polissia, and western Volhynia and incorporate them into the territory of Soviet Ukraine. These new additions to Ukraine were subjected to policies of de-Polonization, and many prominent Polish, Jewish, and Ukrainian landowners and industrialists were deported or executed. Counting on their pact with Hitler, the Soviet leadership was caught by surprise by Germany's attack on the Soviet Union in June 1941. This opened up the Eastern Front and set the stage for some of the most brutal battles of World War II. The victorious German army progressed eastward, and most of Ukraine was occupied by December 1941.[17] The panicked Soviet leaders retreated and transferred much of Ukraine's skilled laborers, intellectuals, and factories—about 850 industrial plants and 3.8 million people in all—eastward behind the Urals. This hasty retreat left much death and devastation in its wake, as prisoners were executed and many inhabitants forcibly deported.[18]

The German occupation was initially welcomed by the Ukrainian population in the western lands because of their resentment toward Soviet policies and their hopes of establishing some form of national sovereignty. The reaction of Ukrainians in the east toward the Germans, however, was more hostile. The initial proliferation of Ukrainian national activities under German rule originated from the aspiration of Ukrainian national organizations for, at least partial, self-determination and resulted in limited and tactical collaboration with German rule.[19] However, with the arrival of Erich Koch as the Reichskommissar of Ukraine in November 1941, German policies toward the Ukrainians became increasingly more brutal and restrictive. Arrests, systematic killings and deportations, collective exterminations, and the continuation of the hated collective farming approach to agriculture provoked resistance from the occupied Ukrainian population. In the first years of Nazi occupation in Ukraine, the Jewish population of the region were annihilated through mass deportations and exterminations in western Ukraine and massive fleeing eastward in eastern Ukrainian lands.[20] During this time, two different resistance movements to Nazi rule arose in Ukraine: the nationalist anti-Soviet movement and the Soviet partisan (guerilla) movement. The Ukrainian Insurgent Army (UPA) was a resistance movement organized by Ukrainian nationalists in 1942 in Volhynia and Polissia. Its fighters numbered just under 40,000, and they fought German forces as well as the Soviet partisans. The Soviet partisan movement gained prominence in 1943 and numbered about 43,000 partisans, who fought the German army and the UPA as well.[21] By 1944 Ukraine was de facto embroiled in civil war between members of UPA and Soviet partisan fighters. The Red Army's victory at the Battle of Stalingrad marked the decisive moment of World War II. Following Stalingrad, the westward-advancing Red Army captured Kyiv in November 1943. The war in Ukraine formally ended in the fall of 1944, after a series of important Red Army victories and German defeats, culminating with the Red Army crossing the Carpathians and taking Transcarpathia. UPA fighters, however, continued to fight the Red Army for Ukrainian independence until 1950.

The immediate postwar years were a time of economic reconstruction, population transfers, and integration of the newly acquired western Ukrainian lands into Soviet Ukraine. Ukraine's losses in the war were staggering, counting over 4 million civilian deaths. Nineteen million were left homeless amid the massive destruction of land and urban infrastructure.[22] The daunting task of economic reconstruction involved building up and strengthening the industrial sector, rebuilding the destroyed collective farms, and a general continuation of collectivization and central planning policies, despite diminishing productivity and famine. The Soviet central government set out to implement specific steps to make the newly acquired western Ukrainian lands conform to a Soviet ideological and socioeconomic framework. These steps included the influx of Russians into Communist Party positions; deportations of dissenting Ukrainians, such as former UPA fighters, intelligentsia, and farmers opposed to collectivization, into Siberia and Central Asia; the abolition of the Greek Catholic Church; and the destruction of all other traditional institutions perceived by the central government as a threat to the concept of a common Soviet identity. Internationally, Ukraine had achieved a degree of name recognition in the postwar years as one of the original founding members of the United Nations. Though it held its own seat in the organization, it was not in a position to formulate a foreign policy independently of the Soviet central government.

The period following Stalin's death in 1953 was a time of political de-Stalinization and agricultural and industrial reform. Though they achieved limited success, these reforms nevertheless afforded the Soviet republics, including Ukraine, an overall increase in the standard of living. As part of the de-Stalinization measures, the central government in Moscow relaxed cultural policy restrictions, enabling the Ukrainian intelligentsia to become more actively involved in developing scientific scholarship in the Ukrainian language and ultimately fostering a new generation of Ukrainian cultural activists by the early 1960s. During this time, many Ukrainian political prisoners incarcerated in Siberia were released and amnestied, easing the country into a post-Stalin era thaw led by Nikita Khrushchev. The final years of Khrushchev's rule, however, saw a reversal of more lenient policies introduced in this period, particularly in cultural affairs. The Brezhnev era brought a reintensified Russification and the rise of dissidents in Ukrainian political and cultural life. In response, the mid-1960s and early 1970s saw renewed restrictions on national expression and waves of arrests and trials. In 1972 First Secretary of the Ukrainian Communist Party Petro Shelest was removed from his position because he was judged to be too soft on Ukrainian nationalism. His removal was followed by an expulsion of thousands of members from the Ukrainian Communist Party for sharing Shelest's autonomist ideas. The most notable dissident group during this time was the Ukrainian Helsinki Group, formed in 1976 following the signing of the 1975 Helsinki Accords. The Ukrainian Helsinki Group was the first civic organization that combined advocacy for civil rights protection, national expression, and Ukrainian independence as a right guaranteed by the Soviet constitution.

On his death, Leonid Brezhnev was succeeded by Yuri Andropov, who died shortly after coming into power, as did his successor, Konstantin Chernenko. The election of Mikhail Gorbachev in 1985 exposed a degree of recognition among party leadership regarding the need for a more innovative direction for the Soviet Union, or at least one that would curtail economic decline. The reform-minded Gorbachev quickly and famously introduced glasnost and perestroika in an effort to revitalize Soviet society. The idea behind glasnost was to introduce openness and allow free discussion about governing in society, while perestroika aimed at restructuring the economy. Glasnost policies provided a space for expressions of national consciousness and their subsequent political changes. One such significant change was the emergence of anti-establishment political movements in ideological opposition to the Communist Party, such as Rukh, the People's Movement for Restructuring in Ukraine, founded in 1989. The first partially free elections for parliament (Verkhovna Rada) in Ukraine were held in March 1990, and candidates of the Democratic Bloc—the opposition to the Communist Party—won approximately 20 percent of the seats. Following the failed coup in Moscow in August 1991, the Ukrainian parliament declared independence. Over 90 percent of the population supported the declaration of independence in a referendum in December of the same year. Several days later, the leaders of Russia, Ukraine, and Belarus formally dissolved the Soviet Union.

The postindependence Ukrainian presidencies of Leonid Kravchuk and Leonid Kuchma were a period of political and economic transition. It was a time of building and reforming institutions and of developing political and ideological diversity. Numerous political parties sprang up in the early 1990s, many with small memberships and limited resources, vying for political gains and resources. Disagreements and conflicts about the division of powers between the president and parliament were a common source of political discord even after the parliament adopted a constitution in June 1996. As dynamic as the politics were in this period, the economy was stagnating. Throughout the 1990s the standard of living plummeted and inflation soared. With the dissolution of the USSR, Ukraine had lost a large market and much of the demand for its industrial output. The mid-1990s brought along rapid privatization, growing deficits, and foreign debt as well as falling agricultural production. By the year 2000 the need for serious economic reforms in Ukraine became apparent. Prime Minister Victor Yushchenko made an attempt to pass economic reforms before being replaced by President Kuchma in early 2001. Increasing public concern about the worsening economic situation and mounting corruption escalated in late 2000, when Socialist Party leader Oleksandr Moroz revealed the existence of tapes suggesting the involvement of President Kuchma in the disappearance and death of opposition journalist Heorhii Gongadze. Protestors organized rallies throughout Ukraine calling for President Kuchma's resignation, inspiring a movement dubbed "Ukraine without Kuchma," which ended in violence and the arrests of hundreds of protesters. In the 2002 parliamentary elections, the Our Ukraine Bloc, led by Victor Yushchenko and consisting of 10 opposition, center liberal, reform-minded parties, won a significant number of votes but was unable to form a government. The 2002 election reinforced the general sentiment of discontent with the government among many Ukrainians and the need for change.

THE PRESENT

Political change came with the 2004 presidential election. The election was, de facto, a standoff between two presidential candidates—former prime minister and opposition politician Viktor Yushchenko and then prime minister Viktor Yanukovych—amid an already charged political climate. In November 2004, following the official announcement of a Yanukovych victory, widespread allegations of electoral fraud, combined with popular demands for change, sparked a mass campaign of peaceful public protests and civil disobedience, which became known as the Orange Revolution, named after the campaign colors of Viktor Yushchenko. A repeated December election resulted in a victory by Victor Yushchenko, who was sworn in as president at the beginning of 2005. Yulia Tymoshenko, another prominent opposition politician and a former deputy prime minister in the 2000 Yushchenko government, became his coalition partner and prime minister, though not for long.

Political infighting and discord among the coalition partners in government and a stalemate between President Yushchenko and the Yanukovych-led parliamentary majority lasted through the next parliamentary election in 2006 and resulted in President Yushchenko dissolving parliament in April 2007. This controversial move was followed by early parliamentary elections in 2007, which ultimately put Yulia Tymoshenko back in the prime minister's seat. The years since the Orange Revolution have mostly brought turbulence to the Ukrainian political scene. Though many Ukrainians may not agree with the politics of the day, the post–Orange Revolution atmosphere in the country reflects Ukrainian aspirations to work for a democratic government and a more pluralist society that can guarantee equality, security, and freedom of speech for all citizens of Ukraine.

NOTES

1. Paul Robert Magocsi, *Ukraine: A Historical Atlas* (Toronto: University of Toronto Press, 1985).

2. Judy Batt and Kataryna Wolczuk, eds., *Region, State and Identity in Central and Eastern Europe* (Portland, OR: Frank Cass, 2002), 67.

3. Taras Kuzio, Robert Kravchuk, and Paul D'Anieri, eds., *State and Institution Building in Ukraine* (New York: St. Martin's Press, 1999), 297.

4. State Statistics Committee of Ukraine, "All-Ukraine Population Census 2001," http://www.ukrcensus.gov.ua/eng/regions/reg_luhan/.

5. World Nuclear Association, http://www.world-nuclear.org/info/inf06app.html.

6. National Cancer Institute, "The Chornobyl Accident: 20 Years of Study_Leukemia Leukemia and Thyroid Cancer," http://chornobyl.cancer.gov/accident.php?lev=0&page=1.

7. Peter J. S. Duncan, "Ukraine and the Ukrainians," in *The Nationalities Question in the Post-Soviet States,* ed. Graham Smith (New York: Longman, 1996), 199.

8. Orest Subtleny, *Ukraine: A History* (Toronto: University of Toronto Press, 2000), 8.

9. Ibid., 9.

10. Ibid., 33.

11. Ibid., 32.

12. Ibid., 70.

13. Ibid., 73.

14. Ibid., 141.

15. Ibid., 344.

16. Magocsi, *Ukraine: A Historical Atlas,* 506.

17. Subtleny, *Ukraine: A History,* 460.

18. Magocsi, *Ukraine: A Historical Atlas,* 624.

19. Subtleny, *Ukraine: A History,* 471.

20. Magocsi, *Ukraine: A Historical Atlas,* 633.

21. Ibid., 635.

22. Ibid., 63.

2

Religion

THE GROWTH OF public religious expression during the perestroika period of the late 1980s signaled the end of atheist policies imposed by the Soviet government. Since independence in 1991, Orthodox Christianity, Catholicism, Judaism, and Islam have experienced a comparative level of religious tolerance and peaceful coexistence. Alongside the major faiths, a growing number of smaller Christian groups, such as Baptists, Pentecostals, and Evangelicals, have contributed to the country's religious mosaic. These communities have a significantly shorter history in the territories of Ukraine than Catholic and Orthodox Christian communities but have had enough of an impact throughout the twentieth century that Ukraine has been referred to as the "Bible Belt of the Soviet Union."[1]

Underscoring the importance of ecumenism in Ukraine, this chapter offers a historical overview of the role religious institutions and identities have played in various epochs and in different political and sociocultural contexts.

CHRISTIANITY IN THE BYZANTINE PERIOD

In 988, Prince Volodymyr the Great (965–1015) accepted Christianity as the official religion of Kyivan Rus'.[2] The population of Kyiv was baptized in the Dnipro River. In his search for a religion to which to convert his pagan empire, Prince Volodymyr sent scouts to the Volga Bulgarians, who practiced Islam; the Germans; and the Greeks.[3] When the scouts

Prince Volodymyr the Great was baptized in Chersonesus and accepted Christianity as the state religion of Kyivan Rus'. Photo by Adriana Helbig.

reached Constantinople, the beauty of the Byzantine rituals overwhelmed them. As described by Prince Volodymyr's scouts in 987 A.D. and recounted in *The Primary Chronicle,* a testament also known as *The Tale of Bygone Years,* composed by various writers from 1040 to 1118 and compiled in its final form by the monk Nestor at the Kyievo-Pecherska Lavra (Kyivan Cave Monastery):

"Then we went on to Greece, and the Greeks led us to the edifices where they worship their God, and we knew not whether we were in heaven or on earth. For on earth there is no such splendor or such beauty, and we are at a loss how to describe it. We only know that God dwells there among men, and their service is fairer than the ceremonies of other nations. For we cannot forget that beauty. Every man, after tasting something sweet, is afterward unwilling to accept that which is better, and therefore we cannot dwell longer here." Then the boyars spoke and said, "If the Greek faith were evil, it would not have been adopted by your grandmother Olga, who was wiser than all other men."[4]

The acceptance of Christianity in Kyivan Rus' helped unite the conquered tribes that constituted the growing state and strengthened the kingdom's political, cultural, and intellectual significance. Kyiv became an important center of education, and many Greek texts were translated into Old Slavonic. Architectural developments and artistic techniques were brought from Byzantium, and the Byzantine style influenced the construction of magnificent architectural monuments such as St. Sophia Cathedral, built in 1037 by Yaroslav the Wise, son of Prince Volodymyr. Today, St. Sophia Cathedral stands in the center of modern Kyiv and, together with the Kyievo-Pecherska Lavra (Kyivan Cave Monastery), has been designated a World Heritage Site by the United Nations Educational, Scientific, and Cultural Organization (UNESCO). St. Sophia is adorned with many mosaics and frescos dating back to the eleventh century, two of which feature the family of Yaroslav the Wise. Yaroslav is buried in a marble sarcophagus inside the Cathedral.

Yaroslav played a crucial role in broadening the political ties of Kyiv's royal family through intermarriage. He married a Swedish princess, one sister married a Polish king, and another married a Byzantine prince. Three sons married European princesses, and three daughters became queens of France, Hungary, and Norway. His granddaughter married Heinrich IV, King of Germany and Emperor of the Holy Roman Empire. It is not surprising that historians often call him the "father-in-law of Europe."[5] Yet such ties were crucial in affirming the relevance of Kyivan Rus' in relation to its Christian neighbors in the eleventh century.

The bell tower of St. Sophia Cathedral in Kyiv. Photo by Adriana Helbig.

Yaroslav the Wise was closely involved in ecclesiastical affairs. At the time of his reign (1036–1054), there were more than 400 churches in Kyiv. He supported the construction of monasteries, which became centers of learning for the urban nobility. In 1051 he appointed Ilarion as the first native metropolitan of Kyivan Rus'. Though this appointment indicates the great strength of the church at this time, the Kyivan metropolitan still ceded power to the Patriarch of Constantinople, from where Christianity was brought to Kyivan Rus'.[6]

The year 1054 in general Christian church history marks the Great Schism between what became western Catholicism and eastern Orthodoxy. At that time, the Christian church had five patriarchs, each governing a particular area, or patriarchate. The patriarchate in the west was located in Rome, and Latin functioned as the language of the church. Greek was the official church language for the four eastern patriarchates, located in Alexandria, Antioch, Byzantium, and Jerusalem. Complex dogmatic and hierarchical disputes between the church in Rome and the churches in the east led to a split into the Latin and Greek branches of Christianity. Kyivan Rus,' which had borrowed its religious form from Constantinople, remained Orthodox and followed its allegiance to the Patriarch in Constantinople.

CATHOLICISM AND ORTHODOXY WITHIN THE POLISH-LITHUANIAN COMMONWEALTH

Following the golden age of Yaroslav the Wise, fighting among descendant rulers contributed to the weakening of the Kyivan Rus' state. Economic decline, brought on by changes in trade routes and the loss of key trading partners such as Constantinople and Baghdad, contributed to further fragmentation.[7] In 1240, Kyiv was completely destroyed during the Mongol invasion. Lands to the west, such as the principalities of Galicia and Volhynia, liberated from Polish control by Volodymyr the Great in 980–990, averted high levels of devastation by the Mongols in 1241. However, Batu (1205–1255), the Mongol leader and grandson of Genghis Khan, summoned Danylo, ruler of Galicia, to appear at his court at Sarai on the Volga and forced him to submit to Mongol rule. Danylo turned to Pope Innocent IV in Rome for aid in launching a Slavic crusade against the Mongols. The Pope sent a royal crown as a sign of his support and a papal viceroy crowed Danylo king in the town of Drohobych in 1253. Though the Pope sent no reinforcements for the crusade itself, King Danylo launched a campaign in 1254 to reclaim Kyiv from the Mongol rulers. His effort failed, and in 1259 the Mongols moved into Galicia and Volhynia. They made King Danylo destroy the fortifications around all towns, making the region vulnerable to future attacks. Nevertheless, Galicia and Volhynia enjoyed relative peace, stability, and prosperity in the thirteenth and early fourteenth centuries. An indication of this is reflected in the actions of Yuriy, grandson of King Danylo, who, in a move against the metropolitan of Kyiv, established a separate metropolitanate in Halych in 1303. Kyiv's former importance had declined so significantly by this time, however, that the Orthodox metropolitan of Kyiv had abandoned the city in 1300.[8] In 1362 Kyiv was incorporated into the Grand Principality of Lithuania, which fought against the Polish for control of Ukrainian lands. Historian Orest Subtelny notes that the Polish proclaimed themselves the "buffer of Christianity" and represented their push to the east as a "crusade against the heathen Lithuanians and the schismatic Orthodox Ukrainians" in hopes of papal support.[9]

Meanwhile, the capture of Constantinople by the Ottoman Empire in 1453 strengthened the ecclesiastical power of the Grand Duchy of Muscovy. In 1569, the Grand Duchy of Lithuania, in attempts to protect its lands from Tatar and Muscovite invasion, united with the Kingdom of Poland and created the Polish-Lithuanian Commonwealth. The Commonwealth was Roman Catholic, and this greatly weakened the position of Orthodox Ukrainian elites within the new state. As the Orthodox Church within the Commonwealth fell into decline, many Ukrainian elites, attracted by the educational and financial opportunities and privileges available to Polish nobility, assimilated into Polish Catholic society. The loss of the elite was devastating for Ukrainian urban and peasant classes. The diminished state of the Orthodox Church prompted certain Orthodox Church leaders to integrate their religious followers into the institutionally stable Catholic Church. Orthodox clergy within the Commonwealth eventually united with the Roman Catholic Church in 1595. Following the Union of Brest, the newly integrated Ukrainian Catholic Church became known as the Uniate Church, the name stemming from its union with Rome. Though the Uniate Church acknowledged Roman papal rule, it retained the Orthodox liturgy and Byzantine aesthetics in its rituals.

An ongoing conflict between Christianity and Islam, however, continued in the frontier territories along the Dnipro River, beyond the borders of Polish influence. Ukrainians escaping from serfdom in the Commonwealth became frontiersmen, fighting Tatars and their Ottoman Turkish overlords to secure the fertile steppes for settlement. Known as Cossacks, they protected Ukrainian towns and villages from constant pillage and destruction by the Tatars. They were comprised of predominantly Orthodox escaped serfs or not yet Polonized Ukrainian nobility.[10] The most famous among them, Dmytro "Baida" Vyshnyvetsky, gathered individual Cossack groups on the island of Mala Khortytsia beyond the Dnipro's southern rapids (*za porohamy*) and organized a democratically ruled settlement for Cossacks, the Zaporozhian Sich.

The Cossacks were involved in numerous insurrections against Polish noblemen and viewed themselves as defenders of the Orthodox faith.[11] They considered the Uniate Church as an example of further Polonization of the Ukrainian people. In 1648 Cossack warriors led by Hetman Bohdan Khmelnytsky waged a revolt against the Polish-Lithuanian Commonwealth. Though the rebellion's primary goal was to gain military control, the battle was cast in religious terms and was fought in the defense of the Orthodox religion against the Catholic Church.[12] The Cossacks fought for the repeal of the Union of Brest and for the reestablishment of the Orthodox Church for Ukrainians living in western territories.

Khmelnytsky's victories were not strong enough to prove a decisive factor in controlling tense Polish-Ukrainian relations. To aid in the Cossack campaign against the Poles, Khmelnytsky had initially relied on Crimean Tatar forces, but their assistance was not constant. Though Khmelnytsky initially bid for the Ottoman sultan's protection of Cossack lands, he signed such an agreement in 1654 at Pereiaslav with Tsar Alexey I of Muscovy. The Pereiaslav Agreement would contribute to very different histories for western and eastern Ukraine (often referred to as Right Bank and Left Bank Ukraine, respectively, divided by the Dnipro River). In 1660, war broke out between Poland and Moscow for control of Ukraine, and by 1686, most of Ukraine was divided up among surrounding powers. Cossack rule in parts of Left Bank Ukraine continued under hetmans, such as Ivan Mazepa (1687–1709), until 1768, when Catherine the Great, ruler of the Russian Empire from 1762 to 1796, destroyed the Zaporozhian Sich in 1709. Western Ukrainian lands came under Austrian rule through the partitions of the Polish-Lithuanian Commonwealth by Russia, Prussia, and Austria in 1772, 1775, and 1795. In 1772 Austria took Galicia and Bukovyna in the west. By 1795, however, the rest of the Right Bank, together with the Left Bank of Ukraine, was incorporated into the Russian Empire and would remain under Russian rule until the twentieth century.

JEWISH HISTORY

The Polish-Lithuanian Commonwealth, against which Khmelnytsky's Cossack army fought, was one of the most religiously tolerant regimes in Europe at the time. It welcomed a large Jewish population, particularly in the region of Podilia, which had belonged to the lands of medieval Rus'.[13] Though Jews were forbidden to own land, they enjoyed the protection of the Polish ruling class, *szlachta,* and worked as estate overseers for the Polish nobles. The majority of people who labored for the Jewish overseers were Ukrainian peasants who had become serfs on the estates of the Polish and Polonized Ukrainian elite. In 1616, over half the crown lands in Ukraine were leased to Jewish entrepreneurs.[14] They collected high taxes from the peasants and demanded six or seven days of hard labor.

The Cossacks aimed to disrupt the hierarchical structure within the Polish-Lithuanian Commonwealth in their rise against the Kingdom of Poland. The Cossack rebellion of 1648 had dramatic political, social, and religious repercussions because it targeted the Polish magnates and their Jewish protectorate. Between 1648 and 1656, tens of thousands of Jews were killed by Cossacks and peasant rebels.[15]

The Cossack rebellions in Ukraine had great effects on the religious beliefs and practices of Jews. In the years following the massacres, a mystic form of Hasidism emerged as a way to help people cope with tragedy and uncertainty. Israel ben Eliezer (1700?–1760), known more commonly as the Baal Shem Tov, which translates as "Master of the Good [Divine] Name," was the movement's informal leader and teacher. A mystic and a person of great faith who practiced the Kabbalah, Baal Shem Tov was known for his good deeds and his powers to heal. He spoke in the language of commoners and tuned in to the growing number of Jews who sought communion with God in ways other than through rabbinical scholasticism. This new approach made the teachings of the Kabbalah accessible to broader strata.

While the Polish-Lithuanian Commonwealth had welcomed Jews, the staunchly Orthodox Russian rulers had always worked adamantly to keep Jews out of the Russian Empire. The partitions of Poland between Russia, Prussia, and Austria, however, brought certain lands of the Polish-Lithuanian Commonwealth under Russian rule. The significant communities of Jews once within the Commonwealth became subjects of the Russian crown. They were forced to obey a decree called the Pale of Settlement, initiated in 1791 by Catherine the Great. This decree forbade Jews to settle in urban centers and forced them to move to small provincial towns, known in Yiddish as *shtetls.* The Pale limited the movement of Jews to territories that include today's Ukraine, Moldova, Belarus, Poland, and Lithuania. It was in existence from 1791 to 1917, until the Russian Empire collapsed in the wake of revolution.

Despite such restrictions, the number of Jews within the Russian Empire rose significantly, particularly throughout the nineteenth century. Of the 5.2 million Jews within the empire, 2 million lived in Ukraine.[16] They constituted 33 percent of the urban population, and in small towns made up as high as 70 to 80 percent of the population.[17] Tight-knit urban Jewish society included rabbis and wealthy owners of distilleries, sawmills, tobacco factories, and sugar refineries as well as petty traders and artisans.[18] Historical animosity, coupled with changes in economic structures and increasing anti-Semitic government policies within the Russian Empire, led to a rise in antagonism against Jews, culminating in a series of pogroms by Russian nationalist groups in 1881 and again in 1903–1905. These destructive attacks contributed to the mass emigration of more than 1.2 million Jews from the Russian Empire to the United States.[19]

Following the breakup of the Russian Empire, and in the anarchy that followed in the territories of Ukraine, it is estimated that approximately 35,000–50,000 Jews were killed in pogroms during 1919–1920. In 1941 Nazi forces massacred between 100,000 and 200,000 Kyiv citizens at Babyn Yar. The majority of victims were Jews: 30,000 were killed in 36 hours. Ukrainians, Russians, Poles, and Roma were murdered as well. The site is commemorated with a large menorah. While in 1941, at the beginning of Nazi occupation, the Jewish population of Kyiv numbered 150,000, by 1942, only 20 survived.[20] As a result of Nazi extermination policies, only 800,000 of the country's 2.7 million Jews remained in the territories of Ukraine by the middle of the twentieth century.[21]

The Jewish community in independent Ukraine is experiencing a cultural, religious, and political revival. They have built new synagogues, schools, community centers, and memorials with the help of aid from Jewish communities in Israel and the United States as well as with the help of the Ukrainian government. Hebrew studies departments have been established at universities in Kyiv and Odesa, alongside the Solomon International University founded in Kyiv in 1993. Seventy-nine synagogues have been established. Significant numbers of Hasidic Jews now travel to Ukraine from the west for the annual Hasidic Jewish pilgrimage to the grave of Rabbi Nakhman of Bratzlav in the town of Uman, 130 miles (210 kilometers) southwest of Kyiv, where pilgrims mark the Jewish New Year at the end of September. A revived interest in klezmer music since the 1980s in the United States and in Jewish-Ukrainian pop culture through American films such as Liev Schreiber's *Everything Is Illuminated,* starring Elijah Wood, help draw cultural and historic connections between Jews in Ukraine, Poland, Russia, and the United States. An increasingly open interreligious dialogue in the postsocialist context has contributed to increasing sensitivities regarding the historical experiences of Jews in the territories of Ukraine.

ORTHODOXY AND CATHOLICISM WITHIN THE RUSSIAN AND AUSTRIAN EMPIRES

When Hetman Bohdan Khmelnytsky signed the Pereiaslav Agreement with Tsar Alexey I of Muscovy in 1654, the fate of Ukrainian Christians became increasingly tied with that of the Russian Orthodox Church. In 1868 the rule of the Orthodox Church in Kyiv was forcefully transferred from Constantinople to the newly formed Russian Orthodox Patriarchate in Moscow. Church leaders in Constantinople considered this move uncanonical. In 2000 Constantinople Patriarch Bartholomew I declared that Ukraine lay within its canonical territory, a position supported by Orthodox Church leaders in Greece, Romania, Bulgaria, and Georgia.[22]

When the Uniate Church found itself within the Russian Empire due to the partitions of Poland in 1772, 1793, and 1795, its members experienced constant pressure to convert to Russian Orthodoxy. Catherine the Great stressed the nominal division of church and state; nonetheless, she viewed Catholics as a political threat to the Russian Empire and wanted to sever ties between the Uniates in the Russian Empire and the Catholic metropolinate in Poland.[23] She recognized the relationship between religion and nationality, which added great fuel to her fervor for controlling the Uniate Church in newly acquired western lands.[24] Russian monarchs who succeeded Catherine followed her policies of religious intolerance and persecution. In 1833, two of the most culturally significant Ukrainian Orthodox monasteries, the Pochaiv Lavra and the Kyievo-Pecherska Lavra (Kyivan Cave Monastery), were transferred to the Russian Orthodox Church. In 1839 Tsar Nicholas disbanded the Uniate Church within the Russian Empire.[25]

In contrast to the fate of Uniates in the Russian Empire, the Uniate Church in the territories of Galicia and Bukovyna, incorporated into the Austrian Empire following the first partition of Poland in 1772, served as a source of Ukrainian consciousness and literacy.[26] Because Austria was a Catholic empire, the government ceded privileges to the Uniates. In 1774 Empress Maria Theresa established the Barbareum Seminary in Vienna, which offered education to the Catholic clergy within the Uniate Church. In 1784 Emperor Joseph, influenced by Enlightenment ideals, ordered the establishment of a school in every rural parish.[27] Following the abolition of serfdom in 1848 in the Austrian Empire (in the Russian Empire, serfdom existed until 1861), the Uniate (Greek Catholic) clergy established hundreds of parish schools for the peasant class.[28] The education of the peasant class through religious institutions offered Catholic clergy opportunities to spread ideas of national consciousness that would influence the nation-building and anti-imperial politics of the nineteenth century.[29] For instance, Mykhailo Verbytsky, a Greek Catholic priest, composed the music for a patriotic poem titled "Shche Ne Vmerla Ukrayina" (Ukraine Is Not Yet Dead), written by ethnographer Pavlo Chubynsky in 1862. The song served briefly as the Ukrainian national anthem in 1917 and officially became the anthem of independent Ukraine in 1992.

One of the most important figures within the Ukrainian Greek Catholic Church was Metropolitan Andrey Sheptytsky (1865–1944), a Polish count who changed his religious affiliation from the Latin to the Greek rite. In 1899 Emperor Franz Joseph named Andrey Sheptytsky Bishop of Stanislaviv (today, Ivano-Frankivsk) in western Ukraine. A year later, the young Sheptytsky was appointed Metropolitan Archbishop. He lobbied for Ukrainian interests with imperial rulers in Vienna and established a free medical clinic by donating his family's holdings to charitable causes.[30]

Under Sheptytsky's strong leadership, rural parish priests became much more involved in urban intellectual circles such as Prosvita (Enlightenment).[31] He also worked to foster understanding between the various ethnic and religious groups. Metropolitan Sheptytsky studied Hebrew to forge closer relations with Jewish communities. During World War II he protected many Jews from the atrocities of the Holocaust, hiding them in his residency in L'viv and in Greek Catholic monasteries. Before he died, he secretly consecrated Josyp Slipyj as his successor as head of the Ukrainian Greek Catholic Church. In 1946 the occupying Soviet government dissolved the Greek Catholic Church. Many priests and faithful were murdered or sent to labor camps in Siberia. The Soviet government forced surviving Catholic priests to annul the Union of Brest, which, in 1595, had joined the Uniate Church with the pope in Rome. The property of the Greek Catholic Church was ceded to the Russian Orthodox Church.

With most of its church leaders and faithful killed, imprisoned, or sentenced to labor camps in Siberia, the Greek Catholic Church became a church in catacombs. It survived in diaspora, particularly in North America and Canada, where many Ukrainians escaping the horrors of World War II eventually found refuge. As the head of the Church following Metropolitan Sheptytsky's death in 1944, Metropolitan Josyf Slipyj was sentenced to prison and forced labor in Siberia. Pope John Paul XXIII worked hard to negotiate Metropolitan Slipyj's release from prison, but such interventions only increased his sentence. In 1963 he was freed and appointed a cardinal in 1965 by Pope Paul VI in Rome. Following his death in 1984, Major Archbishop Cardinal Myroslav Lubachivsky became the head of the Ukrainian Greek Catholic Church. This position has been held by Major Archbishop Cardinal Lubomyr Husar since 2000.

The Greek Catholic Church, which dissolved in 1946, became a church in hiding, with Church leaders such as Cardinal Slipyj working on behalf of Greek Catholics in Rome. In Ukraine, the faithful were under constant fear of persecution but participated in Masses held in secret in forests, apartments, and places beyond the relentless gaze of Soviet government officials. As an institution, the Church survived most prominently in the west among diaspora Ukrainians who fled their homeland in the turmoil of World War II. Large communities of Ukrainian Greek Catholics exist to this day throughout Canada, the United States, Australia, Latin America, and Europe.

RELIGIOUS TENSION AND SUPPRESSION IN THE TWENTIETH CENTURY

Following the collapse of Russian and Austrian imperial rule on the territories of Ukraine, the role of the Orthodox and Catholic churches became even more politicized. In 1921 a group of Ukrainian Orthodox clergy, opposing the Bolsheviks, who had seized power during the Russian Revolution of 1917 and had established rule in the territories of Ukraine, broke away from Moscow and founded the Ukrainian Autocephalous Orthodox Church. The process regarding the founding of this church did not follow canonical law due to the turbulent times during which it was founded. In 1924 Metropolitan John Theodorovych began to establish Ukrainian Autocephalous Orthodox parishes in the United States. Pittsburgh, Pennsylvania, Sound Bound Brook, New Jersey, Minneapolis, Minnesota, Chicago, Illinois, and Cleveland, Ohio, became important centers of Ukrainian Orthodoxy in the United States. In Ukraine, however, the Ukrainian Autocephalous Orthodox Church was dissolved in 1926 and incorporated into the Polish Autocephalous Orthodox Church, which had been established in 1924 by the Patriarch of Constantinople as a revival of the Kyiv Metropolitanate. The aim of the Polish Autocephalous Orthodox Church was to serve the 6 million Orthodox Ukrainians living under Polish rule in the interwar period.[32] In 1995 the Ukrainian Orthodox churches in the United States were brought under the jurisdiction of the Patriarch in Constantinople.

In 1989 the Ukrainian Orthodox Church of the Kyiv Patriarchate was revived; the Ukrainian Autocephalous Orthodox Church followed suit in 1990. By 1992, there were 2,000 Autocephalous churches in Ukraine. However, more than half of the parishes belonging to the Russian Orthodox Church are found on the territories of Ukraine. In 1990 the Russian Orthodox Church began to call itself the Ukrainian Orthodox Church–Moscow Patriarchate. This has led to significant confusion among believers with regard to jurisdiction, though the majority supports a break from the Moscow Patriarchate and unification of all the Orthodox churches under the Ukrainian Orthodox Church–Kyiv Patriarchate (UOC-KP), with an eventual return to the jurisdiction of the Patriarch in Constantinople. Forbidden to practice religion in Ukraine, Patriarch Mstyslav (Stepan Skrypnyk) left Ukraine during WWII and worked to unite the Ukrainian Orthodox Church in the United States. The Ukrainian Orthodox Churches (UAOC) ordained him Patriarch of Kyiv and All Ukraine in 1990, at the age of 92. He died in 1993 and was succeeded by Patriarch Volodymyr (Romaniuk). Patriarch Filaret (Mykhailo

Denysenko), Patriarch of Kyiv and All Rus'-Ukraine, has headed the UOC-KP since 1995.

Tensions between Ukrainian Greek Catholic, Ukrainian Orthodox, Ukrainian Autocephalous, and Russian Orthodox Churches still often run high in Ukraine due to the politicized nature of religion and culture that has emerged in light of very different histories of the western and eastern parts of the country. The visit of Pope John Paul II to western Ukraine in 2001 bore witness to the culmination of these tensions. More than 1 million people greeted the pope during his visit to L'viv. Alexei II, Patriarch of Moscow and All Russia, decried the pope's visit to Ukraine. In 2005, to counter the marginalized status of the Greek Catholic Church in Ukraine and to eradicate the deep historical skepticism toward Catholicism as an agent of Polonization and Westernization, Major Archbishop Cardinal Lubomyr Husar moved the seat of the church from L'viv, in western Ukraine, to Kyiv and took the historical title "Major Archbishop of Kyiv and Halych," meaning a representative of Catholics in eastern and western parts of Ukraine.

THE EVANGELICAL MOVEMENT IN UKRAINE

Protestantism in the Russian Empire goes back to the eighteenth century, but its followers were often persecuted. Anthropologist Catherine Wanner believes this is because "it introduced the possibility that religious practice did not have to be an ascribed attribute of identity bestowed at birth," as was the common attitude toward Orthodox religion and identity throughout the Russian Empire.[33] The notion of being "born again," where a Believer recognizes his or her own sins and accepts Christ, is the single most transformative action in the faith. By spreading the news of the Gospel, Evangelicals aim to show so-called non-Believers the path toward salvation.

Evangelical communities in Ukraine grew steadily throughout the Soviet era and have reached significant numbers in the period since independence. Much has to do with the financial support they have received from Evangelicals in the West, many of whom travel to Ukraine on missionary trips to help foster interest in the religion and financially and morally support the communities of converts throughout the country, particularly in cities such as Kharkiv and Kyiv. Nigerian pastor Sunday Adelaja's Embassy of God church is the fastest growing religious community in Ukraine.[34] Adelaja's church draws support from a wide variety of people, ranging from older-generation Ukrainians to young migrants from Africa.

Despite the successful growth of churches such as Embassy of God, the history of Evangelism in Ukraine has been marked by significant hardship and persecution. Many Evangelicals have moved to the United States as religious refugees, supported by the network of religious communities in the West.

This movement is similar to the emigration of Jews from the Soviet Union to Israel in the 1970s and to the United States with the help of the Hebrew Immigrant Aid Society.[35]

MUSLIMS: THE RETURN OF CRIMEAN TATARS TO UKRAINE

Crimean Tatars are descendants of a very large Muslim population that adopted Islam in the thirteenth century and lived in the territories of the Crimean Peninsula. Descendants of the Golden Horde, they comprised Turkic and non-Turkic groups, ruled by the Crimean Khanate (1441–1783), whose state religion was Islam (Sunni Muslim of the Hanafi School).[36] The Khanate answered to the Ottoman sultan in Istanbul (formerly Constantinople) but pursued autonomous policies. Tatars conducted frequent raids into Ukrainian lands and the frontiers of the steppes to secure their foothold and to capture slaves, often 3,000 at a time.[37] Such actions and the cries of Cossacks in Turkish captivity are often depicted in *dumas,* or epic songs.

In 1774 Russian and Cossack fighters forced the Ottomans to relinquish their power over the Khanate, which was absorbed in 1783 into the Russian Empire under the rule of Catherine the Great. In the first half of the twentieth century, the Crimean Peninsula was part of the Russian Socialist Federation of Soviet Republics (SFSR). In 1954 Nikita Khrushchev transferred the Crimean Peninsula from the Russian SFSR to the Ukrainian Soviet Socialist Republic.

The greatest tragedy befell the Crimean Tatars on May 18, 1944, when the whole population (about 200,000 people), predominantly women, children, and elderly (able men were fighting on the Soviet front), were forcefully transported to the Urals and Central Asia by order of Joseph Stalin, who fabricated charges against the religious-ethnic group regarding their alleged cooperation with the Nazis. Many Crimean Tatars had close familial, ethnic, and religious allegiances with the hundreds of thousands of Crimean Tatars living in Turkey. It is probable that their close relations with Turkey were a stimulating force for Stalin's deportation of the entire ethnic group.[38]

A significant percentage of deportees perished during the harsh journey in cattle cars. According to Crimean Tatar sources, half of those who survived deportation perished as a result of hunger and disease shortly after arrival in Central Asia.[39] The cruelty of forced deportation fueled incredibly strong nationalism among second-generation Tatars born in exile. Though many Crimean Tatars managed to establish successful lives in Central Asia, particularly in Uzbekistan, where an estimated 100,000 reside,[40] many have returned to Ukraine since the fall of the Soviet Union.

Returning Crimean Tatars have worked to reclaim their ancestral homes. Because their lands were taken over by ethnic Russians and Ukrainians forced to resettle the area after World War II, the returning Tatars have staged sit-ins on lands that once belonged to their families. The presence of these squatters led to great violence in Crimea throughout the 1990s. They built shelters, *samostroi,* out of train cars or other scrap materials. Many houses were eventually converted into more appropriate housing and legalized, though many still lack basic amenities.[41] The Mejlis, the Parliament that represents the interests of the Crimean Tatars, has worked to appease tensions between returning Crimean Tatars and the rest of the predominantly ethnic Russian population living on the Crimean Peninsula.

NEO-PAGANISM

Native Ukrainian National Faith

In 1934, at the height of the Stalinist purges that led to the increased Soviet grip on people living in the territories of Ukraine, Professor Volodymyr Shaian, an ethnic Ukrainian, developed a pagan religion grounded in nationalist discourse. His student, Lev Sylenko, brought these beliefs with him when he immigrated to Canada and founded Ridna Ukrainska Narodna Vira (RUNVira, or Native Ukrainian National Faith).

While Sylenko's monotheistic faith grabbed hold among the North American diaspora (the headquarters of RUNVira is in Spring Glen, New York), today's neo-pagan groups in Ukraine draw on both Sylenko's monotheistic and Shaian's polytheistic beliefs, centered around Dazhboh, the sun god. As folklorist Mariya Lesiv points out, due to the lack of sources on old Slavic rituals, many neo-paganists in Ukraine actively create their own rituals.[42] The belief in magic, while having never been fully eradicated by the modernizing Soviet government, has witnessed a revival in the social and cultural turbulence of the postsocialist era. The rituals and beliefs are rooted in the idea of offering a way to construct new relationships toward Ukrainian identity and the nation-state. Unlike transnational pagan movements, those in Ukraine are focused on the territories of Ukraine and in reconstituting a connection to the Ukrainian land and to the Ukrainian culture. As states Lesiv, "the neo-pagans' vision of the Ukrainian nation is connected with its native religion, whose roots were 'buried' (by the Christian church) and now are being rediscovered."[43]

Pagan Rituals in Christian Holidays

The recent rise in both Christian religious practice and neo-pagan rituals has been complemented by a renewed interest in all types of pre-Christian beliefs once followed in the territories of Ukraine. Pagan-based rituals have always been strong and were practiced alongside or interwoven into Christian religious practice and mystic Hasidism, particularly in rural contexts, where belief in the supernatural continues to be strong.

While practitioners of Ukrainian neo-paganism may be relatively few in number, there are numerous pagan rituals that form the basis of the modern Christian rituals in particular. For instance, the *Koliada* is a winter cycle of rituals that corresponds to the celebration of Christmas Eve, which, according to the Julian calendar, falls on January 6. Celebrated with many variations throughout the country, the Christmas Eve dinner for Orthodox Christians and Catholics is symbolic on many levels. One of the unique dishes served during this meal is the *kutia,* a sweet grain pudding made from wheat, poppy seeds, honey, nuts, and dried fruit. In pagan times, *kutia* was made as a meal for dead ancestors. Today, during the Christmas Eve meal, a dish with *kutia* is set aside with a candle for those who have passed away. This practice has been preserved in diaspora communities as well as in Ukraine. Another element taking its roots from pre-Christian origins is the wheat *didukh,* a symbol of the grandfather, *did,* as the ancestral head of the family. Christians interpret the *didukh* as a symbol of the hay on which the baby Jesus lay in the manger. Traditionally, people also put hay beneath the table during the Christmas Eve meal, a special time during which it was believed that animals could talk.

The Pysanka Museum, built in 2000 in Kolomyia, Ivano-Frankivsk region (western Ukraine). Photo by Adriana Helbig.

Easter, in its pagan elements, features the tradition of *hahilky,* spring songs and dances performed by young girls. The songs have Christian and pagan texts and are strongly rooted in the symbolism of the passing of winter and the rebirth of spring. The Easter egg, *pysanka,* from the verb *pysaty,* "to write," heralds back to ancient times, when pagans worshiped Dazhboh, the sun god. The eggs were decorated with symbols from nature to symbolize the rebirth of spring using beeswax, and the eggs were dipped into various colors to create multicolored geometric and floral patterns and symbols. Variations in technique are evident in *maliovanky* (painted eggs), *drapanky* (etched eggs), and modern decorative eggs. *Pysanky,* in their Christian context, represent the rebirth of man, and it is considered good luck to receive a *pysanka.* The designs are interpreted as wishes for love, peace, health, and prosperity. Similarly to *pysanky,* embroidery, whether on wedding towels or as part of traditional dress, was also believed to protect the wearer from evil. Each of the colors and designs on a *vyshyvanka* (embroidery) has special significance and varies from region to region in Ukraine.

Many of the Christian holidays that marked the agricultural and spiritual calendar of peasants in particular (as these were tied closely to the land) were broken at the time of Soviet collectivization and particularly by the harsh policies of the Soviet government toward organized religion and religious beliefs. For instance, holidays such as St. John's Eve, known in Ukrainian as Ivana Kupala, which were preserved among diaspora Ukrainians in North American and Europe but lost among many Ukrainians who lived in Soviet

Ivana Kupala celebrations in Kyiv, July 6, 2008. Photo by Adriana Helbig.

Ukraine, have been revived in independent Ukraine. Ivana Kupala is now often celebrated during festivals organized in cities and villages on July 6. The holiday is associated with magic; herbs gathered during St. John's Eve were believed to have special healing powers. Young girls washed themselves with the dew that had fallen on the Eve of Kupalo and ran barefoot or rolled in the dewed meadows with the belief that this would make them fertile and help with childbearing. One of the main features of this holiday, usually celebrated alongside a river, is the belief that a girl will find her true love. She makes a wreath out of wild flowers and sets it afloat on the river. The young man who finds her wreath is believed to become her destined lover. Other rituals associated with Ivana Kupala include jumping across a fire with one's beloved—if both people jump successfully across the fire, it is believed that they will be together forever. The straw effigy of Maryna, the goddess of spring, is burned during the festivities. President Viktor Yushchenko and First Lady of Ukraine, Kateryna Chumachenko-Yushchenko, have participated in Ivana Kupala festivities in Kyiv. Wearing traditional Ukrainian embroidered shirts and jeans, their participation in revived rituals shows the complex postmodern layering of meanings that inform both religious and secular practices in contemporary postsocialist society. They also show that the relationship between politics, ethnic identity, religious beliefs, and practices continues to weave a complex fabric, as it has for centuries, in the territories of Ukraine.

NOTES

1. Catherine Wanner, *Communities of the Converted: Ukrainians and Global Evangelism* (Ithaca, NY: Cornell University Press, 2007), 1.

2. The first Christian in Kyivan Rus' was Prince Volodymyr's grandmother, Princess Olha, who was baptized in 955 in Constantinople. Her son Sviatoslav, father of Prince Volodymyr, remained a pagan. Volodymyr and Olha are canonized saints.

3. Serge Zenkovsky, *Medieval Russia's Epics, Chronicles, and Tales* (New York: E. P. Dutton, 1963), 66.

4. Ibid., 67–68.

5. Orest Subtelny, *Ukraine: A History,* 3rd ed. (Toronto: University of Toronto Press, 2000), 35.

6. Ibid.

7. Ibid., 39.

8. Ibid., 70.

9. Ibid., 73.

10. Ibid., 109.

11. Ibid., 113.

12. Natalie Kononenko, *Ukrainian Minstrels . . . and the Blind Shall Sing* (New York: M. E. Sharpe, 1998), 134.

13. Moshe Rosman, *Founder of Hasidism: A Quest for the Historical Ba'al Shem Tov* (Berkeley: University of California Press, 1996), 51.

14. Subtelny, *Ukraine: A History,* 124.

15. Subtelny, *Ukraine: A History,* 127–28. See also William Helmreich, Foreword in *The Abyss of Despair,* by Nathan Hanover, trans. Abraham Mesch (New Brunswick, NJ: Transaction, 1983).

16. Ibid., 276.

17. Ibid., 277.

18. Ibid.

19. Ibid.

20. Maryna Makhnonos, "Ukraine Marks Solemn 60th Anniversary of Babyn Yar Massacre," *Ukrainian Weekly,* October 7, 2001.

21. Subtelny, *Ukraine: A History,* 277.

22. Taras Kuzio, "The Struggle to Establish the World's Largest Orthodox Church," *Radio Free Europe/Radio Liberty Newsline, Part I* 4 (2000).

23. Larry Wolff, "The Uniate Church and the Partitions of Poland: Religious Survival in the Age of Enlightened Absolutism," *Harvard Ukrainian Studies* 26 (2002–2003): 172.

24. Ibid., 191.

25. Ibid., 156. Today, Pochaiv Lavra and the Kyievo-Pecherska Lavra (Kyivan Cave Monastery) are functioning monasteries of the Russian Orthodox Church–Moscow Patriarchate.

26. John-Paul Himka, "The Greek Catholic Church in Galicia, 1848–1914," *Harvard Ukrainian Studies* 26 (2002–2003): 245–60.

27. Ibid., 230.

28. Ibid., 246.

29. Wolff, "Uniate Church," 233.

30. Himka, "Greek Catholic Church," 255.

31. Ibid., 266.

32. Kuzio, "Struggle to Establish."

33. Wanner, *Communities of the Converted,* 4.

34. Ibid., 210–48.

35. Ibid., 91.

36. Greta Lynn Uehling, *Beyond Memory: The Crimean Tatars' Deportation and Return* (New York: Palgrave Macmillan, 2004), 33.

37. Subtelny, *Ukraine: A History,* 78.

38. Ibid., 41.

39. Ibid., 38.

40. Ibid., 42.

41. Ibid., 44.

42. Mariya Lesiv, "Glory to Dazhboh: Neopaganism in Ukraine and the Ukrainian Diaspora," paper presented at the 39th national convention of the American Association for the Advancement of Slavic Studies, New Orleans, LA, November 15–18, 2007.

43. Ibid., 7.

3

Language

LANGUAGE IS NOT only a means of communication, but also an indispensable part of personal and social identity. Given the importance of language, it is not surprising that language policies have been at the center of political struggle since time immemorial. Ethnic Ukrainians, whose lands were occupied by foreigners throughout history, repeatedly experienced both official and unofficial suppression of their language. Nevertheless, they kept their language and culture alive, along with the dream of self-determination and independence. This chapter focuses on how that dream was supported and suppressed through changing language policies throughout Ukrainian history.

Ukrainian is the state language of Ukraine, and it is one of the most widely spoken Slavic languages, along with Russian and Polish. Like other languages of the Slavic group, Ukrainian belongs to the Indo-European family of languages, the largest language family in the world. Although geographically, Ukrainian is classified as an Eastern Slavic language, it has a lot in common with Western Slavic and Southern Slavic subgroups. Within the boundaries of Ukraine, the Ukrainian language has three major dialect groups: northern, southwestern, and southeastern. The Ukrainian alphabet is a variation of the Cyrillic alphabet and consists of 33 letters that represent 38 phonemes, and an apostrophe that indicates the hardness of a sound, where otherwise the sound would be soft. The alphabet is primarily phonemic, which means that each letter corresponds to one phoneme.

The proto-Ukrainian language appeared between the sixth and mid-eleventh centuries A.D., when the Common Slavic–speaking tribes to the west of the middle basin of the Dnipro River developed speech features distinct from other Slavic dialects. The accumulation of these distinctive characteristics led to the emergence of the proto-Ukrainian language, which served as the foundation for the development of standard Ukrainian. Standard Ukrainian developed in three distinct stages, which are traditionally classified as Old, Middle, and Modern Ukrainian. Old Ukrainian coincides with the formation and disintegration of the Kyivan state in the tenth to fourteenth centuries. Middle Ukrainian is the language that was spoken from the fourteenth century until the eighteenth century. Finally, Modern Ukrainian is the language that evolved in the nineteenth to twentieth centuries.

Old Ukrainian is the language used in religious and scholarly writings as well as charters, chronicles, and private letters in Kyivan Rus'. The language of all these works is essentially the oldest literary Slavic language called Church Slavonic, with constantly increasing local phonetic, morphological, syntactical, and lexical additions. The concentration of literary life around religious centers kept the language relatively constant. Nevertheless, contact with the Byzantine Empire and the Turkic peoples of the steppe enriched Old Ukrainian with many new words. In the thirteenth to fourteenth centuries, rivalry among princes and the Mongol invasions led to the migration of a large part of the population of the central and northern parts of Kyivan Rus' to the west and the subsequent emergence of western and northwestern dialects.

The period associated with the development of Early Middle Ukrainian coincided with the incorporation of Ukrainian territories into the Grand Duchy of Lithuania and with the rise of the Cossacks. Crimean Tatar incursions pushed Ukrainians westward and northwestward. The Ukrainian language spread uniformly over a vast territory due to the influx of a large part of the Ukrainian-speaking population into a small region, their return to central Ukraine, and their subsequent expansion into southern and eastern territories. Although Ukraine was under Lithuanian rule, the influences of the Lithuanian language were rather insignificant. Polish, on the contrary, served not only as an active source for loanwords, but also as a channel through which Ukrainian borrowed from Latin, German, and Czech. Borrowings from these languages enriched Ukrainian administrative, cultural, and commercial terminology. This process, active for approximately 150 years, brought the Ukrainian vocabulary closer to that of west Slavic languages. Furthermore, many new words of Turkic origin, including military and commercial terms, appeared in the Ukrainian language as a result of regular encounters between Ukrainians and Crimean Tatars.

The Middle Ukrainian period spans from the consolidation of Polish rule in 1569 to the restriction of Ukrainian autonomy under Russian rule in 1720. The most important development during this time period was "the formation, on a vast territory, of a relatively uniform southeastern dialect, which later served as the foundation of Modern Standard Ukrainian."[1] The appearance of a uniform dialect owes to the intermingling of much of the population as a result of political turmoil and migration. By the end of this period the vocabulary, morphology, and syntax of the Ukrainian language were essentially identical to those of Modern Standard Ukrainian.

The southeastern dialectal base of Modern Standard Ukrainian entered scholarly writings in the mid-nineteenth century. However, this progress came to a halt due to a series of anti-Ukrainian decrees issued by the Russian government. These political developments shifted printing in the Ukrainian language to Austrian-ruled Galicia, where Ukrainian came under the strong influence of the local vernacular but maintained its use of the Cyrillic alphabet.

By the time the ban on the Ukrainian language was lifted in 1905, Standard Ukrainian had a synthetic character. When the time came to normalize and codify Standard Ukrainian, opinions diverged between supporters of the ethnographic approach, who advocated the adoption of the vernacular as the standard, and supporters of the school that took into consideration not only tradition, but also the development of the Ukrainian language. In the end, the latter approach gained the upper hand and determined the norms of Standard Ukrainian. Another salient issue was whether Ukrainian and Russian were two dialect systems of the same language, or two separate languages.[2]

Today, Ukrainian is a unified language with certain regional distinctions. The total number of words in contemporary Ukrainian is about 170,000.[3] Ukrainian is rich with loanwords, particularly from German, Polish, Turkish, and Tatar, as well as Europeanisms, including Greek or Latin components. The legacy of Church Slavonic is manifested in poetry and in religious writings. A new wave of loanwords comes from the English language, reflecting Ukraine's growing economy, increased migration, and exponential access to global media and culture since 1991.

HISTORY OF LANGUAGE POLICIES

The complex political history of Ukraine accounts for the language policies in its territories. Except for Ukraine's brief periods of independence, the status of the Ukrainian language was decided by foreign occupiers: the Lithuanians, the Poles, the Russians, the Austrians and the Hungarians, and the Romanians.

Following the disintegration of the Kyivan state, most of its lands were absorbed by the Grand Duchy of Lithuania. The language of the government in the Ukrainian lands was basically a mix of Belorussian and Ukrainian. In Galicia and the Kholm region, which became part of Poland, the language of the government was first Latin and later Polish, and therefore Ukrainian was virtually excluded from the government and the courts. In the lands ceded to Poland by Lithuania, the authorities also imposed the Polish language. Regardless of protests by the Ukrainian nobility, in 1696 the Polish Constitutional Sejm passed a law abolishing the use of Ukrainian in the government. Ukrainian continued to be used only by the church.

Similarly, the Russian authorities pursued a highly restrictive policy toward the Ukrainian language. In 1627–1628 the government ordered the confiscation and burning of books printed in Lithuania in the Ukrainian variant of Church Slavonic. Then, in 1684, all Ukrainian publications became subject to Russian censorship. In 1721 the Russian government forbade the printing of anything in Ukrainian. Only the printing of church books was allowed, though these had to follow Russian standards. Two decrees, issued in 1727 and 1728, enforced these restrictions. In 1735, books printed in Ukraine were banned from churches, and Ukrainians were instructed to follow the Russian pronunciation of Church Slavonic during religious services. In 1863 the Russian government issued a secret circular aiming to suppress the emerging Ukrainian literary language based on the vernacular. The government declared that there could not and would not be a distinct Ukrainian language and banned the printing of educational, scholarly, and religious works in Ukrainian. Equally important, 13 years later, the Russian government went further and issued the Ems Decree (Ems'kyi Ukaz), which banned the staging of Ukrainian plays and readings and the printing of religious, scholarly, and educational literature in Ukrainian. Ukrainian publications could not be held in libraries or imported from other countries. The only publications that were allowed to appear in print in Ukrainian were belles lettres and historical documents, though only in a modified Russian alphabet. At the end of the nineteenth century, censorship relaxed, but Ukrainian continued to be viewed merely as a dialect of the Russian language. A brief period of liberalization occurred after the 1905 Revolution. The publication of Ukrainian periodicals, books, dictionaries, and grammars was allowed, but censorship made publication difficult. In addition, the Ukrainian language continued to be banned from the courts, the church, and educational institutions. With the outbreak of World War I the authorities shut down the Ukrainian press and publishing houses.

In contrast, in the Austrian Empire, the status of the Ukrainian language in Galicia and Bukovyna improved. Nonetheless, despite the favorable policies of the Austrian government, the Ukrainian language played a secondary role. In Galicia, opposition to Ukrainian came from the Polish community. In Bukovyna, the Ukrainian language played a secondary role after German. Hungarian-ruled Transcarpathia was subject to an active process of Magyarization.

Under Ukrainian statehood, the status of the Ukrainian language continued to improve. After the February Revolution of 1917, Ukrainian became official in the government, the military, the courts, and public life. Furthermore, in January 1919, Ukrainian was proclaimed the official language of the Ukrainian National Republic. In the Western Ukrainian National Republic, the Ukrainian language also gained official status. However, Ukrainian governments were short-lived, and their efforts to Ukrainianize some spheres of public life were not particularly successful.

In western Ukraine, during the interwar period, the Poles tried to remove the Ukrainian language from the governmental and educational institutions, despite international agreements to respect the linguistic and cultural rights of Ukrainians. Accordingly, in 1924, Polish became the only official language of the republic. In the areas that were predominantly Ukrainian, Polish was the internal language in governmental institutions, but Ukrainian was also used to communicate with the Ukrainian population.

In Transcarpathia, Czechoslovak authorities allowed the use of Ukrainian in schools, the press, the courts, and the civil service, but in the 1930s the government began to lean toward the Russian language.

Bukovyna and Bessarabia experienced total Romanianization. In 1923 Romanian was declared the only official language, and Ukrainian was banned from the church, civil service, and educational institutions. Between 1929 and 1933, limited use of the Ukrainian language was allowed in elementary schools where Ukrainians were a majority.

Soviet language policies fluctuated. Vladimir Lenin (1870–1924) supported the free development of national languages, but the policy of indigenization was launched only in 1923. Ukrainianization brought the Ukrainian language to the government, the arts, science and education, and public life. Equally important, the Ukrainian language was standardized. However, the process of Russification that started in 1933 reversed many achievements of the previous decade. Ukrainian linguists were accused of separating the Ukrainian language from Russian, and the publication of Ukrainian language and linguistic studies came to a halt. Consequently, Russian became the dominant language everywhere, except in elementary schools and in rural areas. Exceptions were made in the more ethnically conscious regions of western Ukraine, where the Soviet government made concessions to gain popular support for its rule.

After World War II the Ukrainian language continued to be viewed as inferior to Russian. The latter was propagated as the language of interethnic communication in the Soviet Union and the language of Lenin. In urban and industrial centers Ukrainian regressed to the status it had under tsarist rule. At the same time, a law adopted in 1959 allowed parents to choose their child's language of instruction. The struggles of intellectuals in the 1960s and 1970s to gain higher status for the Ukrainian language were suppressed by the authorities. Many of these struggles were vocalized in the popular music and literature of the time. In 1978 the Soviet government passed a resolution aimed at intensifying the learning and teaching of the Russian language. However, in the 1980s, Soviet language policies came under increasing criticism, and in 1989 the Supreme Soviet of the Ukrainian Soviet Socialist Republic declared Ukraine the official language of the republic and set forth a plan for the Ukrainianization of all public institutions of Ukraine.

The 1989 law on languages was reiterated in the 1996 constitution, which, today, remains the principal legal instrument regulating language policies in contemporary Ukraine. Article 10 declares the Ukrainian language the state language of Ukraine and ensures the comprehensive development and functioning of the Ukrainian language in all spheres of social life throughout the territory of Ukraine. It also guarantees the free development, use, and protection of Russian and other languages of national minorities such as Crimean Tatars. Article 11 proclaims that the state promotes the consolidation and development of the Ukrainian nation; of its historical consciousness, traditions, and culture; and also of the ethnic, cultural, linguistic, and religious identity of all indigenous peoples and national minorities of Ukraine. Article 53 states that citizens who belong to national minorities are guaranteed, in accordance with the law, the right to receive instruction in their native language or to study their native language in state and communal educational establishments and through national cultural societies. Finally, Article 138 ensures the operation and development of the state language and national languages in the Autonomous Republic of Crimea.[4] In addition to these regulations, there are laws pertaining to language policies in self-government and judicial administration, education, broadcasting, and advertisement. Although language policies have been a source of tension throughout the postcommunist period, the majority of Ukraine's population, and particularly ethnic Ukrainians, are bilingual in Ukrainian and Russian.

INDEPENDENT UKRAINE

Since 1991, the government of newly independent Ukraine has pursued a policy of Ukrainianization in all spheres of public life. The linguistic issue,

together with Ukraine's political orientation, remains one of the most de-
bated topics in Ukrainian society. Political preferences largely coincide with
linguistic differences. For instance, the Ukrainian-speaking western regions
of Ukraine opt for closer ties with the West, whereas the Russian-speaking
east supports closer connections with Russia. The poles of this opposition
are the cities of L'viv and Donetsk. The absolute majority of L'viv residents
prefer to speak Ukrainian, whereas most Donetsk residents prefer to speak
Russian. Overall, the Ukrainian language is dominant in the western part of
the country and in rural areas across most of the country, whereas Russian is
prevalent in urban areas outside the western part and in the southeastern part
of the country. The labor market clearly favors Russian speakers,[5] and the
Russian language dominates in the business sphere, media, and in technical
professions.[6]

According to the 2001 census, 67.5 percent of Ukraine's citizens claim
Ukrainian as their native language, and 29.6 percent claim Russian. However, there is a clear tendency among scholars to single out the following
groups in the Ukrainian population: Ukrainian-speaking Ukrainians (40%),
Russian-speaking Ukrainians (33% to 34%), and Russian-speaking Russians
(20% to 21%).[7] The reason for the difference in numbers is the incongru-
ence between the concepts of ethnicity, declared mother tongue, and actual
language use. This phenomenon is a legacy of the Soviet concept of nationality, which posits that nationality owes its existence to a distinct language.[8]
Most Soviet citizens interpreted the category of native language as meaning
the language of the group with which someone identifies rather than the
language the individual chooses to speak on a daily basis. For instance, a
person who identifies as Ukrainian but grew up speaking Russian and prefers
to use Russian in daily communication could still claim Ukrainian as his or
her native language. This practice was common in the Soviet Union, and
it remained in the 2001 Ukrainian census.[9] Simultaneously, "people whose
passport certified them to be of 'Ukrainian' ethnic nationality, yet spoke Russian as their first language, would nevertheless associate 'Ukrainian' with their
ethnic identity, at least by force of habit."[10]

The concept of *ridna mova,* or native language, has a central place in Ukrainian nationalist ideology. *Ridna mova* is viewed as a biological phenomenon
transmitted from mother to child. It is shaped by the experiences of ancestors
and passes on the nation's unique world outlook to each new generation. An
"individual is seen to be socialized by a native language that provides him
with moral values and a world view that explain to him his place in time and
space."[11] Moreover, the individual has a moral obligation to protect the native language, and a failure to do so would threaten the language boundaries
of Ukraine.[12] Hence the Ukrainian language is considered to be the primary

marker of Ukrainian national identity, and the supporters of the current language policies view the privileged status of the Ukrainian language as a form of affirmative action.

Accordingly, the dominant nationalist premise in Ukraine is that the language of educational instruction is not a matter of choice, but rather of heritage.[13] Therefore the 1989 Language Law's main article on language of instruction in school, which states that "freedom of choice in the language of instruction in [elementary and secondary] schools is an inalienable right," has been mostly disregarded. Although only half of ethnic Ukrainians prefer to have their children taught in Ukrainian, the proportion of students enrolled in Russian-language schools is steadily falling,[14] which means that children of Russian speakers now learn more Ukrainian than Russian.[15]

Each major ethnic group in Ukraine expresses concerns regarding the status of their language, although with varying degrees of intensity. The status of the Russian language, however, remains one of the most controversial and politically salient topics. De-Russification of Ukraine's public life did not pose a threat to the ethnic minorities with reasonably high linguistic autonomy, such as the Poles, Hungarians, and Romanians, yet it did touch ethnic Russians, Belorussians, Russian-speaking Jews, and Russian-speaking Ukrainians.[16] In an annual survey conducted by the Institute of Sociology of the National Academy of Science of Ukraine in 2005, the number of persons claiming that they predominantly use Ukrainian peaked, and the number of persons claiming that they predominantly speak Russian jumped to its second highest level. These results illustrate the polarization made evident during the Orange Revolution and its aftermath.

The status of the Russian language is an issue that repeatedly gains prominence before elections. Nonetheless, despite the general dissatisfaction of the Russian-speaking population with the language policies of the Ukrainian government, political mobilization of Russian speakers over language issues remains rather weak. In fact, this lack of mobilization is not surprising. In practice, the use of the Russian language is widespread, and no one forbids speaking Russian. The Russian language is widely used by the private and public media. One of the most popular Ukrainian writers is the Russian-born Andrii Kurkov, who writes in Russian. Andrii Danylko, a pop star who is better known under his stage name Verka Serdiuchka, and who sings in a mix of Ukrainian and Russian, was the first to have a disc go platinum. However, though laws ensure the dissemination of the Ukrainian language in the public sphere, these language policies are not always put into practice. For instance, despite the 1993 law on national content and language use in broadcasting, a five-week monitoring of the musical content of the 17 largest commercial radio stations, conducted in 2005, revealed that the share of Ukrainian language music in their musical programs was, on average, less than 10 percent.[17] Some television talk shows have bilingual hosts but primetime television is predominantly in Russian with Ukrainian subtitles. Recently, a number of cities and *oblasts* in Ukraine gave the Russian language an official status in their territories, and other municipal and *oblast* councils are contemplating granting Russian the status of a regional language. Thus the Russian-speaking population would like to see Russian as a second official language mainly because this would show them that they count as much as Ukrainian speakers in Ukrainian politics. At the same time, considering the widespread use of the Russian language, it is not surprising that the defenders of the Ukrainian language believe that granting Russian an official status would undermine and completely overshadow the efforts to revitalize Ukrainian.

Many people, especially those residing in middle-size urban centers or rural areas, speak some combination of Ukrainian and Russian, so-called *surzhyk*. The original meaning of this word is "a mixture of rye and oats, which results in poor-quality bread." In its new meaning, *surzhyk* retains its pejorative connotation but is used to describe all nonstandard language varieties that dissolve the boundary between standard Ukrainian and standard Russian. *Surzhyk* emerged in the eighteenth century, when Ukrainian peasants came into contact with Russian speakers. Industrialization triggered a wave of migration from rural areas to industrial centers. Newly urbanized workers, associating industrialization and modernization with the Russian language, tried to incorporate Russian words into their speech. In contrast, Ukrainian was often associated with rural life and was therefore deemed obsolete.[18]

Contemporary nationalist language ideologists see the development of *surzhyk* as a result of Russian dominance and try to raise the linguistic awareness of Ukrainian speakers. One Ukrainian linguist argues that in a bilingual situation, it is the ability to differentiate between Ukrainian and Russian that decides the level of culture and education of an individual speaker.[19] Given these attitudes, it is hardly surprising that the choice of the *surzhyk*-speaking pop icon Verka Serdiuchka to represent Ukraine at 2007 Eurovision caused the indignation of people who feel that she "denigrates Ukrainian culture with a trashy image and mangling of the Ukrainian language."[20] With *surzhyk* being widespread in most parts of the country, Ukrainian linguistic purists, who have traditionally opted for variants different from Russian, emphasize the need for clear-cut boundaries between the two Slavic languages.[21]

In summary, language policies have been the most vocally discussed issue since independence. This debate is part of a broader discussion on Ukraine's political orientation: whether Ukraine should seek alliances in the East or the

West. While the official policies are oriented at strengthening the position of the Ukrainian language, and much has already been achieved, actual language use continues to reflect the diversity of Ukrainian society. Thus, as Ukraine has historically tried to balance the relationship between its eastern and western parts, the reality of independence has been marked by the coexistence of the Ukrainian and Russian languages.

Notes

1. Encyclopedia of Ukraine, "Ukrainian Language," http://www.encyclopediaofukraine.com/display.asp?AddButton=pages\U\K\Ukrainianlanguage.htm, para. 16.

2. Niklas Bernhand, "Surzhyk and National Identity in Ukrainian Nationalist Language Ideology," *Berlin Osteuropa Info* 17 (2001): 40.

3. Encyclopedia of Ukraine, "Ukrainian Language."

4. Constitution of Ukraine, http://www.rada.kiev.ua/const/conengl.htm.

5. Amelie Constant, Martin Kahanec, and Klaus F. Zimmerman, "The Russian-Ukrainian Earnings Divide," IZA Discussion Paper No. 2330, Bonn, Germany, September 2006, p. 22.

6. Council of Europe, *National Report on Ukraine* (Strasbourg, France: Council of Europe), 10.

7. Yaroslav Hrytsak, "National Identities in Post-Soviet Ukraine: The Case of L'viv and Donetsk," in *Cultures and Nations of Central and Eastern Europe: Essays in Honor of Roman Szporluk,* ed. Zvi Gitelman, Hajda Lubomyr, John-Paul Himka, and Roman Solchanyk (Cambridge, MA: Harvard Ukrainian Research Institute, 2000), 263.

8. Dominique Arel, "Introduction: Theorizing the Politics of Cultural Identities in Russia and Ukraine," in *Rebounding Identities: The Politics of Identity in Russia and Ukraine,* ed. D. Arel and B. Ruble (Washington, DC: Woodrow Wilson Press, 2006).

9. Dominique Arel, "Interpreting 'Nationality' and 'Language' in the 2001 Ukrainian Census," *Post-Soviet Affairs* 18 (2002): 213–49.

10. David I. Kertzer and Dominique Arel, "Censuses, Identity Formation, and the Struggle for Political Power," in *Census and Identity: The Politics of Race, Ethnicity and Language in National Censuses,* ed. D. Kertzer and D. Arel (Cambridge: Cambridge University Press, 2002), 5.

11. Bernhand, "Surzhyk and National Identity," 42.

12. Ibid., 43.

13. Arel, "Introduction."

14. Ibid.

15. Ibid.

16. Viktor Stepanenko, "Identities and Language Politics in Ukraine: The Challenges of Nation-State Building," in *Nation-building, Ethnicity and Language Politics in Transition Countries,* ed. François Grin and Farimah Daftary (Flensburg, Germany: European Center for Minority Issues, 2003), 107–36.

17. Oleh Protsyk, "Majority-Minority Relations in Ukraine," *Journal on Ethnopolitics and Minority Issues in Europe* (JEMIE), Vol. 7, issue 1 (2008).

18. Bernhand, "Surzhyk and National Identity," 41.

19. Ibid., 40.

20. Zenon Zawada and Maria Shevchuk, "Ukrainian Representative at Eurovision 2007 Is Pop Icon Verka Serduchka," *Ukrainian Weekly,* May 13, 2007, 11.

21. Bernhand, "Surzhyk and National Identity," 40.

4

Gender

Equality enjoyed by both men and women in family and at work, in community and in country must become a norm. The search for gender balance is a huge resource to harmonize all spheres of our life. That is not particularly women's business, as it affects us all.

—Kateryna Yushchenko's speech at the presentation of the textbook
The Fundamentals of Gender Theory (2005)

UKRAINIAN WOMEN WERE granted basic political and citizenship rights more than eight decades ago. Nevertheless, life for women in Ukraine has not yet reached a level of complete equality or empowerment. Today, the Ukrainian constitution guarantees equality between the sexes; however, even with these legislative achievements, women still lag behind men socially and financially. This chapter examines the struggle for women's rights in Ukraine, touching on the topics of women's social responsibilities, their opportunities within society, and issues that pertain to human trafficking, abortion, and gay rights.

WOMEN IN UKRAINE

The Soviet Union had an array of remarkable achievements to its credit regarding advancements in gender politics. The Bolsheviks came to power in 1917 with revolutionary ideas about women's roles and proclaimed and imposed gender egalitarianism from above. The Soviet state expected women to perform the roles of mother, full-time worker, and active citizen.[1] On one hand, the new ideologists fought the notion of the traditional bourgeois family. On the other hand, the Soviet state, which suffered massive population losses, was determined to industrialize in a short period of time and needed to boost labor force participation by attracting women. To support women's participation in the labor market, the Soviet state provided subsidies for child care, sick leave, and paid maternity leave for a period of up to three years. Thus women had equal access to health care, child care, education, employment, cafeterias, and laundries. Quotas guaranteed that women occupied a certain number of government positions. These policies led to high levels of women's literacy, educational attainment, and labor force participation. Reportedly, both literacy and participation in the labor force were close to 100 percent. Although the accuracy of these numbers is not confirmed, the general consensus is that the actual numbers were exceptionally high.

Despite these achievements, gender stereotypes lived on, and women were never on an equal footing with men, whether in family or professional life. The man was still believed to be the primary breadwinner and head of the household, and the woman was responsible for child rearing and domestic chores. Thus, in effect, women carried a double burden of both domestic and social duties. In addition to being solely responsible for child rearing and household chores, they also participated in the labor force, held decision-making positions, and earned money. As a result, Soviet women consistently reported less leisure time during the week than did men.[2] The burden that women had to bear kept them away from active participation in public life. In professional life, stereotypes about gender-appropriate occupations put constraints on career choices among men and women alike. For instance, under social pressure, men often opted against the spheres that were traditionally considered female, such as education or nursing.

Regarding their roles as active citizens, women, similar to men, could engage only in "officially condoned civic causes."[3] The only exception to this unwritten rule occurred in the late 1980s, when women became involved in the movement for national rights, religious tolerance, and freedom of conscience. The first women's organizations were the committees of soldier's mothers involved in draft-resistance campaigns. Following this movement, other organizations came together to advocate for cultural revival and moral change. Another wave of women's public activity was caused by the Chornobyl nuclear accident. Thousands of women mobilized to help the victims of the catastrophe and participated in environmental protests.[4]

With independence, men and women gained rights to express their views, pursue their interests, and participate in elections with relative freedom. However, women's public participation at the grassroots level declined after independence.[5]

While the Soviet Union left a rather mixed legacy, gender relations were greatly polarized during Ukraine's transition to capitalism. The social and economic problems that followed independence brought about insecurity in gender relations. Men, trapped in the stereotype of the primary breadwinner, responded with high rates of depression, substance abuse, alcoholism, violence, and suicide. This led to soaring rates of psychological and physical abuse against women. Accordingly, divorce rates soared, while marriage and birthrates plummeted.

Despite the economic turmoil that followed independence, women's levels of educational attainment and participation in the labor force today still remain remarkably high. However, even though Ukrainian women have higher educational levels than men, women tend to cluster in poorly paid professions and earn approximately 70 percent of men's pay.[6] At first glance the pay gap seems wide, yet it is smaller than the gaps within other countries, such as the United States or the Netherlands.[7] The biggest gender gap in pay persists in the financial sphere, while the smallest gap exists in agriculture, where salaries are generally much lower than in other sectors of the economy.

The persistent notion of separate professional spheres has contributed to the pay gap. Many occupations are, to a significant extent, segregated by sex. Men tend to dominate in defense, technology, industry, transportation, construction, and agriculture, while women dominate in education, health care, retail trade, and food processing as well as in social, legal, and financial services. It is important to note that although women hold the majority of jobs in these spheres, men are still primarily the business owners and therefore the ones who benefit the most professionally and financially.

Since independence, drastic changes occurred in the wage structure across different sectors of Ukraine's economy. Owing to the lasting gender stereotype that men, as the ones responsible for the financial well-being of their families, should earn more than women, the changes in wage structure reinforced professional segregation. For example, a decrease in teachers' salaries made the teaching profession almost exclusively female. Male teachers are extremely rare, and they are often regarded as professionally unsuccessful by society's standards. Simultaneously, salary growth transformed finance and banking into two of the most highly regarded fields. Although they were previously dominated by women in the Soviet Union, prestige and high incomes led to a massive influx of men into these careers.

Another reason for lower pay is the glass ceiling that prevents women from getting the highest executive positions, even if they have the relevant professional skills. More often than men, women stay in positions that demand lower professional skills and offer limited opportunities for professional and income growth. Surprisingly, even in the spheres dominated by women, women have difficulties being hired for better-paid managerial positions.

In addition to these setbacks, women experience greater discrimination in hiring, most often due to expected family obligations. Job classifieds often specify the potential candidate's sex and age, and it is hard for women past 40 to get a job. On the other hand, young female candidates might get hired for unimportant positions because employers assume they will become pregnant at some point and will have to leave their jobs. Accordingly, women are dismissed more often than men. Studies also show that many women experience sexual harassment at work. As a result, women are overrepresented in the informal sector, where they engage in noncontractual work. This work allows them to earn an income, but they are less likely to have a pension and other benefits. In the end, women often cannot make ends meet without family help, as their incomes are not enough to allow for self-sufficiency.

In addition to facing challenges socially and professionally, women in Ukraine have also had political setbacks. After the first elections in newly independent Ukraine, women filled only 3 percent of seats in Parliament.[8] In 2002, although one-fifth of parliamentary candidates were women, they filled only 5.1 percent of parliamentary seats, one of the lowest ratios of female representation in the region.[9] Women's representation in politics had seen higher ratios in the past. In marked contrast to today's political scene, in the Soviet period, the proportion of women in Parliament was 24 percent at its lowest level, in 1938.[10] On the eve of independence, women occupied 36 percent of seats in the Supreme Soviet of Ukraine and 50 percent on municipal councils.[11]

Women's participation in politics varies widely by region. In eastern Ukraine, women's level of political engagement is higher than in more rural western Ukraine, where traditional gender norms prevail and political power rests almost entirely with men. Accordingly, in the 2002 elections, the male-female ratio among parliamentary candidates in the eastern Donetsk region was 1 to 1.25, and in the western city of L'viv, it was 1 to 15.[12]

Women's representation in Ukraine diminishes as the levels of political influence and stature increase. For example, the proportion of women and men in the civil service sector is more or less equal. Yet while women constitute a majority at the lowest level of administration, the number of women holding high political office is negligible. This is particularly true at the national level. Yulia Tymoshenko, a key figure in Ukrainian politics, is a notable exception.

According to a recent study of Ukrainian mass media, the rate at which women in politics were reported in the media was even lower than the actual male to female ratio on the political scene. However, this finding was not limited to the political sphere. Men were much more likely to appear in the capacity of an expert, even in the spheres where women dominated, including education and health care. Women were also interviewed in the media several times less than men. Given women's high level of participation in the labor force, there is clearly a gender imbalance in the presentation of the social roles played by women and men. The reinforcement of gender stereotypes by the mass media remains a big problem.

On top of all the problems mentioned previously, women in the country-side face additional challenges. Patriarchal rural society is more demanding of them. The lack of infrastructure in rural areas, including electricity, running water, sanitation, health care, and educational facilities, affects women disproportionately, especially due to their role as domestic workers. As a rule, a woman in the countryside works in an agricultural enterprise, cultivates her private plot of land, does all the household chores, and maintains sole responsibility for child rearing and cooking. The situation has worsened since the collapse of collective farming, as the commercial enterprises established in the transition period can no longer cover the costs of child care and health care facilities.

Violence and Trafficking

As mentioned previously, the social and economic instability of the transition years led to high rates of depression and substance abuse, especially among men. This, in turn, led to increased levels of violence against women. Violence against women occurred in every social group, across all educational levels, and with or without substance abuse. Housing problems and extreme lack of shelter forced women to stay with their abusers. Patriarchal norms and fear of the abusive partner aggravated unsafe situations. Because so many women went through it, oftentimes, victims believed that their experiences were normal, and they were unwilling to report cases of violence to law enforcement authorities. Consequently, most cases of violence have gone unregistered, making domestic violence the most unreported crime.

Violence against women has taken other forms as well. Economic hardship and geographic location have made Ukraine highly vulnerable to human trafficking and forced labor. Many victims of trafficking are women who come from low-income families and need to provide financial support to their dependents. On the other hand, victims of trafficking appear to have weaker family ties. Pimps prey on 16-year-old teenagers newly released from orphanages.[13] Lack of opportunities at home as well as the attractiveness of Western incomes force many women to seek opportunities to leave the country. In a survey by the International Organization for Migration (IOM), the option "to find a better job" was given as the main reason for leaving the country, while Western lifestyles did not appear as significant pull factors.[14] Lacking foreign language skills, information on foreign job markets, and the financial resources necessary to cover visa and travel costs, women become easy prey to trafficking networks, which make migration appear trouble-free. Women seeking a better life are often misled by false information on migration laws and are offered work as housemaids, nannies, waitresses, models, or dancers. Their travel is organized through travel agencies.

The key recruitment channels have been acquaintances and advertisements in the mass media. A study of Ukrainian newspapers demonstrated that each newspaper carried 5 to 20 doubtful advertisements,[15] for example, "A well-paid job abroad for a respectable agency" or "Single, tall and pretty? Want to work abroad as model, choreographer, or gymnast?"[16] In addition, women have been recruited by marriage agencies, at photo studios, and at auditions. Still, because a recruiter receives between $200 and $5,000 for each woman, acquaintances end up as the primary recruitment channel.[17] A most disturbing phenomenon is the so-called second wave, when a victim returns home and recruits other women. An IOM study revealed that some women who fell prey to fraud and deception are ready to go abroad again,[18] which reflects their bleak prospects at home.

Sadly, most victims do not realize that they will be forced into prostitution until after their arrival at their destinations, where they become subject to violence, debt bondage, and confiscation of travel documents. Servicing hundreds of clients, women suffer from sexually transmitted infections, injuries from violence, and even torture, depression, and substance abuse. Victims often do not seek help because of their mistrust of public authorities, which developed in their home country, and because of blackmail by pimps. Some pimps have even been reported to pose as policemen.[19] In the end, if and when discovered by the police, victims of trafficking are most often treated as criminals, either for prostitution or for breaking immigration laws. Victims of trafficking are arrested or detained pending deportation, with almost no services available to assist them. This experience contributes to the women's trauma.[20]

The full scale of the problem remains unknown due both to the fear of social stigma that makes trafficking victims reluctant to share their stories and to the secrecy that surrounds the transnational trade of human beings. However, available data put numbers in the hundreds of thousands. The Ukrainian Ministry of the Interior estimated in 1998 that 400,000 women had been trafficked from the country during the preceding decade, and the IOM estimated that 500,000 women had been trafficked between 1991 and 1998.[21] Independent research and nongovernmental organizations place the actual numbers much higher. Nevertheless, even available numbers position Ukraine as one of the major suppliers of global commercial sex markets.

International attention has recently been drawn to the tragedy of sexual slavery. Victor Malarek's book *The Natashas: Inside the New Global Sex Trade* (2003) and David Cronenberg's movie *Eastern Promises* (2007) have helped to uncover and expose the sex industry. The film, starring Viggo Mortensen, Naomi Watts, and Vincent Cassel, tells the story of a British midwife (Naomi Watts) who unravels a human trafficking gang when she seeks relatives of a sex slave baby named Tatiana. The book by the Canadian journalist Victor Malarek provides a more in-depth portrayal of the global sex trade. Malarek, who spent years researching the trafficking of women from Eastern Europe to expose an international human rights tragedy of epic proportions, tells the story of a young, unemployed Ukrainian woman named Marika. An employment agency informs Marika that a waitress position has been arranged for her in Tel Aviv. Marika flies to Egypt, from where Bedouins transport her across the desert to her destination country. On arrival, Marika learns that she has been purchased for $10,000 and that she needs to pay off a $20,000 debt by working as a prostitute. Marika stays in a locked apartment with a guard in the hallway and, over four months, services hundreds of "soldiers, husbands, and religious men."[22] Marika's story is only one of many thousands of stories of shattered lives.

Feminism

The pioneers of Ukrainian feminism were outstanding nineteenth- and twentieth-century literary figures and public intellectuals, among them Natalia Kobrynska, Olena Pchilka, Lesia Ukrainka, and Olha Kobylianska. Each of these prominent intellectuals popularized feminist ideas through her writings. Natalia Kobrynska devoted much energy to fighting for women's educational opportunities, communal kitchens, and day care centers. She spearheaded the notion of equality between the sexes, and the title of one of her short stories, "The Spirit of Time" (1884), became symbolic of the new feminist movement. Olena Pchilka wrote the novel *Women Friends,* about the emancipation of womanhood. In 1887 Pchilka and Kobrynska edited and published the almanac *Pershyi vinok* (The First Garland), a pioneering collection of works by women of letters from eastern and western Ukraine. The almanac became one of the first publications in Europe to be produced by women. What may come as a surprise is that two other feminists, Lesia Ukrainka and Olha Kobylianska, were deeply influenced by the apparently misogynist philosophy of Friedrich Nietzsche. Kobylianska's female protagonists were strong, self-sufficient characters, and her men were feeble. At the time, "the very attempt to show a man who was inadequate in his social role was a serious challenge to the patriarchal norm."[23] The women portrayed by Ukrainka and Kobylianska dream of free love, but at the same time, they show "fundamental fear of any relationship with a man, a terror of patriarchal confines."[24] In Kobylianska's philosophy, satisfaction from a physical relationship with a man is a woman's essential right.[25]

The prominent modern-day feminist and writer Solomea Pavlychko wrote that Kobylianska's early works were "programmatically" and inherently feminist and frightened men.[26] A cofounder of the Society of Ruthenian Women in Bukovyna, Kobylianska made a speech called "On the Idea of the Women's Movement." At the time, women still were confined to traditional marriages and had no opportunities for a formal career. In turn, female writers experienced social neglect. Portraying the lives of their contemporaries, feminists called for action to address the plight of Ukrainian women and to raise their status in society.

The feminists of modern literature are undoubtedly Solomea Pavlychko and Oksana Zabuzhko. Pavlychko is noted, in part, for revitalizing the feminist consciousness in Ukrainian literature. Zabuzhko writes on a wide range of themes, spanning from erotica to politics, with a critical view of men running as a thread through all her works.

A woman looks at an advertising billboard with the cover of *Korrespondent* magazine depicting Ukraine's Prime Minister Yulia Tymoshenko as "Person of the Year 2007" in Kyiv. SERGEI SUPINSKY/AFP/Getty Images.

Despite many efforts to change the status of Ukrainian women, changing cultural attitudes requires time. In contemporary Ukraine, women are viewed as mothers and sex symbols, the latter being perhaps a reaction to the repression of sex-related themes in Soviet popular culture. Since the early 1990s, pornography has become readily accessible, and women are socially expected to accent their physique through fashion. Politicians usually turn their attention to women's issues twice a year—on International Women's Day and on Mothers' Day—and women are celebrated as wives and mothers.

A top political figure, Yulia Tymoshenko has revolutionized the notion of womanhood in Ukraine. Wearing the hairstyle of *Berehynia* (Hearth Mother), a female spirit in Slavic mythology who, since independence, has been transformed to symbolize the guardian of the Ukrainian nation, Tymoshenko mediates between the female as nurturer, sex symbol, tough politician, and savvy businesswoman.

ABORTION

The history of current abortion legislation in Ukraine begins with Vladimir Lenin (1870–1924), who viewed abortion as a woman's basic right and believed that no woman should bear a child against her will. Joseph Stalin (1879–1953), who considered population growth to be an engine of economic growth, forbade abortion, except in special cases, such as danger to the mother's life or health or hereditary disease.

In 1955, two years after Stalin's death, the Soviet Ministry of Health made abortion legal again, though state ideology continued to treat "childrearing as a woman's primary mission in life."[27] People were encouraged to marry young, but at the same time, they were not taught about contraception, which made abortion a popular method of birth control and led to high levels of infertility.[28]

The newly independent Ukraine inherited the Soviet abortion law. Abortion rates were quite high, mainly due to inadequate family planning services and a lack of awareness. In 1995 the level of abortions in Ukraine was close to 4 times higher than in the United States. A survey published in 1999 demonstrated that almost 40 percent of all women aged 15 to 44 had had at least one abortion, and 18 percent had had at least two abortions.[29] In 2003 the Ministry of Health reported that there were 72.8 abortions per 100 live births.[30]

In recent years, Ukraine has witnessed a growing antiabortion movement, especially among religious denominations, scientists, and teachers.[31] As a consequence of awareness campaigns, abortion rates are in decline. Perhaps the most significant decrease has been in abortions among teenage women.[32]

Yet even with falling abortion rates, Ukraine's birthrate remains below two children per woman, which, if it stays at this level, will eventually lead to a decline in population.

In response to the looming demographic crisis, exacerbated by a massive out-migration to the West, the Ukrainian government has undertaken measures to increase the population. These measures include financial incentives and appeals to the younger generation to have children. Young women receive considerable sums of money to have babies, and a husband's masculinity is judged in part by his number of children.

HOMOSEXUALITY

In the Soviet Union, homosexuality was penalized under law, and the disclosure of one's homosexual orientation could lead to social ostracism, forced medical treatment, and even imprisonment. However, soon after independence, the Ukrainian Parliament decriminalized homosexuality.

Although Ukraine is one of the more progressive former Soviet republics in matters concerning homosexuality, the overall social attitude toward nonheterosexual behavior, whether homosexual, bisexual, or transsexual, is unsympathetic at best. Nevertheless, the acceptance of homosexuality in Ukrainian society is clearly increasing, albeit slowly.

The First Ukraine International Lesbian and Gay Conference convened in 2000 in Kyiv. There are a few gay bars and nightclubs, gay Web sites, and a few gay and lesbian publications. The gay magazine *One of Us* is distributed through subscription and is sold in kiosks all over Ukraine. In September 2003 a small gay pride demonstration was held in the Ukrainian capital. Elton John performed a free charity concert in 2007 on Kyiv's Independence Square in support of Ukrainian children suffering from AIDS. This performance stirred controversy, with the Union of Orthodox Ukrainians stating that holding Elton John's concert would be blasphemous.[33] The concert was still a huge success, bringing together 200,000 people, including President Viktor Yushchenko, former President Leonid Kuchma, and other top public figures.[34] It was an important step in raising HIV/AIDS awareness in Ukraine, which has the most severe AIDS epidemic in Europe.[35]

Like elsewhere, tolerance toward homosexuality is higher in large urban centers than in the countryside. Accordingly, Kyiv and Kharkiv, Ukraine's two largest cities, have the most developed gay infrastructures. In addition, homosexuals from all over the former Soviet Union come to the resort town of Simeiz, known for decades as the homosexual capital of Ukraine. Still, even in Kyiv, homosexuals steer clear of openly gay behavior. Many homosexuals find each other through classified ads, thereby avoiding the public eye.

SUMMARY

Almost two decades into independence, Ukrainian women and men continue to redefine their roles in personal and public life. While Ukrainian women share many of the same challenges women all over the world face, they can build on a history of active participation in society. This foundation makes their struggles unique, yet no less deserving of attention. As can be seen, even with the existence of vocational opportunities and formal political equality, in reality, women still do not enjoy the ability to compete for positions of status or rank. Men are also adjusting to new socioeconomic realities, as is reflected in the men's health crisis. A clear transformation in social attitudes is appearing in the increasing acceptance of homosexuality. This higher acceptance in turn precipitates increased opportunities for conversation and awareness about formerly social taboos, such as HIV/AIDS. Movements in sexuality and in issues of abortion confirm that change is evidently happening not only in the economic and political spheres, but also in the ways in which men and women relate to each other.

NOTES

1. Alexandra Hrycak, "The Dilemmas of Civic Revival: Ukrainian Women since Independence," *Journal of Ukrainian Studies* 26 (2001): 135.

2. Nora Dudwick, Radhika Srinivasan, and Jeanine Braithwaite, *Ukraine: Gender Review* (Washington, DC: World Bank, 2002), 25.

3. Hrycak, "Dilemmas," 135.

4. Ibid., 136.

5. Ibid.

6. Dudwick et al., *Ukraine: Gender Review,* 30.

7. Ibid.

8. United Nations Development Programme, *Gender Issues in Ukraine: Challenges and Opportunities* (Kyiv: United Nations Development Programme, 2003), 10.

9. Ibid., 9.

10. Ibid.

11. Dudwick et al., *Ukraine: Gender Review,* 59.

12. United Nations Development Programme, *Gender Issues,* 10.

13. "Slave Trade Endures into the Twenty-first Century," *San Francisco Chronicle,* July 2, 2000, 8.

14. International Organization for Migration, Information Campaign against Trafficking of Women from Ukraine, research report, July 1998, 9.

15. Dona Hughes, "The 'Natasha' Trade: The Transnational Shadow Market of Trafficking in Women." Published under the rubric "In the Shadows: Promoting Prosperity or Undermining Stability?" *Journal of International Affairs.* Vol. 53, No. 2 Spring 2000, pp. 625–51.

16. International Organization for Migration, Information Campaign, 16.

17. Hughes, "In the Shadows."

18. International Organization for Migration, Information Campaign, 17.

19. Ibid., 15.

20. Hughes, "In the Shadows."

21. Ibid.

22. Patrick Belser, *Forced Labour and Human Trafficking: Estimating the Profits* (Geneva, Switzerland: International Labor Organization, 2005), 1.

23. Solomea Pavlychko, "Modernism vs. Populism in Fin de Siècle Ukrainian Literature: A Case of Gender Conflict," in *Engendering Slavic Literatures,* ed. Pamela Chester and Sibelan Forrester (Bloomington: Indiana University Press, 1996), 10.

24. Ibid.

25. Ibid., 12.

26. Ibid., 13.

27. Hrycak, "Dilemmas," 138.

28. Ibid., 139.

29. Oleh Wolowyna, "Abortion in Ukraine: A Health Crisis," *Ukrainian Weekly,* September 3, 2000.

30. United Nations Population Fund, *Country Programme Document for Ukraine,* Rep. DP/FPA/DCP/UKR/1, October 18, 2005.

31. Tamara Govorun and Borys M. Vornyk, "Contraception, Abortion, and Population Planning," http://www2.hu-berlin.de/sexology/IES/ukraine.html#9.

32. http://www.podrobnosti.ua/health/2005/03/17/188273.html.

33. "Elton John's Free Concert in Kiev May Destroy Ukrainian Society with Its Gay Propaganda," *Pravda,* July 6, 2007, http://english.pravda.ru/society/show biz/07-06-2007/92958-orthodox_elton_john-0.

34. ABC News, "Elton John Rocks for Charity in Kiev," June 17, 2007, http://www.abc.net.au/news/stories/2007/06/17/1953467.htm.

35. World Health Organization, "Update: Ukraine," December 2006, http://www.who.int/globalatlas/predefinedReports/EFS2006/EFS_PDFs/EFS2006_UA.pdf.

5

Education

UKRAINE'S HISTORY OF education spans a millennium, from the intellectual advances in Kyivan Rus' to the Bologna process initiated in 1999. Throughout each century, this history remained closely intertwined with politics, religious influences, and language policies. Education administration was greatly dependent on the interests of those in power and varied widely by region. Foreign occupiers influenced education policy, jeopardized Ukrainian cultural integrity, and put the very survival of Ukrainian culture at stake. Today, Ukraine is an independent nation-state experiencing a cultural revival reflected in the Ukrainianization of the country's educational content. Simultaneously, this newly independent state recognizes that success depends largely on the quality of its educational system. Asserting a place in the information age, Ukraine is introducing ambitious reforms expected to improve the quality of education and to bring it closer in tune with European educational structures.

KYIVAN RUS'

The emergence of education and literacy in Kyivan Rus' was linked with the acceptance of Christianity and the introduction of Cyrillic script. As elsewhere, education and literacy were initially privileges of the elite. The clergy were educated at Episcopal cathedrals, and the nobility were taught at home by private teachers. Knowledge of foreign languages was highly appreciated in princely courts, and an ideal European monarch was expected to speak five languages. Prince Volodymyr the Great required children of the elite to attend school and to learn how to read. His son, Prince Yaroslav the Wise, provided stipends for the clergy to teach reading and writing in the church. These efforts helped minimize illiteracy rates among city dwellers. While church bookmen used Greek in their daily work, Galician-Volhynian rulers in western Ukrainian lands used Latin, an early sign of Western European influence on education. Despite efforts to educate the general population, the Kyivan state did not leave a strong education structure, and the collapse of Kyivan Rus' led to a decline in educational activities.

MID-FOURTEENTH TO EIGHTEENTH CENTURIES

Although it was still limited in scope, basic education eventually became accessible to a broader range of people. Wealthier families could hire private tutors, and the rest of the general population slowly gained access to elementary education through a network of parochial schools. However, a lack of educational institutions on a higher level forced many aspiring students to continue their studies abroad, most often at the Latin universities in Krakow and Prague or in Western Europe.

The sixteenth and seventeenth centuries saw a rapid spread of Protestant and Catholic schools, in particular, those founded by the Jesuit order. While Calvinist schools taught in Polish, German, or Latin, Jesuit colleges instructed in Polish and Latin and taught Ukrainian as a subject. The Jesuit order founded colleges and academies throughout Ukrainian territories. Jesuit schools consisted of two levels, including a lower level with five grades and a higher level with two grades. The Ukrainian nobility often sent their sons to Jesuit colleges, and many Ukrainian clergy were graduates of Jesuit seminaries. Through Jesuit schools, many Ukrainians were converted to Roman Catholicism.

Striving to counteract the denationalizing influence of other churches, the Orthodox Church made efforts to improve the quality of its own educational institutions. One of the most prominent schools was the Ostroh Academy, established in 1576 under the leadership of the writer Herasym Smotrytsky. A bastion of the Orthodox faith, the school had an enduring influence on education and was transformed into the Ostroh National Academy in 2000.

The Ostroh Academy became a model for brotherhood schools. The first school of this kind was established by the L'viv Dormition Brotherhood in 1586. It was governed by school statutes and articles of law and also served as a model for other brotherhood schools in the Polish-Lithuanian Commonwealth. Brotherhood schools were open to students from all social strata and judged students by performance, rather than by lineage. This included orphaned and poor students living in student residencies and *bursas*. The Kyiv Epiphany Brotherhood School was founded in 1615 and later merged with the school established at the Kyievo-Pecherska Lavra (Kyivan Cave Monastery) by Metropolitan Petro Mohyla. This school became the first Ukrainian institution of higher learning and eventually developed into the famous Kyiv Mohyla Academy. In the beginning, teachers in brotherhood schools lectured in Church Slavonic and taught Greek as a second language. Greek teachers were brought from Greece, and brotherhood schools received strong support from Greek patriarchs, which explains why brotherhood schools were also called "Greek schools." However, by the mid-seventeenth century, the Greek language was fully replaced by Polish and Latin. Ukrainian was used only for examinations and later for teaching the catechism. In addition to languages, these schools taught dialectics, poetics, rhetoric, homiletics, church singing, arithmetic, geometry, and astronomy. Brotherhood schools were the first to publish Church Slavonic and Ukrainian grammar books and contributed to the growth of national and religious consciousness, and the Ukrainian culture in general.

The leading center of education in the seventeenth to eighteenth centuries was the Kyivan Academy, which appeared as a result of a merger between the Kyiv Epiphany Brotherhood School and the Kyivan Cave Monastery School. Petro Mohyla established the school in 1632 and sought to apply the intellectual thought of contemporary Europe to the defense of the Orthodox faith. Mohyla conceived the new institution as an academy capable of teaching philosophy and theology, while supervising a network of secondary schools. The Orthodox academy would compete with Polish academies run by the Jesuit order. In response, the Polish authorities prohibited the academy to teach philosophy and theology and gave it a status equal to a secondary school. In 1694 the institution received full privileges of an academy, and in 1701 Peter the Great recognized it officially as an academy. The structure, teaching methods, and curriculum emulated those of Jesuit schools, and with the support of the progressive clergy, Latin and Polish were instituted as the languages of instruction. A typical student would start with a five-year program based on a liberal arts curriculum, designed to develop public speaking skills, rather than instill merely fact-based knowledge. The student would then continue with a three-year higher education program in philosophy and, finally, a four-year program in theology. Many accomplished Ukrainian authors and churchmen served on the faculty of the Kyivan Academy, and many of its graduates continued their education in European universities.

The 1667 Treaty of Andrusovo, a truce signed between the Duchy of Muscovy and the Polish-Lithuanian Commonwealth, acknowledged Russia's control over Left Bank Ukraine and led to the emigration of many leading scholars to Muscovy. As a result of this emigration, brotherhood schools and the Kyivan Academy experienced a decline. In the Hetmanate, where Orthodox academies endured years of fluctuating success, two important schools were established in Chernihiv and Pereiaslav. In addition, the Hetmanate had a strong network of parochial schools financially supported through contributions collected by students. Nonetheless, the educational establishment with the most modern program of the time was the Kharkiv College, established in 1727 in Sloboda (free) Ukraine.

In Right Bank Ukraine, still under Polish control, the influence of the Orthodox Church at the turn of the eighteenth century declined. In response to this decline, the Uniate Church undertook efforts to expand its reach and assumed responsibility for education. The Uniates established a seminary, where Church Slavonic and Ruthenian served as the languages of instruction, in addition to Latin. In eastern Transcarpathia, the church was allowed to set up schools and teach Church Slavonic, Greek, Latin, Hebrew, and other languages. Uniate educational institutions emulated the Jesuit model of education.

END OF THE EIGHTEENTH CENTURY TO WORLD WAR I

After Russia annexed Right Bank Ukraine in 1793–1795, Polish schools continued to function until the Polish uprising of 1830. After this uprising, Polish schools were replaced by Russian schools. In 1804, four-year gymnasiums were established in gubernatorial centers and placed under the jurisdiction of universities. The secondary education system also included boarding schools, cadet schools in Kyiv and Poltava, and finishing institutes for daughters of the nobility in Kyiv, Kharkiv, Poltava, Odesa, and other cities. Rather than send their children to Russian schools, peasants preferred having their children taught by a *diak,* a layman in Ukrainian Orthodox and Catholic churches who assisted with church services and taught reading and writing. In the 1820s, some landowners set up Lancastrian schools for their serfs. These schools were modeled on the educational system developed by Joseph Lancaster, where advanced students taught less advanced students, enabling a small number of adult masters to educate large numbers of students at a low cost.

The institutions of higher learning consisted of universities and lyceums. The first university in Russian-ruled Ukraine was established in 1805 in Kharkiv, and the second almost three decades later in Kyiv. The most prominent lyceums were the Richelieu Lyceum established in 1817 in Odesa and the Nizhen Lyceum established in 1825.

The death of Nicholas I in 1855 and the end of his restrictive policies for Ukrainian schools was followed by the rapid development of Sunday schools. Classes in these schools were taught in Ukrainian and, because of a shortage of Ukrainian textbooks, in Russian. In 1862, however, the Russian authorities closed down the Sunday schools, and a year later, a circular of the Minister of Internal Affairs prohibited the publication of books in Ukrainian. A new system of elementary education was introduced in 1864. It consisted of one- and two-classroom schools under the jurisdiction of the Ministry of Education, literacy schools under the authority of the Holy Synod, and three-year parochial schools.

Zemstvo schools, organized by self-governing bodies, provided elementary education at first, and later expanded to include secondary and vocational schools. These institutions were established after the tsarist agrarian reforms of 1864 and existed until 1917. There were over 4,000 *zemstvo* schools by World War I. The efforts to introduce Ukrainian into *zemstvo* schools were unsuccessful, as the government did not trust them for ideology and instead provided support to more primitive parochial schools. Besides *zemstvo* schools, reestablished Sunday schools continued to serve as important educational institutions. These schools provided tuition-free general and vocational education. Technical institutions of higher learning, including polytechnic and veterinary schools, began to appear in the 1870s.

The first training school for teachers in Russian-ruled Ukraine was the Provisional Pedagogical School, founded in Kyiv around 1862. The first pedagogical seminary was opened 7 years later, and a pedagogical institute 12 years later. Pedagogical institutes had a higher standard of education than seminaries. On the eve of the 1917 Revolution, there were 33 seminaries for teachers and 8 pedagogical institutes.

The first Ukrainian student organization was founded at Kyiv University in 1895. After the 1905 Revolution, and due to the influence of student *hromadas* (organizations), some professors began to lecture in Ukrainian, though they were soon forbidden to do so. Although on the eve of the revolution the number of Ukrainian student organizations was approaching two dozen, most of these were underground.

Extramural education and literacy societies spread in the late nineteenth century. Public readings in Russian were organized in Poltava in 1861, but later, their success fluctuated. In 1898 Ukrainians living in St. Petersburg founded the Philanthropic Society for Publishing Generally Useful and Inexpensive Books, which published autodidactic materials in Ukrainian.

Kuban had separate Russian schools for Cossacks and non-Cossacks. Only the former were free. Instruction in Ukrainian was introduced in 1917, but only in the elementary schools. Two Ukrainian gymnasiums were opened and two seminaries for teachers were Ukrainianized, but most schools remained Russian.

Galicia

In Galicia, Austria's annexation in 1772 put a temporary halt to the Po-lonization of schools. The authorities introduced three types of state-run schools: the six-grade normal school, the four-grade major school, and the trivium school. While six- and four-year schools taught in German, most trivium schools taught in Polish and Ruthenian. Trivium schools pro-vided the most accessible elementary education; urban-based schools taught in German.

In 1774 Empress Maria-Theresa founded the Barbareum, a seminary for Greek Catholic priests. In addition to systematic theological educa-tion, the Barbareum provided a way to expose young Galician priesthood candidates to Western culture.[1] Seven years later, Joseph II, a despotic but enlightened ruler, introduced compulsory universal education for all lo-calities with 100 residents of school age. Landowners, who in Galicia were mostly Poles, became the caretakers of these schools, which were supple-mented by the state treasury. Five gymnasiums teaching in Latin opened their doors, and soon only the graduates of these gymnasiums could qualify for the priesthood.

In 1783 a Greek Catholic theological seminary opened in L'viv. L'viv Uni-versity followed suit, adding Latin to its languages of instruction. For those priesthood candidates who did not read Latin, a temporary institute, the Studium Ruthenium, was established at L'viv University. Another important clerical institution, the L'viv Dormition Brotherhood, was reorganized into the Stauropegion Institute, a prominent cultural and educational center that had its own printing press, bindery, and bookstore. It published textbooks for elementary and secondary schools and the Studium Ruthenium ran a school and a dormitory.

The death of Joseph II in 1790 brought about a decline in his educational policies. Greek Catholic priests were barred from teaching religion in public schools, L'viv University was demoted to a lyceum, compulsory universal ed-ucation was repealed, and trivium schools teaching in Ruthenian were closed down. This decline lasted until 1817, when L'viv University was reopened with German as the language of instruction. In the same year, a group of churchmen in Peremyshl founded an institute for sextons and teachers. As a result of their efforts, the government accepted the idea of school instruction in Ruthenian and entrusted the Ukrainian schools to the Greek Catholic clergy. The Peremyshl group began the publication of Slavonic Ruthenian textbooks.

An important new development was the appearance of Halytsko-Ruska Matytsia, an educational and literary society based on Serbian and Czech models. It was established by the Supreme Ruthenian Council in L'viv in 1848. The society promoted the cultural and educational development of Galicia through the publication of books. A year later, the chair of Ruthenian literature was established at L'viv University. H. Shashkevych, chairman of the Department of Galician Public Schools and Gymnasiums of the Education Ministry in Vienna, was a prominent contributor to the development of Ukrainian scholarly terminology.

In 1855 Franz Joseph I placed the schools under the supervision of the consistories, which gave the Greek Catholic consistory in L'viv a greater voice in the running of Ukrainian schools. A year later, the Ukrainian language was no longer a compulsory subject in the secondary school system, and in 1867, when the Poles took over the control of Galicia, instruction in Ukrainian became considerably restricted. Although six years of schooling became compulsory for all children, most villages could afford only one- or two-grade schools. Although on the eve of World War I, 97 percent of Ukrainian children in Galicia attended Ukrainian-language schools, educational opportunities were still very limited, and one-third of the population over the age of nine was illiterate.

In the same year, the Provincial School Board, consisting of four Poles and one Ukrainian, was established in L'viv, and the German language was replaced by Polish in secondary schools and at L'viv University. Ukrainian could be used as a language of instruction only in the lower grades of the Academic Gymnasium in L'viv. Six years of schooling became compulsory for all children.

A highly influential association, the Prosvita Society, was founded in 1868 in L'viv with the goal to preserve and develop Ukrainian education and culture. In 1869, education was separated from the church, although the Uniate Church continued to influence educational policy. The two languages of Galicia—Polish and Ukrainian—became mandatory for the faculty members of L'viv University in 1871. Despite the newly introduced regulations, the university remained Polish speaking.

On the eve of World War I, two-thirds of elementary schools in the Ukrainian part of Galicia were Ukrainian, and virtually all Ukrainian children attended Ukrainian schools. Although one- and two-grade schools dominated in Ukrainian villages, there were also a few Ukrainian language four-grade schools and two private Ukrainian senior elementary schools for girls. As for gymnasiums, there were only six state eight-grade classical Ukrainian gymnasiums. Thus, whereas the Poles in Galicia had one gymnasium per 60,000 inhabitants, the Ukrainians only had one per 500,000. All teacher's seminaries were bilingual. There were no state Ukrainian vocational schools. In response, the Ruthenian Pedagogical Society (1881) and the Provincial School Union (1910) set up private Ukrainian schools. Thus, prior to World War I, there were 16 private Ukrainian elementary schools and 13 secondary schools, including 9 gymnasiums, 3 teacher's seminaries, and 1 lyceum.

The Galician student movement, which dated back to the Theology Students Association formed in L'viv in 1830, experienced a rapid expansion toward the end of the nineteenth century. Ukrainians were unhappy with the Polish domination of postsecondary education. L'viv University had the highest percentage of Ukrainian staff, but Ukrainian professors comprised only 10 percent of the faculty. By 1916, as a result of student protests, the Austrian authorities agreed to found a Ukrainian university, but the project came to a halt due to the war.

Bukovyna

In Bukovyna, educational opportunities before the Austrian annexation were limited to the monasteries providing instruction to candidates for priesthood. Under Austrian rule, Bukovyna generally followed the Galician educational model. The Ukrainian language was first taught at the German gymnasium in Chernivtsi in 1851. The German Chernivtsi University, established in 1875, had three Ukrainian chairs: in language, literature, and theology. The Ruska Shkola educational society was founded in 1887 and published school textbooks and the newspaper *Ruska shkola.*

Elementary schools teaching in Ukrainian spread slowly in towns because much of Bukovyna's urban population was Jewish and supported German schools. In 1896, there were 165 Ukrainian state-supported schools, including 34 bilingual Ukrainian-German and Ukrainian-Romanian schools. In the same year, Ukrainian or Ukrainian-German gymnasiums were opened in several towns. A private Ukrainian teacher's seminary for women was founded in Chernivtsi in 1907, and a Ukrainian-language division was set up at the state teacher's seminary three years later.

On the whole, Ukrainian schools in Bukovyna were more successful than in Galicia because the Austrian authorities did not favor the Romanians as they favored the Poles. By 1910–1911 Bukovyna had 224 Ukrainian schools, compared to 177 Romanian, 82 German, 12 Polish, and 8 Hungarian schools. Ukrainian schools were supervised by Ukrainians.

Transcarpathia

In Transcarpathia, the bishops laid the foundation for a strong educational system, but the death of Bishop Andrii Bachynsky in 1809 led to the interruption in state support for Ukrainian schools and their consequent decline.

Efforts to improve Ukrainian education were undertaken by Bishop N. Popovych of Mukachiv; O. Dukhnovych, the author of the first primer written in the vernacular; and O. Dobriansky, the founder of the Society of St. Basil the Great, which published schoolbooks.

The establishment of the Austro-Hungarian Empire in 1867 led to the Magyarization of Transcarpathia. The Ruthenian language remained only as a subject and was replaced by Hungarian as the language of instruction. Early on, the Ruthenian language remained the language of instruction in parochial schools, but the 1907 law introduced by the Hungarian minister of education left only bilingual Ruthenian-Hungarian schools. The education policy of the Austro-Hungarian Empire led to an illiteracy rate of 60 percent in Transcarpathia, which undermined the educational progress achieved previously.

1917–1939

In 1917–1921, several Ukrainian and foreign authorities assumed responsibility for education. The Soviet government banned religious instruction and, with a view to industrialize the country, placed emphasis on technical education. Access to education, including higher education, improved greatly. The first congress of Ukrainian teachers convened in Kyiv. A Ukrainian Pedagogical Academy was founded, alongside a number of Ukrainian schools and institutions of higher education. The newly founded Society of School Education began to develop and publish Ukrainian textbooks. As a result of the Soviet policy of indigenization adopted by the Bolsheviks after the revolution, Ukrainianization swept the Ukrainian Soviet Socialist Republic (SSR) and its educational system. This policy was more successful in rural areas, where, by 1925, 82 percent of schools became Ukrainian speaking.

By 1926–1927, more than 9 out of 10 rectors of institutions of higher learning were members of the Communist Party, and various measures were applied to the educational system to strengthen political control: two-year programs at special departments for workers (*robitfaky*) were geared toward the creation of politically reliable cadres, and many vocational schools came under the jurisdiction of various branches of industry. In 1929 the language of instruction in most *robitfaky* was Ukrainian, and more than half of their students were members of the Communist Youth League of Ukraine or the Communist Party. Institutes of people's education, which sprawled across Ukraine, were geared toward preparing political agitators and teachers. Less than one-third of these institutes taught in Ukrainian.

A four-grade school became compulsory by 1925 and a seven-grade school by 1930 in urban areas. Primary and secondary education was free, except for the children of merchants, clergy, and well-to-do peasants. Most vocational schools charged tuition, but children of poor peasants and workers were exempt.

In 1928, technical education in the Union of Soviet Socialist Republics was standardized, and *tekhnikums* were reduced to the status of secondary schools. Ukrainians were underrepresented in vocational schools, and in 1929–1930, at a time when Ukraine's population was 80 percent Ukrainian, Ukrainians accounted for only half of the enrollment. Continuous changes in the educational system and teaching methods had an adverse effect on higher education, and very few students actually graduated.

The cultural society Prosvita was very active in the early years of Soviet rule but was dissolved in 1922. Some of its branches were transformed into Soviet cultural institutions such as village centers and reading houses. A literacy program, initiated in 1921, was implemented through a network of educational centers that conducted compulsory reading lessons for adults up to the age of 50. The illiteracy rate dropped from 36 percent to 12 percent between 1926 and 1939.

The policy of Ukrainianization came to an end in 1933, and the proportion of Ukrainian students and enrollment levels in Ukrainian schools started to decline. In 1936, institutions of higher learning were brought under the Committee for Higher Education in Moscow. The People's Commissariat of Education of the Ukrainian SSR remained in charge only of the lower and secondary schools, preschool education, and some *tekhnikums.* The history of Ukraine was no longer taught as a subject in secondary schools, and a positive view of tsarist imperialist policies again dominated history curricula. In 1938 Russian became compulsory at all levels of schooling. Less than half of institutions of higher learning used Ukrainian as a language of instruction.

Ukrainian Territories under Poland

Galicia, occupied by Poland in 1919, joined a unified system of education and administration for all Polish lands. Although six, and later, seven years of schooling were compulsory, the proportion of children enrolled in schools in Ukrainian territories as well as the number of seven-grade elementary schools were slightly lower than the average for Poland as a whole. In 1924 Poland introduced a law that required that Polish and Ukrainian schools in certain areas be unified into bilingual schools and that the language of instruction in specific areas be decided through referenda. However, as the Polish teachers and the Polish language became dominant, large numbers of Ukrainian teachers were either dismissed or transferred to Polish territories. By 1939 the number of Ukrainian schools in Galicia dropped from 2,420 in 1922 to 352 and in Volhynia from 443 in 1923 to 8.[2] At the beginning of the 1930s, all eight teacher's seminaries were closed down. Ukrainian was no longer taught as a subject in schools, and in some regions, the teaching of Ukrainian was forbidden. Only 7 percent of Ukrainian children could attend Ukrainian schools by the late 1930s. The only state-supported Ukrainian gymnasiums were those that remained from the time of Austrian rule. In 1926 the Ridna Shkola society assumed responsibility for all matters pertaining to Ukrainian education in Galicia. Ridna Shkola's efforts led to an increase in the number of Ukrainian secondary schools and raised school standards.

Although the Polish government was obliged by an international agreement to establish a Ukrainian university by 1924, it did not honor this agreement. Ukrainian university courses organized in L'viv were banned by the Polish authorities and continued to function clandestinely as the underground L'viv Ukrainian University until 1925. The L'viv Ukrainian Higher Polytechnic School functioned in a similar way until 1925. The dissolution in 1925 of the Ukrainian underground schools forced Ukrainians to attend Polish educational institutions, yet the number of Ukrainians admitted into these institutions was limited. The only Ukrainian school of higher learning recognized by the Polish authorities was the Greek Catholic Theological Academy in L'viv, established in 1928. At different times and in different areas, Ridna Shkola, Prosvita, and the Ridna Khata educational societies worked to developed Ukrainian schools, but their efforts were not supported by the Polish authorities.

Transcarpathia

Transcarpathia was incorporated into the Czechoslovak Republic in 1919, which led to positive developments in education. Between 1916 and 1938, the number of Ukrainian elementary schools increased from 34 to 492,[3] and Ukrainian education institutions became a majority. With the founding of short-lived autonomous Carpathian Ruthenia (Karpats'ka Ukrayina) in 1938, the School Administration in Uzhhorod was turned into the Ministry of Education.

Bukovyna and Bessarabia

In Bukovyna, the Romanians imposed a state of emergency and began to Romanianize the Ukrainian schools. The government lifted the state of emergency only in 1928 and for the following five years allowed the partial use of Ukrainian as the language of instruction in the Romanian schools of Bukovyna. At the same time, Bessarabia enjoyed greater educational autonomy.

WORLD WAR II

The Soviet annexation of Western Ukraine in 1939 resulted in the provisional extension of the Soviet educational system to Galicia, Volhynia, northern Bukovyna, and Bessarabia. In Hungarian-ruled Transcarpathia, the number of Ruthenian schools decreased considerably. At the same time, the Ukrainian territories incorporated into the *Generalgouvernement*[4] had a wide network of schools teaching in Ukrainian. In 1941, there were over 900 Ukrainian schools, administered by the Ukrainian Central Committee in Krakow and the Ukrainian Teachers Union. Over 4,000 elementary schools teaching in Ukrainian functioned in the *Generalgouvernement* after the incorporation of eastern Galicia in 1941. In 1942–1944, there were 12 gymnasiums and 9 teacher's seminaries, none of which had existed under the Polish regime. At L'viv Technical Institute and at state vocational schools, classes were taught in German, although most students were Ukrainian. As for the territory of the *Reichskommissariat* Ukraine, the German regime did not allow Ukrainian general schools above the fourth grade, with some vocational schools being an exception to the rule.

The Soviet government established 71 Ukrainian schools for Ukrainian evacuees in the Russian Soviet Federative Socialist Republic and 64 Ukrainian schools in Kazakhstan. In the meantime, 32 institutions of higher learning were evacuated from the Ukrainian SSR and continued to function as separate establishments. Evening schools, called "schools for working youth" in urban localities and "schools for peasant youth" in rural areas, were established in 1943–1944 for young people deprived of educational opportunities during the war period.

1945 TO INDEPENDENCE

In the aftermath of the war, the Soviet system of education was geared toward eliminating labor shortages. Accordingly, there was a rapid increase in the number of vocational correspondence schools, night schools, and other educational opportunities for adults. At the same time, the number of institutions of higher learning dropped. Almost half of students in Soviet Ukraine were enrolled in correspondence schools or night schools and worked the rest of the time. At one point, following Nikita Khrushchev's reforms, the proportion of full-time students dropped to one-third. Industrial occupations, engineering, and the military were a priority, whereas the importance of social sciences and humanities decreased further, creating a sharp contrast between achievements in science and the humanities. A limited number of students were enrolled in finance, economics, and law.

The Soviet government stated that two-thirds of teachers in the newly incorporated western Ukraine were unqualified to teach in Soviet schools. These teachers had to go through ideological retraining that would weaken their nationalist, anti-Soviet spirit. In addition, within six years after the war,

A secondary school classroom in Lviv, Ukraine, where 11-year-old students are studying foreign literature. Jeff Greenberg/Art Directors & Trip Photo Library.

about 35,000 teachers were brought to western Ukraine from eastern Ukraine. Owing to the demographic changes during the war, western Ukraine had the highest percentage of Ukrainian schools. Most of the educational institutions created initially taught in Ukrainian, but by 1952 they were forced to switch to Russian.

A number of changes were introduced to the educational system in the 1950s. To help parents stay active in the labor force, the government established fee-charging boarding schools and extended-day schools, where children could stay longer during the day. The education reforms of 1959 introduced 8-year compulsory schools and 11-year general education labor-polytechnic schools. Secondary school graduates, with the exception of the top 20 percent, were obliged to spend a minimum of two years in the labor force before applying for university study. The Ukrainian language and literature were no longer compulsory subjects in the Russian schools of the Ukrainian SSR.

Another practice introduced in the Soviet Union was called "distribution." University graduates were sent to work in places far from their hometowns. On one hand, the state introduced professional distribution to modernize the countryside, and on the other hand, it was done to break bonds of tradition. Graduates of universities and vocational schools were obliged to work for three years wherever they were assigned, oftentimes outside of Ukraine. Most students received monthly stipends, but the Communist Youth League had the right to increase or decrease the amount. In the late 1960s Ukraine had 25 percent fewer students per 10,000 inhabitants than Russia. In 1974 a secret order was issued requiring that no more than one-fourth of the freshman class at universities in western Ukraine be drawn from the local population. Political dissent grew among students in the 1960s–1970s and was repeatedly suppressed.

Some prominent characteristics of the Soviet educational system were its central planning and administration, uniform requirements, and the absence of private institutions. The Ministry of Education of the Soviet Union developed policies and determined the curriculum and its content. In the institutions of higher learning, all students, regardless of their major, were obliged to study Marxist-Leninist philosophy, the history of the Communist Party and the Soviet Union, political economy, scientific communism, scientific atheism, Marxist-Leninist ethics and esthetics, and a foreign language.[5] The notion of the collective was the cornerstone of the educational theory. The primary goal of education was to develop a so-called new socialist personality that would build a communist society.

TRANSITION YEARS

The newly independent Ukraine inherited the Soviet system of education with all its strengths and weaknesses. Education was accessible to all, but the content was encyclopedic and not oriented toward the development of critical thinking and other essential competencies. As elsewhere in the Soviet Union, there was a strong focus on the sciences, and little emphasis was placed on the humanities and social sciences. Virtually all subjects were compulsory, and subject-based knowledge was taught with little focus on broad competencies such as decision-making, management, teamwork, and conflict resolution skills. The learning process was based on the excessive memorization of facts. The academic curriculum lagged behind the requirements of the new labor market. Vocational education lost its relevance, and general education had a strong focus on the elite. Consequently, in the early years of independence, the educational content was overloaded with frequent reviews of textbooks.

The Ukrainianization of the curriculum and the development of humanities and social sciences became the cornerstone of the transformation process. The old ideological material was removed, and new material was incorporated, including much of what was excluded during the Soviet era. Textbooks on Ukrainian history were dramatically improved and expanded. Literature textbooks were replenished with works by previously unknown Ukrainian writers, and Russian literature was moved to a foreign literature section. Programs in history, philosophy, economics, law, sociology, and religious studies were revised, and new subjects, including civic education and environment, were introduced. Foreign language study was introduced during the second year of primary school.

The Constitution of Ukraine and Ukrainian law define what languages of instruction are to be used in educational institutions. The number of educational institutions teaching in Ukrainian has increased considerably since independence. In support of cultural rights of different linguistic groups, Ukraine has educational institutions teaching in Russian, Romanian, Hungarian, Crimean Tatar, and Polish in the areas of compact residence of these minority groups.

Today, the Ukrainian educational system includes preschool, general secondary education, and higher education, with postgraduate and doctoral programs. There is a developed network of institutions offering extracurricular activities, vocational training, and continuous education. The leading institution in education management is the Ministry of Education and Science of Ukraine, which is assisted by the Supreme Certification Commission and the State Accreditation Commission. For every second child in Ukraine, education starts with preschool. A network of crèches and kindergartens created during Soviet times helps parents stay active in the labor force, although this network does not function as well as it did before independence. Preschool is followed by general secondary education, which begins at the age of six and has recently made a transition to the 12-year model. Regular schools generally have neighborhood units assigned to them, while specialized schools, gymnasia, and lyceums, as a rule, have no neighborhood units assigned and may admit students from the entire city. One in five schoolchildren is also enrolled in an institution providing extracurricular activities. General secondary education is followed by vocational training or higher education. Vocational schools train students in two or more related professional areas, which is designed to facilitate future employment. Vocational schools carry an important social function, as many of their students come from underprivileged backgrounds. Most students in these schools are male. Higher educational institutions offer full-time, part-time, and distance learning. The number of university students per 10,000 inhabitants has increased from 170 to 190 during the years of independence.[6] In addition, Ukraine has a well-developed system of in-service training departments. In-service education is beneficial in a transitional society like Ukraine because it is market-oriented and more flexible in response to rapid changes in social, economic, and technological conditions. Distance learning is successfully developing and improving, alongside with the development of information technologies.

The state guarantees that its citizens have the right to education in state educational institutions free of charge, regardless of gender, race, ethnic group, social and financial status, specialization, philosophy, party membership, religious preferences, state of health, and place of residence. It also guarantees the right of each citizen to obtain full general secondary education. Legal instruments adopted during independence have become the foundation for the development of new curricula and educational content:

the content should be based on common human values and scientific principles, intercultural approaches, secular character of education, integrated system principles, unity of education and training, human, democratic and civic values, tolerance among nations and nationalities in the interests of an individual, family, society and state.[7]

In spite of the existing laws, there has been a slight drop in enrollment and educational attainment since independence. Enrollment is decreasing at the primary level and is low at the upper secondary level.

A number of serious problems in education persist. As a result of the economic problems experienced by Ukraine since independence, the funding for education has been insufficient, and teacher salaries are inadequately low (see Table 5.1). The average pay of workers in education-related fields is between 1.5 and 2 times less than the subsistence minimum and is 2.5 times less than provided for by effective legislation. Inadequate incomes result in the loss of professional motivation and deteriorating performance.

Given the existing conditions, the teaching profession has lost much of its prestige. Teachers are forced to take additional jobs in education or in an unrelated field to supplement their income. The most qualified and

Table 5.1
Dynamics of Teachers' Incomes between 1996 and 2001

	1996	1997	1998	1999	2000	2001
Average teacher income in Ukraine as a percentage of the average income in Ukraine	94	88	84	79	67	72
Average teacher income in Ukraine as a percentage of the average income in industry	77	72	70	65	50	53

Source: From Ministry of Education and Science of Ukraine, *Reform Strategy for Education in Ukraine: Educational Policy Recommendations* (Kyiv: KIS, 2003), 146.

promising young professionals leave educational institutions for companies that can provide better pay. As a result, the average teacher age is increasing, turnover is high, and pedagogical staff are lacking at every level.

In addition to the decreasing popularity of the teaching profession, a lack of efficiency has reduced the amount of time teachers spend with students. Usually, a teacher stays at school only for lessons and not during the entire workweek. A study conducted by the Organization for Economic Cooperation and Development (OECD) demonstrated that Ukrainian teachers work 17 percent fewer hours annually than the average for OECD countries.

Education quality has also been compromised by a lack of teaching aids, equipment, and quality textbooks. Despite relatively high prices, textbooks are visually unattractive, overloaded with material, and their content often does not meet acceptable standards.

One Soviet legacy is the existence of elite general secondary schools in most cities. Enrollment in these schools was not highly competitive, which allowed children living in the same neighborhood to study there. These schools offered intensive instruction in certain subjects, with a primary focus on foreign languages. The elimination of the Iron Curtain and the opportunity to communicate openly with other countries made foreign language study vital. A network of specialized schools with emphasis on early foreign language study began to grow as a result of these changes.

After Ukraine gained independence, different types of general secondary school emerged, including gymnasia, lyceums, and different types of private schools. Elite school costs rose due to the increased number of school hours per week in standard classes and to classes being split into groups. Smaller class sizes meant that funds could be injected into the development of the school and teaching processes. Often, parents provided additional funds on a private basis. This resulted in an increase in the cost of education in these schools in comparison with ordinary schools. The difference in the cost of education is determined by the types of curricula. As a rule, instruction in specialized schools, gymnasia, and lyceums is based on a six-day-week curriculum, and ordinary schools are based on a five-day week. Additional fees are paid if classes are split into two groups for more intensive study in certain subjects. In addition, these schools tend to have a larger number of staff members, with an additional deputy principal, a laboratory assistant, and, in some gymnasia, a class counselor and mentor positions.

In addition to financial complications, other challenges are created by the selective approach adopted by elite secondary schools for enrolling children. As previously noted, the closed entrance examination procedures followed by the majority of elite schools make it difficult for children from low-income families to gain access to education in these schools. The current educational system increasingly favors privileged urban populations in the financially better off parts of the country. These populations are better able to access higher-quality upper secondary general education and enroll at tertiary institutions. The result is a contrast between privileged groups, who continue to progress through elite secondary programs and move on to higher education, and less privileged groups of students dropping out of school with incomplete secondary education or less. This trend exacerbates existing socioeconomic inequalities. Above all, finding a solution to this problem should contribute to the consolidation of Ukrainian society and the realization of the key principle of the National Doctrine for the Development of Education: equal access to a high standard of education. Equal access to quality education will in turn help the development of Ukraine's human capital.

The current quality assurance and monitoring mechanisms in the educational system have proved ineffective and are undergoing reform. In the domain of higher education, the accreditation of all institutions is the responsibility of the Ministry of Education and Science, which determines official knowledge standards for each subject and minimum financial, material, and technical requirements. The accreditation and licensing processes suffer from a lack of transparency. As a result, many private higher education institutions have sprawled out across the country since independence. Unlike many state higher education institutions, private institutions are quite flexible, are better adjusted to the market, and offer new and trendy majors such as business, management, law, economics, and international relations. The quality of education in these institutions, however, is often low, and it is sometimes argued that they simply provide diplomas for tuition. At the same time, large, established institutions are always in demand and do not have incentives to innovate. Admissions, grading, and learning processes are often riddled with bribery. Institutions vary widely in the way they select students because there is no standard system of admission.

The increase in returns from education in Ukraine is very slow, and this is especially palpable in comparison with neighboring Russia, which, for many years, shared institutions and policies. In 2002 the estimated returns from schooling in Ukraine were 2 times less than in Russia. The likely reasons for these low returns are a lower demand for educated labor, limited labor mobility, higher separation costs, and the larger role played by trade unions in Ukraine.[8]

In 2002 Ukraine introduced the National Doctrine for the Development of Education, the country's first attempt at an educational development strategy for the next quarter century. The doctrine, suggesting new policies in education, science, and intellectual property, lays the groundwork for an innovative educational model that aims to raise a generation of young people possessing the knowledge, skills, and competencies essential for lifelong learning and competitiveness in the international job market.

Most important, with the increased reality of international mobility and with the European Union a direct neighbor, Ukraine is now a participant in the Bologna process, a European reform process that aims to standardize academic degrees throughout Europe by 2010. The three priorities of the Bologna reforms are the introduction of a three-cycle higher education system divided into baccalaureate, masters, and doctoral studies; quality assurance; and recognition of qualifications and periods of study. In addition, the Bologna process aims to decentralize the higher education system, to develop new financial mechanisms, and to give more academic freedom to students and faculty. This transformation aims to facilitate international mobility, attract non-European students to European universities, and assure a broad, high-quality, and advanced knowledge base as well as further development of Europe as a stable and tolerant community. Ukraine's decision to join the European Higher Education Area is a significant step toward the modernization of its national educational system, integration into the information society, and full participation in the European community.

NOTES

1. T. Mackiw, "150 Years Ago: The Ukrainian National Awakening in Halychyna," *Ukrainian Weekly,* November 8, 1998.

2. Volodymyr Kubijovyc, ed., *Ukraine: A Concise Encyclopaedia* (Toronto: University of Toronto Press, 1963), 158.

3. Ibid., 801.

4. The general government (*Generalgouvernement*) refers to a part of the territories of Poland under German military occupation (that were occupied in September 1939) during World War II by Nazi Germany but not directly annexed to the Third Reich.

5. Nobuo Shimahara, Ivan Z. Holowinsky, and Saundra Tomlinson-Clarke, eds., *Ethnicity, Race, and Nationality in Education: A Global Perspective* (Mahwah, NJ: Lawrence Erlbaum Associates, 2001), 221.

6. Speech by M. Zhgurovsky, Minister of Education of Ukraine at World Conference on Higher Education, United Nations Education, Scientific, and Cultural Organization, Paris, October 5–9, 1998.

7. Ministry of Education and Science of Ukraine, *Reform Strategy for Education in Ukraine: Educational Policy Recommendations* (Kyiv: KIS, 2003), 17.

8. Yuriy Gorodnichenko and Klara Sabirianova Peter, "Returns to Schooling in Russia and Ukraine: A Semiparametric Approach to Cross-Country Comparative Analysis," *Journal of Comparative Economics* 32 (2005): 346.

6

Customs, Holidays, and Cuisine

UKRAINIAN DAILY HABITS, attitudes toward family and community, celebrations, and holidays are a dynamic and complex mix of historical tradition, necessity, and aspirations for the future. Ukrainian customs trace their origins back to pre-Christian, Orthodox, and Catholic traditions as well as the country's geopolitical position on the crossroads of Eastern and Western cultures. Ukraine is a modern European country with a daily cosmopolitan rhythm firmly rooted in the past.

CUSTOMS

The overall impression of visitors to Ukraine is that its people are very hospitable and welcoming, though not always at first glance. On the street Ukrainians do not smile often or much, in particular to strangers. They are, however, ready and eager hosts. In Ukrainian everyday life, visiting family and friends is the main form of social interaction. Exchanging visits and socializing at home is an expression of caring for one's family, friends, neighbors, and guests. Traditionally, bread and salt were offered to guests, with bread symbolizing the cultural permanence of Ukrainian hospitality derived from its rich soil and salt a promise of enduring friendship. When guests were offered bread and salt by their host, tradition required them to break a piece of bread, dip it in the salt, and eat it, after lightly bowing in thanks. Today, the phrase "to greet with bread and salt" in Ukrainian is used to describe a heartfelt and generous reception of guests without an actual offering of bread and salt.

Ukrainians place great emphasis on community and family. Traditionally, individuality has not been a highly praised quality. Ukrainian values of community are rooted in centuries of working together and cooperating with family, neighbors, and villagers in farming the land, producing food, and surviving hard times. Moreover, decades of conformism, fostered during the Soviet era, reinforced positive values in the idea of belonging to community and society, a necessary mechanism for cultural and individual survival in contexts of political and economic transition and uncertainty. More recently, growing Western influences, particularly the emphasis on consumerism and material culture promoted in the media, are changing the traditional Ukrainian orientation away from community and the fear of sticking out and toward individual accomplishment. Ukrainian sense of community has translated well among the diaspora in the West. North American Ukrainian communities in particular reflect and foster this spirit through numerous groups, societies, organizations, and associations that work to preserve Ukrainian culture and traditions and organize the communities politically.

As an extension of the Ukrainian focus on community and sharing, there is generally less sense of the boundaries of personal space than in more reserved and individualistic cultures in the West. Ukrainians tend to stand closer to each other when they speak, and it is not uncommon for people to bump or brush against each other when walking down the street or standing in (an often disorderly) line. Ultimately, there is always room for one more person at a Ukrainian dinner table or an already packed means of transportation. This sense of reduced space and tighter quarters is partly based in the traditional Ukrainian cohabitation of several generations living under the same roof in villages and working together in the fields. In the past, sharing living quarters with extended family was a function of necessity and survival. In Soviet times and in more recent years, housing shortages and dire economic circumstances compelled many urban Ukrainians to divide their small living spaces among two, or often three, generations. With an increasing number of people moving from villages to the cities after independence, housing in cities such as Kyiv has become particularly expensive. It is common for close friends to be treated like family, while having more casual acquaintances is not as frequent. With an invitation for coffee or dinner, Ukrainians will gladly open up their homes to guests, whether they are family, lifelong friends, or visitors. Everyday socializing typically happens over food and drink, even if only over coffee. Ukrainians most often visit each other at home, spending time eating, drinking, toasting, joking, and chatting about family, children, and life in general.

Food in Ukraine is considered a tradition and an opportunity to spend time
with loved ones, as much as it is a necessity. Ukrainians generally prefer to eat
at home when possible: breakfast between 7:00 A.M. and 10:00 A.M., lunch
(or dinner) between noon and 3:00 P.M., and supper between 5:00 P.M. and
8:00 P.M. With the exception of the wealthier class, restaurants are reserved for
special occasions. Traditionally, lunch is the main meal of the day, but with
increasingly demanding work schedules, it is getting harder for urban professionals to eat a hearty meal in the middle of the day. A range of Ukrainian-
style fast food places have arisen to accommodate this need. In spite of this,
Ukrainians still primarily value the quality and freshness of their food. For
most, soaring food prices are an important consideration.[1] Much of the
everyday food is still purchased at the local market (*bazar*). These markets
offer a larger selection of fresher and better-quality food than most shops or
supermarkets in urban areas. In the past, markets were not only places for
trading goods, but they were also the heart of the town. Still today, these
assemblies of merchants selling fresh fruits and vegetables, meats (fresh and
cured), pickled goods, preserves, dairy products, and flowers are not so much
shops as they are events. Going to the market is a necessity, a daily or weekly

Women shopping at a vegetable stall in a market in Kyiv. Michael O'Brien/Art
Directors & Trip Photo Library.

routine, and/or a pastime for virtually every Ukrainian homemaker, working mother, housekeeper, grandmother, and family member. Most major cities have central markets, such as the Bessarabka Market, which is the oldest and best known in Kyiv.

The Ukrainian sense of community and inclusion has easily extended to their fellow Ukrainians, though foreigners have historically been looked upon with a degree of suspicion and caution. For decades, most ordinary Ukrainians have had minimal contact with foreigners because of the Soviet government's restrictions on travel. Since Ukrainian independence, particularly in the last several years, an influx of foreigners eager to take advantage of business opportunities and wishing to explore countries of the former Soviet Union as tourists has positioned foreigners as relatively common in Ukrainian everyday life, particularly in cities. Many aspects of Ukrainian life, ranging from business, travel, and education to popular culture, music, and film, have been, for better or worse, permeated by foreign influences. Accordingly, attitudes of Ukrainians toward foreigners have evolved from caution to curiosity and now mainly focus on cultural and business exchange.

While also evolving in a positive direction, the relationship between ethnic Ukrainians and the largest minorities in Ukraine has been complicated and, at times, conflicting. In areas where the Russian minority exhibits a lesser degree of cohesion and regional concentration, namely, in western Ukraine, they are exposed to varying degrees of social discrimination. Similarly, ethnic Ukrainians, particularly from western Ukraine, experience such discrimination in larger cities in eastern and southern Ukraine. Such dynamics are being addressed through conventional political action. Crimean Tatars, an ethnic minority with a strong group identity and regional concentration, enjoy a significant degree of political representation due to their geographic concentration in Crimea, the only region of Ukraine granted autonomous status. The Jewish minority, historically and at present the second largest ethnic minority in Ukrainian lands, has, throughout history, experienced bouts of repression, persecution, and anti-Semitism. Today, some discrimination on a small scale still occurs, though compared to some other transitional post-communist countries, there is relatively little neo-fascist activity.[2] Notably, increasing involvement of minorities in political life as well as legislative initiatives such as the 1992 Law on National Minorities, hailed as one of best in the region by the Council of Europe, have helped change popular attitudes toward minorities and have increasingly encouraged stronger inclusion and tolerance.[3]

The breakup of the Soviet Union and subsequent transition years caused significant political, economic, and social tribulations, which, over the last decade and a half, have profoundly altered the lives of Ukraine's citizens.

Communist ideology was built on the premise that the government provides for all citizens, particularly those in need, especially pensioners and the disabled. Many Ukrainians today still hold on to these expectations, though they are echoes of the past.[4] A worsening economic situation, eroding job security, declining pensions, and decreasing unemployment benefits during the 1990s have caused a steady loss of confidence in the providing role of government. Another source of eroding confidence in government is corruption, which is very much on the minds of Ukrainians. The judiciary, political parties, and police are perceived by the general public to be the most corrupt, and citizens' confidence in the government to effectively combat corruption is quite low.[5] This ambiguous view regarding the role of government permeates everyday life in Ukraine.

The rise of a small wealthy class has contributed to conspicuous changes in Ukrainian lifestyle. During the Communist era, the *nomenklatura* was a de facto upper class, but their privileged position was derived from facilitated access to everyday consumer goods and luxuries, not as easily or at all available to others. More recently, among the Ukrainian upper class, much like among the same classes in other countries in transition, displays of wealth have become much more extravagant, and the difference between ordinary citizens and the privileged few has become vast and stinging. Seeing such unbridled wealth, enormous social differences, and significant political leverage of the oligarchs continues to remind ordinary Ukrainians of their own often precarious economic situation as well as their inability to rely on the government for help. Since 2000, the improving economic situation and overall well-being in the country has contributed to a diminished fear of uncertainty, though the distinction between the wealthy and the poor is still evident throughout the country.[6]

Traditionally, Ukrainians have always had strong ties to the land. Not surprisingly, in the country historically designated as the breadbasket of Europe and subsequently the breadbasket of the Soviet Union, the majority of the people were peasants surviving and living from tending the land. Many Ukrainian traditions, much of its folklore, art, and literature are rooted in village life, cycles of harvest, and religious rites. In recent history, urbanization and industrial growth drew much of the population into cities. Many people still have relatives in the villages and through this preserve a tenuous connection to the land. Some own dachas (country homes or summer cottages), to which they retire over the weekends and during holidays and vacations. During communism, dachas provided the Ukrainian urban population with a private fruit and vegetable garden through which people affordably supplemented their diet. Today, they serve a mostly recreational purpose, offering city dwellers a way, albeit temporary, to connect with nature.

A village house from the turn of the twentieth century, Kharkiv region. Photo by Adriana Helbig.

DAILY LIFE, FAMILY, AND RELATIONSHIPS

City-dwelling Ukrainians spend a significant portion of their typical weekday at work and much of the rest of the day at home with their families. More often than not, a weekday begins around 8:00 A.M., when children's school starts, while a typical adult workday begins at 9:00 A.M. Lunch breaks from work are normally taken between 1:00 and 2:00 P.M. School ends by noon or 2:00 P.M. at the latest, but many children stay later for optional after-school activities. The workday normally lasts until 6:00 P.M. The growth of new professions, such as management consulting, public relations, and stock trading, as well as the proliferation of foreign companies in Ukraine, have contributed to changes in work ethics and a reorganization of time. However, many uniquely Ukrainian idiosyncrasies still hold. Overall, Ukrainians are conscientious workers but tend to rely more on the group and less on individual accomplishment and thus have a different concept of personal responsibility in business than more individually based cultures. A number of holidays (nine official state holidays and about two dozen other holidays and days of celebration) transect the Ukrainian year, allowing for days off from work and anticipated opportunities for extending vacations and deadlines alike. In business as well as in their private lives, Ukrainians have a somewhat flexible sense of time. Being a bit late (five minutes or so) for an appointment is not considered noteworthy and is quite acceptable, particularly when taking into consideration the increasing problem with traffic that often brings movement to a standstill throughout the day. After a long day at work, a common thread in the lives of many Ukrainians is the tendency to devote their free time to family, both immediate and extended, and to dear friends, who are considered as part of the family.

A picture of an average Ukrainian family will include parents, children, and, more often than not, grandparents as well. Three generations often find themselves under the same roof in Ukraine due to practical and traditional reasons. Many children remain in their parental home well into their twenties. Housing shortages during Soviet times and in the immediate transition years caused apartments to be passed down from generation to generation, so that children, after getting married, often remained living with one of the parents. Furthermore, since in many families both parents work, the grandparents become de facto caregivers to the children. The usual babysitter is the *babtsia,* or grandmother. *Babtias (babushka* in Russian) are a ubiquitous presence in Ukrainian daily life. They help the parents tend to the children, and they cook for and feed the family (and sometimes their guests). The children often fondly remember their grandmothers telling wonderful stories based on historical events, their own, often harsh life experiences, and folklore. Because of the small pensions many retirees receive in Ukraine, *babtias* can sometimes be seen selling food or flowers at the market to supplement their incomes. Traditionally, the extended family has always been important in Ukraine. The agricultural tradition and village life mandated that each member of the household be engaged in working in the fields, growing food, or maintaining the household. Surviving hard times and prospering depended on everyone in the family accepting his or her role and working for the common good. Many modern Ukrainian families still live by this principle.

Marriage is very much the basic family unit in Ukraine, with the vast majority of the population married by the time they reach their thirties. Almost 50 percent of all Ukrainian women are already married in their early twenties, while only about one-quarter of all men the same age are. The picture reverses as Ukrainians age. Among women over 70, barely one in four is married, while two out of three are widowed. At the same age, 7 out of 10 men are married, and only one-quarter of them are widowers.[7] Furthermore, many women find themselves without a partner at a later age, and not surprisingly so, since the life expectancy of an average Ukrainian woman is 73 years, while for a man, it is 61.[8] This leaves older women particularly vulnerable and exposed to dramatic social, demographic, and economic changes. In the last several decades Ukraine has suffered a dramatic decrease in its population due to a drop in birthrates and a rise in death rates. Since the 1960s, there has been a general increase in the incidence of divorce as well as an increase in unmarried couples living together.

An advertisement aimed toward foreigners looking for Ukrainian wives, 2006. Jim Goldberg, Magnum Photos.

Attitudes toward sex have been changing in the last several decades as well, particularly since the 1990s. Though sex is still considered a fundamentally private and personal affair, ideas regarding sex in postsocialist society have become increasingly more open. Premarital sex is considered significantly more permissible in Ukraine today, and there is a proliferation of eroticism and sexuality in popular culture, particularly since the dissolution of the Soviet Union. Furthermore, a relatively recent introduction of sex education in schools has contributed to forming healthier and more open attitudes toward sexuality among younger people. In the former Soviet Union, homosexuality in society was largely considered to be deviant behavior. As with many other social issues, this has been changing since independence. Though many homosexuals in Ukraine still hide their sexual orientation out of fear of still-present prejudice, today, there is increasing awareness and, to a degree, acceptance of homosexuality in society as well as some political activism.[9]

FOLKLORE, TRADITIONAL ARTIFACTS, AND SUPERSTITIONS

Folkloric tradition in Ukraine is incredibly rich and closely intertwined with Ukrainian art, literature, music, myths, storytelling, and some daily customs, particularly in the countryside. Folk songs, tales, and stories as well as folk sayings are the most common and observable oral elements of Ukranian folklore. Throughout history, oral tradition has served Ukrainians as a collective memory bank, preserving and celebrating their sense of identity and belonging by reminding them of a glorious past. Oral folklore commemorated important personal and family events and passed on unassailable life truths and widespread values. In a way, Ukrainian oral folk tradition is like a comforting, omniscient, proud, advice-dispatching grandmother.

Ukrainian folk songs are musical commemorations and celebrations of special events and people's daily lives. Occasions as diverse as the harvest, a christening celebration, and the baking of the wedding bread called for particular folk songs. Folk songs are an integral part of many festivities. Christmas in Ukraine is celebrated by singing carols, which provide an aural framework to the festivities. Song themes reflect the nature of their intent and focus on natural occurrences; cycles of the harvest and the seasons; family occasions and village life; holidays, rituals, and pagan traditions; and historical events and personalities. Ukrainian folk songs often depict joyful aspects of love such as two young people falling in love or a young maiden finding a fiancé and preparing for and awaiting her wedding day. They can also be quite mournful, speaking of loss, sorrow, unrequited love, and tragic destinies. Most folk songs are imbued with traditional symbolism, evoking elements of nature, such as flowers, plants, and animals, and infusing them with meaning.

Folktales are another important expression of Ukrainian oral folklore. These delightful stories of clever little foxes, fierce she-dragons, honorable princes, and fair maidens, the Wind, rivers, and Christmas spiders, have, throughout centuries, enchanted generations of Ukrainians, particularly children. These stories are mesmerizing and educational, entertaining and inspiring. Animal folktales put familiar domestic or wild animals in human situations, in which they humorously expose their weaknesses or demonstrate wit, bravery, and camaraderie in resolving problems. Moral stories tell of virtuous individuals who, despite their natural limitations or disadvantaged class or position in society, manage to excel and become admired in their communities. Legends and fairy tales evoke a magical and mythical world of kingdoms and wonders, where beauty, honor, and grace meet evil and dishonesty, most often with a happy ending. Some folktales breathe life into inanimate objects and natural phenomena, weaving stories with the purpose of explaining how the natural world and human societies came about. Ukrainian folktales, however, are not only favorites of children—they are a treasure chest of Ukrainian mythology, beliefs, and values. They reveal

Ukraine's complex history in their pagan motifs, Christian themes, and foreign influences.[10]

Folk sayings are an element of folklore that have faded but have not disappeared from everyday life. These bits of popular wisdom packaged in catchy phrases are used from time to time in conversation to illustrate or underline a point. Some folk sayings are more prophetic, while others are more anecdotal; some resonate with humor, while others echo popular wisdom and goodhearted warnings. Numerous folk sayings, for example, caution men against the complex nature of women and potential pitfalls and benefits of building a home with one ("Play neither with horse nor wife if you wish not to be kicked"). Others, as simple as "He who licks knives will soon cut his tongue," carry a tone of good-natured forewarning with a hint of playfulness. A well-timed saying uttered with good intentions conveys much more than an ordinary prosaic conversation. Though not as common in everyday speech, folk sayings have remained in Ukrainian daily life. For example, the saying "If you chase two hares at the same time, you will catch neither of them" inspired the plot of a popular comedy movie from Soviet times and lives on in the name of a restaurant in Kyiv called Chasing Two Hares (*Za Dvoma Zaitsiamy*).

Colorfully painted Easter eggs, *pysanky,* and embroidered ceremonial towels, *rushnyky,* are the most familiar and common material expressions of Ukrainian folklore. People created and preserved these objects as reminders of the past and in honor of tradition. *Rushnyky* are woven cloths decorated with stylized floral, animal, and geometric patterns most commonly embroidered in red and black. The combination of colors of the embroidery is a traditional indication of the region from which the *rushnyk* comes. *Rushnyky* are an important part of Ukrainian family rituals and are used in courtship, marriage ceremonies, funeral services, and as protection for the home. At weddings, the couple stands on a *rushnyk* during the religious ceremony. Young women present their fiancés with elaborately decorated *rushnyky* as tokens of their devotion. *Rushnyky* are also visibly displayed in homes, often draped over icons for protection. Today, *rushnyky* are predominantly used on special occasions such as religious holidays, family celebrations, and traditional festivals. The motifs and patterns on *pysanky,* the elaborately painted Easter eggs, reveal important pre-Christian symbolism of the sun, spring, and rebirth. This tradition of decorating eggs has lasted from pagan times. Today, *pysanky* are an integral part of a Ukrainian traditional Easter celebration, where they are given as gifts to family and friends as emblems of good wishes.

A significant number of superstitious beliefs survive in Ukraine today, many of which trace their roots to pre-Christian times. A belief in a multitude of pagan gods, capricious and mysterious, produced a complex set of rules for humans to obey. Many superstitions, such as the evil eye, are residuals from pagan days of old. Though superstitions may seem highly illogical or nonscientific to outsiders, they make sense to many Ukrainians, who often feel compelled to act on them. For instance, a young, single woman must not sit on the corner of the table lest she postpone her marriage; people should not shake hands in a doorway as it is believed to bring bad luck; one should sit quietly for a few moments before going on a trip; a half-empty bottle should not be left on the table since this is bad luck; whistling indoors will cause one to lose money; and an even number of flowers are an appropriate gift only for a funeral. Though many Ukrainians laugh at these superstitions, they still abide by them, just in case.

SPORTS

Ukrainians follow a variety of sports closely and are proud of their accomplished athletes. Ukraine has a long and successful history of achievement in international sporting competitions, many of which were won under the banner of the Soviet Union. During Soviet times, the consistent official policy in support of sports not only brought good results to the Soviet sports teams, which often included Ukrainian athletes, but it also built up infrastructure and helped foster the development of prospective young athletes in the constituting republics. Since independence, athletes from Ukraine have continued to achieve notable international results. In the 2008 Olympic Games in Beijing, Ukrainian athletes won 27 medals (7 gold, 5 silver, and 15 bronze) in sports as diverse as fencing, diving, shooting, cycling and wrestling.

As in many other European countries, soccer is the most popular sport in Ukraine. Throughout the country, people of different ages enthusiastically play and follow the game. The first official soccer match on Ukrainian territories was held in L'viv on July 14, 1894, kicking off Ukrainian soccer history. In 1942 the entire Start team (made up mostly of Dynamo Kyiv players) was allegedly detained and shot to death after beating Flakelf, representing Nazi forces in occupied Kyiv. In reality, there is conflicting evidence and testimony as to what really happened during and after the so-called Death Match. The Ukrainian Premier League was founded in 1991, and the first games were played the following year. Since the Ukrainian national team began to compete on the international stage in the early 1990s, it has been well respected by its opponents. Ukraine and Poland were selected to co-host the 2012 UEFA Euro (European Soccer Championship). This will be the first time that countries from the former eastern bloc host this competition. The most internationally recognizable names in Ukrainian soccer are Oleg Blokhin and Andriy Shevchenko. Both were awarded the European Player of the Year title, though Blokhin was active much earlier, during Soviet times. Shevchenko, on the other hand, is a national hero in modern Ukraine, where he is widely admired for his achievements. Nationally, the most important teams are Dynamo Kyiv, Shakhtar Donetsk, and Dnipro Dnipropetrovsk. In recent years the Ukrainian league has become a destination of choice for many African players, who are attempting to use it as a stepping-stone toward Western European leagues.

Another team sport followed by Ukrainians is hockey. However, the international results of the national team have mostly not matched fans' enthusiasm for the game. Ukrainians were among the first nations to begin playing professional hockey in the early twentieth century, but as of 2007, the Ukrainian hockey team ranked fifteenth in the world.

Boxing is a sport followed by many in recent years. Notable boxers who have successfully competed in the international arena are brothers Vitali and Volodymyr Klitschko. In the last few years, Volodymyr Klitschko held the International Boxing Federation, World Boxing Organization (WBO), and International Boxing Organization world heavyweight titles, while his brother Vitali is a former World Boxing Council and WBO heavyweight champion. Vitali Klitschko pursued an unsuccessful bid to become mayor of Kyiv in 2006 and entered the race again in 2008 in the midst of early local elections called because of corruption accusations against his former opponent. Aside from their successes in competitions, the two brothers are known for combining their passion for sports with their humanitarian work supporting athletic programs for young people.

Other remarkable Ukrainian athletes are pole vault champion Sergey Bubka and gymnast Larisa Latynina, both sports legends in their own right. Bubka holds 35 world records and countless medals, including one Olympic gold, and is widely regarded as the best pole-vaulter of all time. Latynina holds the record for the athlete with the most Olympic medals, having been awarded 18 (9 gold medals, 5 silver, and 4 bronze) during the span of her career. Figure-skating champion Oksana Baiul is a Ukrainian athlete whose successes are often fondly remembered, particularly among Ukrainians abroad and in the United States, where she now lives. She is among the first Ukrainian Olympic athletes to win a gold medal as a member of an independent Ukrainian Olympic team. Her remarkable life story of overcoming adversity as a young girl and reaching sports heights as a teenager (as the 1993 World Figure Skating Champion and the 1994 Winter Olympic Gold medalist) served as inspiration to many Ukrainians. Her story is inextricably linked with Viktor Petrenko, who took Oksana in as a young orphan in Odesa and helped her reach her potential as a world-class ice skater. Petrenko won the gold medal in ice-skating at the 1992 Winter Olympics as a member of the Unified Team, when athletes from former Soviet countries competed together as one team for the last time.

Most Ukrainians keenly follow and support their favorite athletes, delight in their triumphs, and eagerly await new successes.

HOLIDAYS AND CELEBRATIONS

Celebrations of traditional and religious holidays as well as family celebrations have a special place in the lives of Ukrainians. Most holidays are elaborate affairs and wonderful opportunities for family and friends to get together. Orthodox Christian holidays are widely celebrated, especially since the dissolution of the Soviet Union and a virtual reintroduction of religion into people's lives. A survey regarding holiday popularity conducted in Ukraine in the mid-2000s revealed some interesting trends. New Year's, Easter, and Christmas were by far the most popular holidays, celebrated by close to 100 percent of those surveyed.[11] While Christmas and Easter are the most important Christian holidays, the popularity of New Year's makes sense when put in the context of the recent past. The Soviet regime banned religious holidays, and though many chose to celebrate at home in small family settings, New Year's became the publicly acceptable display of the end of the year festivities. Each of the Ukrainian celebrations has its own ceremonies, rituals, and rites, normally involving special foods, singing, and dancing. Celebrations differ somewhat, depending on the region and family preference, but generally contain the same basic elements. Music is present at all the celebrations, even solemn ones. Singing is most common at Christmas, when carolers celebrate the birth of Christ in song. Dancing, on the other hand, is obligatory at both traditional and more modern wedding celebrations. Traditional dishes, prepared for special days and holidays, are often the most intricate part of all Ukrainian celebrations.

Religious Holidays

As in many other Christian Orthodox churches, the Ukrainian liturgical calendar is based around the Julian calendar. This calendar was introduced by Julius Cesar in 45 B.C. as an effort to reform the quite inaccurate, previously used Roman calendar. The Gregorian calendar, introduced in 1582 by Pope Gregory XIII, was intended to correct the inaccuracies of the Julian calendar and to further standardize the Church's liturgical schedules. The principal difference between the two calendars lies in the 14 days that currently mark the divergence between the same dates in the two calendars. In other words, Christmas falls on December 25, according to the Gregorian calendar, and on January 7, according to the Julian. While it spread relatively quickly through the Catholic and even Protestant countries, most Orthodox nations did not easily accept the Gregorian calendar, some not until well into the twentieth century. Russia began observing the Gregorian calendar following the October Revolution, and soon after, it became the official calendar of the Soviet Union. During Soviet times, the suppression of religious practices and the intent to reform traditional ways of life in Ukraine resulted in the Gregorian calendar being used in the secular, public, official, and urban spheres, while the Julian calendar remained in the religious, rural, and traditional spheres.

Christmas (*Rizdvo*) is, next to Easter, the most revered and observed religious celebration in Ukraine. In the Orthodox rite, it is an elaborate affair involving food, music, and traditional rituals, which last from Christmas Eve to the day after Christmas. On the evening of January 6, Christmas Eve festivities begin with the Holy Supper—*Sviata Vechera.* Elaborate rituals and customs accompany *Sviata Vechera,* many of which originated in pagan times and became a part of the Christian celebration. Though most are no longer practiced in urban contexts, the Ukrainian Christmas Eve rituals are fascinating and reveal a rich and long tradition. The table for dinner is sprinkled with hay and covered with embroidered cloth and a centerpiece consisting of a large *kolach,* traditional braided circular bread lined with candles and straw. The table is usually set with an extra place for an unexpected guest or for a deceased relative. The dinner begins once the children notice the first star in the night sky. The first (and the last) dish of the *Sviata Vechera* is the *kutia,* an ancient ceremonial dish present in many Orthodox traditions made with boiled wheat kernels, honey, poppy seeds, and sometimes nuts and raisins. A separate serving of *kutia* is placed on the window or sideboard with a candle in remembrance of family members who have passed away. Another item of remembrance is the *didukh,* a sheaf of grain in the corner of the room, usually under an icon, symbolizing the spirits of ancestors. The meal itself is traditionally meatless and contains 12 (or 9 or 7) dishes, including meatless beet soup (*pisnyi borsch*), fish, cabbage rolls, filled dumplings (*varenyky*), dried fruit compote, and doughnuts (*pampushky*) with preserve fillings.

After dinner, carolers sing Christmas carols, *koliady,* to begin their rounds of neighboring homes, where their songs are rewarded with treats, food, and drink. The most popular carols are "Boh predvichnyi" (The Eternal God) and "Nebo i zemlia" (Heaven and Earth). As with many other elements of the Ukrainian Christmas rituals, themes and origins of carols are a combination of pagan and Christian traditions. *Kolach, kutia,* borsch, and many other traditional dishes are common at Christmas Eve dinner tables, though regional and family variations are not uncommon. The table decorations and the number and choice of dishes still reflect tradition in most Ukrainian households, while *didukh* is sometimes replaced by the Christmas tree. Christmas Day celebrations continue with people attending religious services and another festive meal with plenty of sweet baked goods. The celebrations conclude the day after Christmas, with family and friends exchanging visits and good wishes.

Easter (Velykden') in Ukraine, as the celebration of Christ's resurrection, is the most important Christian holiday. It fuses the dignified restraint of Lent with joyous spring festivities on Easter Sunday. Spring revelry and ritualistic eating and singing are elements of pre-Christian celebrations relating to the rebirth of nature, while exacting Easter religious rites are anchored in Christian tradition. Celebrations effectively begin during Holy Week, the week before Easter, despite the solemn mood and fasting traditionally observed by Ukrainians during this period. During Holy Week, people refrain from singing and dancing and other joyful activities since it is a time of sorrow. Today, most Ukrainians fast and observe these rules only on Good Friday. On Easter Sunday morning, Ukrainians attend religious services with a basket of food to be blessed (*sviachene*) in hand. After being blessed in church, the basket containing foods like sausages, hams, horseradish root, cheese, butter, salt, hard-boiled eggs, millet, dyed cooked eggs (*krashanky*), and *pysanky* is taken home and served to the family. As remnants of ancient pagan rituals, Ukrainians give each other gifts of *pysanky* at Easter, share Easter food, and sing traditional spring songs (*vesnianky*) outdoors as a farewell to winter and a welcome to spring. Today, many of these ritualistic customs connected to Easter are celebrated with some variation in urban Ukraine.

Family Celebrations

The traditional Ukrainian wedding ceremony is the most elaborate and complex of all family celebrations. The intricate wedding rituals require the involvement of not only the immediate families of the bride and the groom, but also their extended families, neighbors, and villagers. Weddings call for serious planning and preparation as well as observance from all those involved. Weddings were traditionally held on Sundays in late winter and early spring or in the fall in reverence for harvest cycles and other rural customs. The origins of the Ukrainian wedding ceremony likely had symbolic significance and reach far into the pre-Christian pagan past. Since the introduction of Christianity, the traditional wedding was more like a staged play with three acts: preparation for the wedding, the marriage ceremony, and postwedding activities. The first act traditionally began with inquiries and matchmaking, rituals aimed at assessing the suitability of the bride and groom for each other. The groom's representatives, the groom, and his matchmaker visited the bride's family bearing gifts of salt, bread, and alcohol in hope of securing the bride's hand. When the groom and his emissaries were served a pumpkin, it was a sign of rejection from the bride. If the matchmaking was successful, the bride and groom were betrothed in front of their relatives and their hands were symbolically bound together in their agreement to marry. In fact, the Ukrainian word for engagement, *obruchennya,* literally means "the act of binding hands together," as in this ceremony. The bride, with her bridesmaids, and the groom, in the company of his best man, then proceeded to personally invite their respective guests to attend the celebrations by presenting them with a loaf of bread. In preparation for the ceremony, married female members of the wedding party baked and decorated the *korovai* (ritual wedding bread) from the flour given by everyone in the wedding. The night

Traditional wedding cake, *korovai,* decorated with dough birds symbolizing the young couple, family, and friends. The periwinkle wreath symbolizes love and purity. Photo by Adriana Helbig.

before the wedding the bride spent with her bridesmaids and her friends singing sad songs in anticipation of the bride's separation from her family and the unbraiding of her long braid—a symbol of her virginity.

On the day of the wedding, the bride's hair was braided and wrapped around her head in the shape of a wreath. After the bride and the groom were dressed in their wedding costumes, they were blessed by their parents before moving on to the church accompanied by musicians and singing guests. At the church the priest blessed the couple and led them to the central table in front of the *iconostas*. The best man and the maid of honor held lit candles in their hands during the ceremony, and once the couple was crowned, they walked around the table three times. After the ceremony the bride and the groom returned to their respective homes. The groom gathered his relatives and his wedding party and went to fetch the bride at her parents' home, where her relatives would playfully try to substitute other women for her. The groom would pay a ransom of food and drink to take the bride to the wedding feast. After the distribution of gifts at the wedding feast, the *korovai* was ceremonially cut and handed out to the couple and their parents, and then to the extended family and guests. After the evening meal the couple went together to their new home—the groom's house—where they were greeted by the bride's parents-in-law. The first wedding night was by no means the conclusion of the wedding celebrations.

The third act consisted of postwedding activities. They began with the bride's family visiting the groom's home, where a fake bride, a little old lady or even a male relative in disguise, welcomed them. For the week following the wedding, guests continued their celebrations, filled with silliness and pranks, throughout the village. The exact scenario for this detailed and convoluted wedding play varied by region, though most included some or all of these elements. The ceremony became more refined with time, but singing, dancing, and food remained central for the festivities. Special wedding songs accompanied all segments of the wedding ceremony and were sung by all participants. The most common themes sang of the potential difficulties in the life of the new couple, the hostile mother-in-law, the loving mother, and the love between the bride and the groom. Though Ukrainian wedding songs are the most abundant lyrical folk songs, they have been substituted in modern wedding celebrations by popular songs. Traditional wedding songs, however, are often performed on the stages as part of a traditional folk repertoire.

During Soviet times, such traditional wedding ceremonies were frowned upon as symbols of archaic, nationalist customs. The Soviet government prescribed ways to conclude marriage with a civil registration that incorporated no elements of religion or tradition. Over the years, many people in the cities came to accept these new rules because it was easier to obey them and harder

The mother-in-law removes the bride's headdress and ties a scarf to symbolize her married status. L'viv, May 17, 2008. Courtesy of Kateryna and Serhii Pobihailo.

to break them. The traditional wedding ceremonies survived in the rural communities and among country folk, where they were more entrenched in everyday sociability and where Soviet rules were easier to bend. Since independence, despite concerted efforts by some groups and individuals advocating a return to pre–Soviet era Ukrainian traditions, traditional weddings are rarely practiced in full in Ukraine. In some villages, it is still possible to come across traditional wedding rituals, but in most urban areas, very few elements of tradition remain in wedding ceremonies. The groom sometimes comes to the bride's house to ask her parents for her hand in marriage as a way to formalize their engagement, a custom that reveals a trace of tradition. These days, the length of the engagement is used to plan for the wedding, which normally consists of a civil and/or church ceremony followed by a dinner and reception. On the day of the wedding the groom sometimes comes to the bride's house, but before he is allowed to see her, he has to pass a series of tests and pay ransom for the bride. This ritual is one of a handful of generally practiced wedding traditions. For many Ukrainians since independence, getting married in a church has become a part of the revival and preservation of Ukrainian cultural traditions. Though it has little in common with the traditional and elaborate wedding celebration, the modern Ukrainian wedding is an equally joyous affair, with plenty of singing, dancing, and feasting.

Christening is another important familial celebration in Ukrainian culture and has been regaining prominence as a religious custom since independence. The symbolism of the christening is the rebirth of a child into the Christian faith, but the ritual likely has its origins in pagan times as a cleansing rite designed to ward off evil. Children in Ukraine are christened in the first couple of years of their lives. As part of the Orthodox christening ceremony, the child being christened is blessed, then has his or her head, hands, and feet anointed with oil, and is finally immersed in water three times. Sometimes, when the child being christened is very young, he or she will receive his or her first haircut at the end of the christening ceremony. Though many people may be present at the christening, the godparents normally have the most prominent role. They are either family members or close friends who, through the act of becoming godparents, make a commitment to care for their godchild. Following the church ceremony, family and friends celebrate with food and drink.

Funerals, though sad and solemn occasions, also bring families together and are an important part of Ukrainian family customs. The traditional Ukrainian burial rites were quite elaborate and particular, such as placing the body of the deceased in the house with the feet facing the door, knocking the coffin against the entrance three times in farewell as it is carried out of the house, and lowering the coffin into the grave in a way that it faces the sunrise. Traditionally, the funeral was followed by a meal and accompanied by funeral chanting and lamentations (*holosinnia*). The first course of the funeral meal was *kutia,* cooked wheat with honey symbolizing resurrection and eternal life. Ukrainian funerals today have lost many of their folkloric rites but retain Orthodox Christian elements. Special prayers and requiem services will normally last for three days following the passing of the deceased, and on the third day, the funeral is held. During the 40 days following the death, the loved ones pray intensely for the deceased's soul. On the fortieth day, when the soul is believed to be assigned a place in heaven or hell, family members and friends gather to eat, drink, and toast to the deceased and gather at the cemetery in commemoration.

Other Holidays

Several holidays with roots in Soviet times are still observed in Ukraine today with an intriguing combination of nostalgia and resentment. The most controversial is, without a doubt, the October Revolution Day on November 7. During the Soviet era, November 7 was a state holiday commemorating the Bolshevik Revolution. It remained an official holiday in independent Ukraine until 2000, when President Kuchma abolished it. Commemorations of this day have sparked some political controversy since 2000. Ukrainian leftists and Communists, many older people, and pensioners observe November 7 by organizing and attending popular rallies and demonstrations. Attending November 7 events for many Ukrainians, particularly older pensioners, is an expression of their nostalgia for the past and their belief that life was better in Soviet times, particularly economically. For leftist and Communist politicians in Ukraine, the October Revolution Day presents an opportunity to highlight their political views and to rally for public support and votes. A prominent holiday from the days of the Soviet Union that is still very present in the everyday lives of Ukrainians is Women's Day, celebrated on March 8. Originally a pan-Communist holiday designed to salute the accomplishments of women in socialist society, Women's Day in contemporary Ukraine is celebrated with small tokens of appreciation given by men to all the women in their lives such as roses or assistance with housework. Labor Day or May Day was also widely celebrated in the Soviet Union, as in many other communist countries. Massive parades and demonstrations in support of worker solidarity attended by workers, collective farmers, and students in Soviet Ukraine were characteristic of May 1 celebrations. These days, Ukrainians mostly celebrate this day off work by resting and enjoying spring weather. Victory Day, celebrated on May 9, is a day of remembrance of World War II and its victims, which numbered in the millions in Ukraine. It was an official holiday in the Soviet Union, commemorating the Soviet victory over Nazi Germany. In modern Ukraine, Victory Day it is still an occasion marked by the remembrance of war victims and veterans' sacrifices and a widely observed holiday.

A few new Ukrainian holidays have been introduced since independence: Independence Day, observed on August 24, and Constitution Day, on June 28. Not surprisingly, Constitution Day marks the signing of the Ukrainian constitution in 1996, and though no particular ceremonies are associated with this day, concerts are common in town squares throughout Ukraine. Independence Day, as the most important state holiday in Ukraine today, honors the proclamation of Ukrainian sovereignty. Celebrations of Independence Day range from parades displaying national military prowess, to popular festivals, concerts, and colorful fireworks. The time since independence has not only brought new holidays but also breathed new life into some old ones, such as Ivan Kupalo Eve, celebrated on July 6. This traditional Ukrainian folk holiday is a relic from the pre-Christian period, which over time became incorporated into Christianity as the Day of St. John the Baptist. Originally dedicated to the cult of the sun and its pagan gods, Ivan Kupalo celebrations revolve around singing and dancing and themes of romance and marriage with an orgiastic quality. Carousing in nature, particularly in and around

Carpathian Mountain Hutsuls enjoy Independence Day celebrations in Kyiv, 2001. Photo by Adriana Helbig.

water, and symbolic courtship rituals remain central to Kupalo Eve. Because of its traditional folkloric elements and religious overtones, commemorations of this holiday were restricted mostly to the countryside during Soviet times but have a renewed significance in modern Ukrainian society. Many Ukrainians today embrace and rejoice in Kupalo Eve's unique combination of celebrating midsummer, a distinctly pagan custom, and honoring St. John the Baptist, an iconic figure in early Christianity. As many other elements of Ukrainian tradition, this holiday has changed with the times but is strongly rooted in tradition.

FOOD AND DRINK

Throughout history, Ukrainians have taken pride in the preparation, consumption, and symbolism of their food. Ukrainian cuisine shares some commonalities with its neighbors, such as Poland and Russia, as well as traditional Jewish cuisine from Eastern Europe. Though it has a definite regional flair, Ukrainian cooking reflects uniquely Ukrainian traditions and tastes. Food has always been more than just sustenance for Ukrainians. Preparation of elaborate traditional dishes is a ritual in itself and has a prominent place in most holiday celebrations, in particular religious festivities and family gatherings. Cooking and eating in Ukraine are opportunities for family and friends to get together, and Ukrainians take advantage of it often. Both festive and daily, Ukrainian cuisine is hearty and based around a range of wholesome and natural ingredients with some favorite tastes, herbs, and spices. Meat, flour, cabbage, potatoes, and beets are among the most common ingredients and are often prepared stewed, baked, and stuffed. Though they sound simple and basic, these ingredients create a variety of exciting and delicious dishes. Several Ukrainian foods, such as *borsch* and dumplings (*varenyky*), have both a daily and a festive version, while some, such as *kutia,* are decidedly festive.

Beverages and alcoholic drinks are inescapable companions to the Ukrainian gastronomic tradition. A popular traditional Ukrainian drink is *kvas.* It is a mildly alcoholic or nonalcoholic drink made from fermented rye (sometimes wheat or barley) bread. Supposedly, *kvas* traces its roots to the times of Kyivan Rus', and the preference for it in many Slavic countries may indeed be a testimony to its ancient origins. In Ukraine it comes in homemade and manufactured varieties and can be flavored with berries, fruit, and birch syrup. *Kvas* is rich in vitamin B, and some believe in its restorative qualities, particularly as a hangover cure. Ukrainians favor sweet beverages, such as fruit juices and *kompot,* a drink made from boiled fruits. However, beer is the alcoholic beverage of choice for most Ukrainians. Beer consumption in Ukraine has been on the rise in recent years, likely because of increasing consumer incomes, accessibility, and marketing campaigns. In Ukraine, beer is viewed as a fun, light drink suitable for daily and causal consumption. Vodka (*horilka*), on the other hand, is perceived as the more serious drink. Drinking *horilka* is somewhat of a social event as it is consumed with friends for special occasions, sometimes with business partners, and often as part of celebrations. Plenty of toasts to friendship, health, love, family, and successful cooperation, depending on the occasion, accompany drinking *horilka.* Though it is often consumed straight, *horilka* can be flavored with berries, fruit, and hot peppers.

Daily Food

Traditionally, a cooked midday meal is the most important meal of the day, normally involving soup, a meat dish, a side dish or salad, and often dessert. In this age of fast food, many urban, working Ukrainians find it more and more difficult to keep this custom, so many eat this way only over the weekend. Homemade Ukrainian dishes require a bit more effort but are well worth it. Though the cuisine is diverse and imaginative, certain Ukrainian dishes have become typical favorites. Once known as the breadbasket of Europe, it is not a surprise that bread and other dough-based foods are fundamentals of Ukrainian cuisine. Ukraine produces a variety of grains, including rye, buckwheat, oats, and millet, which are then used to bake an incredible variety of breads ranging from plain white bread, rye bread, fried bread puffs, *babka* (traditional Easter bread), honey bread, and crescent rolls. In Ukraine, simpler breads are served for everyday meals, while many of the more elaborate ones are desserts or ceremonial foods for special occasions.

One of the most recognizable and well-liked Ukrainian dishes is *borsch*, an elaborate and hearty beet soup made with or without meat, depending on the region and occasion. The popularity of *borsch* reflects the general Ukrainian liking for soups and stews. Much of the international *borsch* recognition comes from its popularity in Russian and Jewish cuisine, the latter made available through kosher food companies such as Manishevitz. Though beets give *borsch* its characteristic red color, cabbage, potatoes, tomatoes, parsley root, carrots, onion, and garlic also find their way into the mix. It is most commonly made with beef but can contain chicken or pork, or can be prepared only with vegetables. Traditional wisdom has it that true *borsch* should contain 22 ingredients. *Borsch* is a common first course in ordinary family meals as well as an important part of festive meals, such as Christmas Eve dinner. Dumplings (*varenyky and halushky*) are quite ubiquitous in much of Ukrainian cooking. *Halushky* are dumplings made of egg, flour, and butter (or pig fat), sometimes with ham and cottage cheese added to the dough. *Halushky* are cooked in boiling water and served with sour cream. *Varenyky* are stuffed dumplings made with a variety of fillings such as cottage cheese, meat, mushrooms, potatoes, and cherries, served with sour cream and cooked in boiling water. According to superstition, if the cook counts *varenyky* while making them, they will overcook and the filling will seep out. Both *varenyky* and *halushky* have their more elaborate festive versions and are eaten for Christmas Eve and Easter. *Holubtsi,* stuffed cabbage rolls, are another Ukrainian favorite. Cabbage leaves are stuffed with meat and rice, and occasionally with mixed vegetables or mushrooms. A variety of other stuffed vegetables, stewed meat, meatballs, sausages, potato pancakes, roll-ups, and patties are among the most common Ukrainian daily dishes. Ukrainian desserts usually contain some combination of sugar, eggs, flour, cheese, sour cream, fresh and dried fruit, honey, and nuts. These ingredients make assorted delicious desserts ranging from apple and cheese cakes, apple, plum, and berry pies, and stuffed apples and apricots to carrot and cheese *babkas,* honey bread, and cookies.

Holiday Food

Holiday menus are complicated affairs in Ukraine, requiring planning and lengthy preparation. Many holiday dishes are in fact more intricate variations of everyday foods such as honey bread, *borsch, varenyky, holubtsi,* fish in aspic, meat in aspic, sausages, and vanilla *babka*. Other dishes, however, are reserved only for special occasions and have become gastronomic symbols of holidays. *Kutia* is one such dish. As a symbol of fertility and abundance, it is served as the first and last dish of *Sviata Vechera* and has ceremonial significance in predicting the following year's harvest, protecting livestock, and remembering deceased family members. *Kolach,* another festive dish, is traditional bread eaten at the Christmas Eve dinner and on other religious and family feasts. A symbol of prosperity and good luck, it is braided and circularly shaped, sometimes stacked and usually served with a candle in the middle. At the Christmas Eve dinner table, each person dips a piece of *kolach* in salt and honey and offers the traditional Christmas greeting of "Khrystos razhdayet'sia" (Christ is born). The *korovai* is the most impressive of all Ukrainian festive breads. It is a tall, elaborate wedding bread decorated with flowers and birds sculpted from dough. These elaborate festive food traditions have been preserved in Ukraine, particularly in the countryside, as well as among Ukrainian diaspora communities in the West.

NOTES

1. O. O. Biloukha and V. Utermohlen, "Healthy Eating in Ukraine: Attitudes, Barriers and Information Sources," *Public Health Nutrition* 4 (2001): 207–15.

2. Orest Deychakiwsky, "National Minorities in Ukraine," *Ukrainian Quarterly* 50 (1994): 371–89.

3. Center for International Development and Conflict Management, "Minorities at Risk Project," University of Maryland, http://www.cidcm.umd.edu/mar/.

4. International Foundation for Electoral Systems and USAID, *Attitudes of Ukrainians Prior to 2007 Rada Elections,* August–September 2007, http://www.ifes.org/publication/c02e 80ae0eb56679827e3a5c38b27f15/Ukraine%20Exec%20Summary.pdf, p. 6.

5. Transparency International, *Report on the Transparency International Global Corruption Barometer 2007* (Berlin: Transparency International, International Secretariat), http://www.transparency.org/policy_research/surveys_indices/gcb/2007.

6. Anders Aslund, "Revolution, Red Directors and Oligarchs in Ukraine," *Ukrainian Quarterly* 60, Vol. 60, Number 1–2 (Spring-Summer 2004): 5–18.

7. State Statistics Committee of Ukraine, "All-Ukrainian Population Census 2001," http://www.ukrcensus.gov.ua/eng.

8. World Health Organization's country information on Ukraine, http://www.who.int/countries/ukr/en/.

9. Tamara Govorun and Borys M. Vornyk, "Ukraine," in *The International Encyclopedia of Sexuality,* ed. Robert T. Francoeur, vol. 20 (New York: Continuum, Vol. I–IV 1997–2001, Chapters 3, 5, 6, and 9), http://www2.hu-berlin.de/sexology/IES/index.html.

10. D. Snowyd, *Spirit of Ukraine: Ukrainian Contributions to World's Culture* (New York: United Ukrainian Organizations of the United States, 1935).

11. Natalia Kostenko, Tatyana Androsenko and Ludmila Males, "In Search of Holidays: The Case of Ukraine," in *National Days/National Ways: Historical, Political, and Religious Celebrations around the World,* ed. Linda K. Fuller (Westport, CT: Praeger, 2004).

7

Media

MEDIA IN UKRAINE are characterized by their role during the Soviet era, the turbulent post-Soviet transition years, and the Orange Revolution. Historically, the Ukrainian press has flourished at times of national revival and awakening. Conversely, it was repressed during periods of restrictive cultural policies implemented by different occupying forces. Media policies during the Soviet era, in particular, left profound marks, without which it would be impossible to understand the media in Ukraine today. Ukrainian independence from the Soviet Union allowed for an unfettered development of media for the first time in modern Ukrainian history. Since independence, however, media in Ukraine, often instrumentalized by powerful political and economic interests, have been fighting to carve out an independent and institutionally protected space. Journalists have managed to claim this space with only a degree of success. Despite an existing legal framework designed to protect the independence and professionalism of the media in practice, many issues, such as political pressure, monopolistic ownership, and economic hardship, prevent the establishment of stable, sustainable, and fully free media. In the midst of tense political fluctuations and power shifts in recent years, courageous but often isolated journalists resisted censorship and intimidation. They helped propel the Orange Revolution, during which people protested media censorship. The development of a relatively unfettered Internet media space in the late 1990s and early 2000s offered an outlet for government critique and created a renewed sense of trust among Ukrainians toward their media as sources of accurate and independent news.[1] Despite many unresolved issues and the tenuous evolution of the media, the Ukrainian media scene is dynamic and diverse. Numerous newspapers and radio and television stations, both national and local, as well as a growing Internet presence keep Ukrainian citizens entertained and informed by offering a wide range of news sources.

History of Media in Ukraine

Historically, the first newspaper published in the Ukrainian language, *Zoria halytska,* appeared in May 1848 as part of the Ukrainian national awakening movement in Galicia. It was the time of the "Spring of Nations" revolutions throughout the Austrian Empire, which helped ignite Ukrainian demands for national recognition. *Zoria halytska* was published in L'viv by the Supreme Ruthenian Council, the first Ukrainian political organization. The increase in Ukrainian political activity at the time sparked an extraordinary expansion in Ukrainian publications and journals.[2] The first Ukrainian periodical in the Russian Empire was *Osnova,* published in 1861 in St. Petersburg. Started by a group of notable Ukrainophile intellectuals, including Taras Shevchenko, Panteleimon Kulish, and Mykola Kostomarov, and backed by the financial support of a few wealthy Ukrainian landowners, *Osnova* became the means for rousing national sentiment and a discursive forum for Ukrainian intelligentsia during its brief existence. *Osnova* published many controversial and thought-provoking articles on the subject of Ukrainian national identity and the fate of the Ukrainian people. For example, Kostromarov's article "Dve russkie narodnosti" (Two Russian Nationalities) proposed that the Ukrainian and Russian people were in fact two distinct nationalities, a novel and nationalistic proposition at the time. *Osnova* also published "Confession," an article by a Polonized Ukrainian noble discussing the future of Polonized nobles and the need for them to rejoin the Ukrainian people.[3] The latter decades of the nineteenth century and the early years of the twentieth century witnessed the appearance and disappearance of numerous similar publications in the Ukrainian lands under the rule of the Russian and Austrian Empires. The existence and longevity of these publications depended directly on financial and political fluctuations as well as changes in the degree of tolerance afforded Ukrainian nationalistic sentiment in both empires.

From the early years of the Soviet Union, the Communist Party leadership understood that control over processes of collecting and distributing mass information would be one of the prerequisites of a successful revolution. They saw a centralized, party-controlled press and its ability to organize and ideologically affect the masses as the key to creating and maintaining revolutionary momentum. Several policies designed to put this belief into practice were enacted immediately after the revolution. A Decree on the Press was introduced in 1917, outlawing any press outlet that dared to express opposition and insubordination to Soviet rule. That same year, a Revolutionary Tribunal on the Press was formed to investigate crimes committed against the people through the use of the press. Finally, in November 1917, Soviet leadership introduced a state monopoly on advertising, severely restricting access to funds for privately owned media. These steps achieved a de facto subordination of the Soviet media to the Communist Party in the early years of the Soviet Union that allowed for decades of repressive media policy.[4]

The media organs in Soviet Ukraine were exposed to much of the same treatment as those in the other Soviet Republics. State control information flows and content ensured the dominance of Communist Party ideology. Under Soviet rule, media in Ukraine ceased to be a tool of national expression and became an instrument for processes of socialization and indoctrination aimed at turning Ukrainians into Soviet citizens. The Soviet era, however, was not a monolithic period regarding mass media. Phases of complete media control were interspersed with those of more relaxed controls, though not of in-depth reform.

In the 1920s the Soviet Communist Party instituted a policy of promoting education, literacy, and cultural activities in the indigenous languages of the republics of the Soviet Union with an aim of uniting different ethnic and linguistic groups behind a common communist ideology. Ukrainianization, a version of this policy in Ukraine, led to an increased use of the Ukrainian language in education, publishing, and in the cultural sphere. The media in Ukraine played an important role in Ukrainianization, sparking an upsurge of Ukrainian-language newspapers and publications.

Stalin's rule brought the cult of personality into the media sphere, turning the media into a tool for exerting and strengthening his personal power. In the period of de-Ukrainianization, in the 1930s, the number of Ukrainian language newspapers dropped drastically. In 1931, 90 percent of all newspapers published in Ukraine were in Ukrainian. This figure dropped to 70 percent in 1940.[5] World War II and German occupation in Ukraine brought a brief respite from Stalin's Soviet censors but did nothing to liberate the Ukrainian media. In fact, following an initial spike in the number of Ukrainian-language publications, the Nazi regime suppressed all elements of Ukrainian nationalism in the press. In 1942 Ivan Rohach, editor of the short-lived newspaper *Ukraïns'ke Slovo,* was arrested by the Gestapo and executed at Babyn Yar. The postwar years brought Stalinism back into the Ukrainian media space. Stalin's death, followed by Khrushchev's thaw, livened up the Soviet media space and introduced a degree of relief from strict

Stalinist media controls. However, the fundamentals of Soviet media policy and its subordination to the Communist Party did not change despite such interludes of perceived official lenience.

Several key strategies were used by the Communist Party to control and supervise the media throughout the Soviet era. The Party controlled access to media facilities, licensing, and finance, allowing only complying media outlets to survive. Furthermore, most of the editors and senior journalists in the Soviet Union as well as ordinary journalists were members and appointees of the Communist Party and were guided by it in selecting content for their media reporting.[6] For journalists, underground publications constituted the only opportunity to express dissent, usually at the risk of job security and personal safety. When political in nature, these underground publications in Ukraine often conveyed opposition to the official policy toward nationalities and elaborated on questions regarding the position of ethnic Ukrainians in the Soviet Union.[7] Official political instruction and guidelines, self-censorship, and overt censorship provided the Communist Party with absolute control over domestic media outlets. Restricted access to foreign press sources and international news rounded up the picture of the media sphere in Soviet times.[8]

The process of transformation of Soviet media and, by extension, the media in Ukraine began in the mid-1980s, when Gorbachev introduced the policy of glasnost, aimed at, among other things, loosening control over the media. Glasnost introduced pluralism and increased access to different media sources in society. In the second half of the 1980s, commentaries and criticisms about the deteriorating economic situation, strikes, ethnic clashes, and nationalist tendencies in the republics began appearing in Soviet media. The only remaining taboos in the media were criticisms directed at the general secretary of the Communist Party and Lenin. The Soviet media space was significantly freed by allowing increased criticism in the media and greater access to information during glasnost. The collapse of the Soviet Union disintegrated the system of controls and brought degrees of liberalization to the media in the republics of the former Soviet Union.

RECENT DEVELOPMENTS

The period immediately following the Ukrainian declaration of independence in 1991 witnessed a rapid expansion of media outlets and provoked jubilation among Ukrainian journalists. Censorship and policies of strict regulatory, financial, and administrative media controls already relaxed during glasnost fell away even more. Considering the sheer number of state-building and international issues on the agenda of the president and parliament in the early years of Ukrainian independence, it is not surprising that the media were given significantly free reign. Journalists took advantage of the professional freedom afforded to them by the newly independent Ukrainian state. Many young people entered the profession, while seasoned journalists attempted to adjust to the new rules of the game.

The first law defining the legal ground rules for regulating the media sector and allowing private ownership of media outlets, the Law on Information, was adopted in 1992. With this law, owning private newspapers, radio stations, and television channels became a possibility, which many powerful individuals and interest groups in Ukraine began to take advantage of. Already by 1993, there were 499 television and 343 radio stations and companies in Ukraine, though many of them were de facto inactive.[9] Regardless of the widening media space and the deluge of privately owned media, however, the state retained formal control over approximately 10 percent of print and broadcast media in this period. Despite this seemingly small percentage, the actual influence of the state-owned media was much greater due to the significant number of inactive registered private media at the time and the broad coverage of its state-owned counterpart.[10] Russian language media and media from Russia were very prominent in Ukraine immediately following independence. By 1993, however, the share of media produced in Russia began to decline as part of efforts by the state to curtail the influence of Russian media. Ukrainian media outlets that transmitted and printed in Russian retained a loyal audience. Six percent of all publications in Ukraine in 1992 were published in Russian.[11] Such was the vibrant and eclectic media space flourishing in Ukraine in the first half of the 1990s.

In the mid-1990s, the situation began to change. The first indication of censorship and media control occurred during the 1994 presidential election campaign, when incumbent President Leonid Kravchuk shut down HRAVIS television station, which supported his opponent Leonid Kuchma, for allegedly improper licensing.[12] Although President Kuchma won the election, the trend toward lessening media freedom increased. Significant financing and state subsidies for state-owned media systematically weakened the market position of the private media, particularly newspapers. In 1996, for instance, the state budget allocated more than $7 million to three government-run newspapers.[13] During this period, politicians recognized television stations as a source of political power due to their broad reach to audiences and their increasing profitability. By 1996 the political control of the executive branch of government over broadcast media was consolidated, with all state-owned radio and television run by a state company and controlled by a government agency.[14] The state's reach expanded to non-state-owned media as well. At this time, the influence of a group of wealthy individuals close to President Kuchma, Ukraine's oligarchs, began to strengthen, and by the late 1990s, all six national television stations were owned by the state or individuals close to the corridors of power.[15] Deliberate pressures on the media designed to interrupt or even shut down their operations were fomented by President Kuchma's increasingly autocratic tactics and mounting corruption in the country. The independence and even existence of certain media venues was sabotaged through methods ranging from lawsuits, tax audits, and other bureaucratic channels applying pressure on printing houses. Calls from government officials requesting positive coverage or reprimanding editors and journalists for critical coverage became common and further encouraged self-censorship. Most owners of media companies lacked the will or the power to stand up to the president. This trend of increasing censorship and tightening media control in the late 1990s escalated with the presidential election in 1999. During this period the Committee to Protect Journalists designated Ukraine as having no genuinely independent major news media.[16]

President Kuchma's reelection in 1999 was followed by an effort on his part to consolidate his power and exert stronger influence over the Verkhovna Rada, Ukraine's parliament, under the pretext of wanting to end legislative deadlock between the executive branch and the parliament. This consolidation of power involved a renewed attack on the media. The already existing controls—through direct ownership, pressure on owners, criminal and civil code revisions that allowed defamation suits, and other forms of pressure on dissenting media outlets—were supplemented by instances of intimidation and physical attacks on journalists. In September 2000, Heorhii Gongadze, an independent journalist and founder of an Internet site called "Ukrainska Pravda" (Ukrainian Truth) strongly critical of the government, disappeared. Two months later, his beheaded body was found outside of Kyiv. In November 2000, Oleksandar Moroz, leader of the Socialist Party, accused President Kuchma in a speech in parliament of being responsible for Gongadze's murder. This public accusation was a spark that ignited the popular protest movement "Ukraine without Kuchma." Another element that contributed to the prevailing sense of censorship in Ukrainian media in the early 2000s was the widespread use of *temnyky* in broadcasting. *Temnyky* were unsigned instructions from the presidential administration that directed broadcast editors and journalists toward acceptable topics for broadcasts and away from undesirable ones. Though *temnyky* were common knowledge among journalists in 2002 and 2003, the government denied their existence and attributed the existence of censorship to owners of media outlets and foreign governments.[17]

During this period, the government did allow small-circulation and limited-reach media, in particular printed media, as well as a small but vibrant

Internet media scene to survive while remaining critical to the government, but mostly utilized their existence as proof of government leniency toward domestic media. The revelation of the president's involvement in a politically motivated murder was a turning point in the perception of the Ukrainian public as a sign of the regime's increasingly repressive measures. In 2002 the Worldwide Press Freedom Index ranked Ukraine as 112th (out of 139 countries) in terms of journalistic freedom.[18]

THE ORANGE REVOLUTION

The Orange Revolution turned the Ukrainian political and media scene upside down. The period immediately preceding the 2004 presidential elections was extremely difficult for media personnel. Constraints on journalistic freedom intensified through an even wider distribution of *temnyky*, increased propaganda, and reduced information content and TV coverage increasingly limited to a single viewpoint. At the end of October 2004, three days before the election, approximately 40 journalists from five television stations declared they would not follow *temnyky* any longer. The following day, many more journalists joined in this declaration. This gesture caused a small shift in media coverage, though not a momentous change in the media's effect on the public. Internet media took the initiative in organizing the "Orange Ribbon" campaign, encouraging people in Kyiv and elsewhere to wear orange ribbons in open protest against President Kuchma and as a sign of disagreement with biased media coverage and falsification of election results. Orange was the campaign color of opposition leader Viktor Yushchenko and discourses of free speech were closely intertwined with his potential election. Some anchors took to wearing orange on television while reading biased news reports. By this time, Yushchenko's supporters were using mobile television screens and rented satellite channels to transmit their message, bypassing the official television channels, as Channel 5 was the only one broadcasting revolutionary events. The first serious changes in broadcasting content were sparked by an unusual event. On November 25, Natalia Dmytruk, a sign language interpreter on state television, signed her own message, instead of translating the anchor's text on election results. She said not to trust the official results from the Central Election Commission and expressed her support for Viktor Yushchenko. From this moment, the television coverage on all channels focused on the previously ignored unfolding events of the Orange Revolution and on Yushchenko. This ushered a period of unprecedented openness in Ukrainian broadcast media. Furthermore, Internet media experienced a record increase in readership due to a great extent to its role in the Orange Revolution.[19]

November 24, 2004, the third day of protests on Independence Square in Kyiv. Photo by Adriana Helbig.

LEGAL FRAMEWORK

The media's legal status is prescribed by the Ukrainian Constitution, and over a dozen laws regulate different aspects of the media space, ranging from regulatory bodies to language. Article 34 of the Ukrainian Constitution guarantees freedom of thought, speech, and expression as well as the right to freely collect, store, use, and disseminate information.[20] The Law on Information from 1992 regulates types of information activities, the rights and responsibilities associated with the provision and usage of information, and the protection of the right to information and responsibility for the breaches of information laws.[21]

Several agencies are in charge of the functioning of the media and information. In parliament, it is the Rada Committee for the Freedom of Speech and Information, while in the government, the responsibility falls on the State Committee for Information Policy, Television, and Radio Broadcasting and the State Committee for Communication and Information. The National Council for Television and Radio Broadcasting is a body responsible for withdrawing and granting broadcasting licenses, with eight members coappointed by the parliament and the president.[22] This was the most contentious regulatory body during the late 1990s and early 2000s because of its ability to impose pressure through licensing regulation. Ukrainian media laws are harmonized with international provisions and allow for the application of European Conventions and decisions of the European Court.[23] Despite this relatively well developed legal and regulatory framework theoretically guaranteeing the Ukrainian media a high degree of independence and a level playing field for competition, the actual situation has been much more complicated. A significant number of gray areas and loopholes in the regulations, exacerbated by a regular lack of implementation, allowed the government to impose pressure on the Ukrainian media throughout the 1990s and prior to the Orange Revolution. To an extent, various degrees of external pressures on the media extend to the present day. This elaborate legal framework regulating the Ukrainian media sphere has often served as a shady alibi that allows the Ukrainian leadership to verbally support, but not practice, their claims of respecting the freedom of the press.

MEDIA IN UKRAINE TODAY

The media scene in Ukraine, changed significantly by the Orange Revolution, has displayed a greater freedom of information and increased access to a greater variety of news sources and points of view. However, while outright media censorship is no longer present, many issues remain unresolved. President Yushchenko's election promises included a commitment to reform the media sector and foster development of a free and sustainable media. Most of his election pledges, however, have yet to come to fruition. Transforming the remaining state-owned media into a public broadcasting system remains one of the most important goals in reforming Ukrainian media. Powerful oligarchs have retained much of the media ownership, which allows them to shape public opinion. Transparency in media ownership is still not adequate.

Television

Television is the most influential media in Ukraine, particularly the television channels with national broadcast reach. The vast majority of television stations are regional, which prevents them from wielding the same amount of nationwide influence. Main television networks with national coverage are UT-1, Inter TV, Studio 1+1, STB, Novyi Kanal (New Channel), ICTV, 5 Kanal (Channel 5), and TRK Ukraina. UT-1 is owned by the National Television Company of Ukraine (state owned) and has almost 100 percent coverage of the Ukrainian territory. Its ratings, however, are not very high (ranking 10th). Inter and Studio 1+1 are the most popular television channels, with ratings of around 24 and 17 percent, respectively, and high national coverage. Not surprisingly, they also divide the majority of advertisement revenue. As of 2004, Inter and Studio 1+1 were controlled by Viktor Medvedchuk, chairman of the (United) Social Democratic Party of Ukraine and one of former President Leonid Kuchma's closest allies. The New Channel has ratings of around 7 percent, and ICTV and STB have around 6 percent each. In the period preceding the Orange Revolution, STB and ICTV were owned by Viktor Pinchuk, former President Kuchma's son-in-law. STB was originally founded with U.S. Agency for International Development funding with the goal of establishing an independent television station but was later privatized and exposed to systematic harassment by the government. Channel 5 was considered the only independent television channel in the period immediately prior to and during the Orange Revolution. By attracting talented opposition-minded journalists and broadcasting independent news, it gained a unique reputation despite its low coverage and lack of resources. Feature films, serial dramas, and soap operas are the most common programming on private television channels, while state-owned UT-1 airs more news and current affairs programming. Several Russian channels are broadcast via satellite and on some of the national and regional television stations. The popularity and broad audience reach of television in Ukraine have resulted in television being most affected by government censorship and other forms of pressure since independence.[24]

Print

The situation with print media in Ukraine is quiet different from the television sector in terms of ownership, degree of openness, and the influence they exert on the public. Print media are owned by a variety of entities, ranging from wealthy oligarchs to media conglomerates, political parties, trade unions, government agencies, and nongovernmental organizations. This diverse funding network contributes to a wide spectrum of viewpoints in print media. The newspapers in Ukraine have experienced an overall drop in circulation since independence, mostly due to rising prices of production and the lowering purchasing power of the Ukrainian public. Only four Ukrainian daily newspapers devoted to the news and current affairs have a circulation greater than 100,000 copies—*Fakty i Kommentarii* (761,000), *Vecherniye Vesti* (500,000), *Silski Visti* (430,000), and *Ukrayina Moloda* (163,000). These high-circulation newspapers represent well the diversity of political views in the Ukrainian print media space. *Fakty i Kommentarii* is a Russian and Ukrainian-language newspaper covering news and current events without much analysis. It is owned by Viktor Pinchuk and has in the past supported former President Kuchma and Viktor Yanukovych. *Vecherniye Vesti* is a Russian-language daily controlled by politician Yuliya Tymoshenko and has been critical of both Viktor Yushchenko and Viktor Yanukovych. *Silski Visti* is a Ukrainian-language daily targeting the rural population and supporting Oleksander Moroz, the leader of the Socialist Party and one-time opponent of President Kuchma and, more recently, an ally of Viktor Yanukovych. Finally, *Ukrayina Moloda,* a Ukrainian-language paper, targets a younger audience and has supported Yushchenko, while being critical of Yanukovych. Other important publications include *Segodnya,* a Russian-language tabloid focusing more on human interest stories and less on politics, though it has been loyal to Yanukovych; *Zerkalo Nedeli,* a widely respected weekly publication containing independent reporting and analysis; and *Den,* a Russian and Ukrainian daily newspaper with a circulation of 62,000 that offers a neutral point of view.[25] Compared to other European countries, the number of national print media in Ukraine is relatively small in terms of number and circulation.[26] Regional and local newspapers have been more popular and sustainable in Ukraine mostly due to their content, which is more appealing to local audiences and has lower costs of distribution. Numerous Russian-language publications contribute to the diversity in the Ukrainian press, comprising 22 percent of registered print media.[27] This diversity of opinion among Ukrainian publications survived even during periods of heaviest censorship, most likely because of their relatively limited reach and influence over audiences.

Other Media

Ukrainian radio is often omitted in the discussion of pre- and post–Orange Revolution media space and influence. However, many radio stations experienced censorship and restrictions in the period preceding the Orange Revolution. Public Radio, for example, was denied a license to broadcast and was pushed off the air at this time. And conversely, radio became increasingly important during the Orange Revolution. The most prominent presence on the Ukrainian radio waves is the National Radio Company of Ukraine, with its three channels and 100 percent national coverage.

Last, but not least, the Internet is a relatively new addition to the media scene in Ukraine, albeit an essential one. In the early 2000s, the Internet became a platform for publishing dissenting opinion, uncensored articles, and unofficial versions of events, providing a space for all that was left unsaid in the mainstream media. The events surrounding the disappearance and murder of Heorhii Gongadze catapulted his Internet site "Ukrainska Pravda" into the political orbit and created greater interest in Internet media. In the months leading up to the Orange Revolution, awareness of the Internet as an alternative to mainstream media exploded. A proliferation of Web sites maintained by political candidates and parties was matched by up-to-date political coverage and commentary on the Internet. In September 2004, Ukrainian news sites had 6.3 million visitors. By December 2004, they had 20 million.[28] This unprecedented growth of Internet media influence took place despite the relatively poor infrastructure of Internet outlets. Internet penetration in Ukraine is relatively low, at only about 12 percent. This is due mostly to a lack of telecom infrastructure, the high cost of connections, and low computer ownership. There are only several hundred active and updated operational Web sites in Ukraine.

The inherent speed of Internet sites, their imperviousness to censorship, and their organizational potential jump-started the Internet as an engine for change. The Internet's role as a facilitator of political change during the Orange Revolution has extended today to become a channel for attracting young people. It functions as a social networking tool that is quickly becoming a dynamic and fast-paced engine of creativity and ideas.

The Ukrainian media scene has experienced momentous changes in the last two decades. Having evolved from a state-owned, ideology-espousing institution of Soviet times to an important factor in political change, the Ukrainian media today are diverse and relatively free. There are, however, many issues that prevent the media from becoming true drivers of change in a democratizing Ukraine. Lack of transparency in media ownership, particularly in broadcast media, makes it difficult at times to grasp the frequent hidden agendas of individual media outlets. Many major television stations and newspapers display strong political affiliations, and Ukrainians often have to reach out beyond a single source to acquire a balanced and fair point of view. The lack of economic sustainability also hampers the growth of a viable independent media industry. However, positive trends, such as the increasingly important and creative role of the Internet and an increasing presence of investigative journalism, have the potential of further supporting the development of Ukrainian media and evoking higher levels of trust in diverse media forums among the Ukrainian public.

NOTES

1. International Foundation for Electoral Systems and U.S. AID, *Attitudes of Ukrainians prior to 2007 Rada Elections,* August–September 2007, http://www.ifes.org/publication/c02e80ae0eb56679827e3a5c38b27f15/Ukraine%20Exec%20Summary.pdf.

2. Paul Magocsi, *A History of Ukraine* (Seattle: University of Washington Press, 1998), 406–13.

3. Ibid., 367; Orest Subtleny, *Ukraine: A History,* 3rd ed. (Toronto: University of Toronto Press, 2000), 280–81.

4. Brian McNair, *Glasnost, Perestroika and the Soviet Media* (New York: Routledge, 1991), 18, 35–36.

5. Subtleny, *Ukraine: A History,* 423.

6. McNair, *Glasnost,* 49.

7. Open Society Archives, "Records of Radio Free Europe/Radio Liberty Research Institute (RFE/RL RI), Samizdat Archives, 1968–1992," http://www.osa.ceu.hu/db/fa/300.htm.

8. Library of Congress, "A Country Study: Soviet Union (Former)," http://lcweb2.loc.gov/frd/cs/sutoc.html.

9. Andrei Richter, "Ukraine," in *Business as Usual: Continuity and Change in Central and Eastern European Media,* ed. David L. Paletz and Karol Jakubowicz (Cresskill, NJ: Hampton Press, 2003), 305.

10. Marta Dyczok, "Was Kuchma's Censorship Effective? Mass Media in Ukraine before 2004," *Europe Asia Studies* 58 (2006): 220–21.

11. Richter, "Ukraine," 309.

12. Dyczok, "Was Kuchma's," 222.

13. Richter, "Ukraine," 306.

14. Ibid., 307.

15. Dyczok, "Was Kuchma's," 222.

16. Committee to Protect Journalists, *Ukraine Report 1999,* http://www.cpj.org/attacks99/europe99/Ukraine.html.

17. Human Rights Watch Report, "Negotiating the News: Informal State Censorship of Ukrainian Television," *Human Rights Watch* 15 (2003): 13–16.

18. Reporters Without Borders, Worldwide Press Freedom Index, 2002. http://www.rsf.org/article.php3?id_article=4116.

19. Olena Prytula, "The Ukrainian Media Rebellion," in *Revolution in Orange: The Origins of Ukraine's Democratic Breakthrough,* ed. Anders Aslund and Michael McFaul (Washington, DC: Carnegie Endowment for International Peace, 2006), 117.

20. Constitution of Ukraine, "Chapter II: Human and Citizens' Rights, Freedoms and Duties," http://www.rada.kiev.ua/const/conengl.htm#r2.

21. Richter, "Ukraine," 301–2. Separate laws regulate printed mass media, TV, and radio broadcasting (with distinct laws for private and public broadcasting) as well as the licensing, advertising, and media coverage of government and information agencies.

22. Human Rights Watch Report, "Negotiating."

23. IREX, Europe and Eurasia, "The Development of Sustainable Media in Europe and Eurasia," *Media Sustainability Index* (MSI), 2008. http//www.irex.org/programs/MSI_EUR/index.asp.

24. Information about ownership and ratings from Human Rights Watch Report, "Negotiating"; Prytula, "Ukrainian Media"; Dyczok, "Was Kuchma's"; and http://www.prioritet.tv/pages/reiting.php.

25. Circulation figures and basic information about newspapers from BBC News Europe, "The Press in Ukraine," http://news.bbc.co.uk/2/hi/europe/4073375.stm, and Human Rights Watch, *Ukraine Report.*

26. Human Rights Watch, *Ukraine Report,* 10.

27. Ukrainian-language publications make up 38 percent, and bilingual publications 20 percent, according to Human Rights Watch, Ukraine Report.

28. Prytula, "Ukrainian Media," 108–11.

8

Literature

UKRAINE'S LITERATURE IS a reflection of its turbulent history. With Ukrainian lands under constant foreign rule, ethnic Ukrainian writers were exposed to various linguistic influences such as Russian, Polish, German, and Yiddish. Historically, they developed strong ties with Russian and Polish literary circles, reflecting as much a vibrant cultural exchange as the political realities of the day. In the nineteenth century, Ivan Franko, a prominent Ukrainian writer and critic, distinguished "the national from the international"[1] in the works written by Ukrainian authors, delineating the development of a distinctly Ukrainian literary tradition in the wake of a rising national consciousness.

THE OLD PERIOD: ELEVENTH TO FIFTEENTH CENTURIES

Writing spread in Kyivan Rus' with Christianization in the late tenth century. Most early writers were monks, and literary works were ecclesiastical and historical in nature. Chronicles were the main literary genre. They were comprehensive works that included various literary genres and later became the most important historical sources for the political and cultural life of Kyivan Rus' such as *The Primary Chronicle* ascribed to the monk Nestor.

According to information in *The Primary Chronicle,* copyists and translators were brought together by Prince Yaroslav the Wise to translate church service books that came from the Southern Slavs (Bulgarians and Macedonians) and Western Slavs (Czechs and Slovaks). These borrowed and translated literary works laid the foundation for early Eastern Slavic literature, which ranged from sermons to heroic epics. The oldest dated Eastern Slavic manuscript is the *Ostromyrova Yevanhelia* (Ostromir's Gospel). Written by Deacon Hryhory for his patron Ostromir in 1056–1057, the book reflects political and cultural relations between Kyivan Rus' under the rule of Yaroslav the Wise and its European neighbors.

Early Ukrainian works in verse, which were influenced by Byzantine poetry, have survived in the present day only as fragments, due to early phonetic changes in the Old Church Slavonic and Old Ukrainian languages. The metrical form of these verses was destroyed through the disappearance of some vowels.

One of the earliest literary genres was the sermon. The most important sermons of this era were written by St. Theodosius, one of the founders of the Kyivan Cave Monastery, and by Metropolitan Ilarion, the first non-Greek Metropolitan of Kyiv. The sermons by St. Feodosii, written for monks, were based on texts from Holy Scripture and expressed his ideas of monastic life. The sermons written by Metropolitan Ilarion compared the Old and New Testaments and praised Prince Volodymyr the Great and his descendants. Noteworthy for their simple phrases, epithets, and rhythmical language, these monumental works glorified Christianity and the notion of the single great state as it existed under Yaroslav the Wise.

Bylinas, or *starynas,* were old epic narratives that depicted heroic events of the past, sorcerers, and heroes: Volga Vseslavych, Prince Volodymyr the Fair Sun and his uncle Dobrynia, Volodymyr Monomakh, Alesha Popovich, Stavr Godinovich, the Scandinavian bard Solovei Budymyrovych, Elijah Muromets, and others.[2] Although not much is known about the form of the old epics, the characters of *bylinas* have been popularized in paintings, films, and animated cartoons and are well known today to most Ukrainians, Russians, and Belarusians of different ages.

Another popular genre was the *life,* the germ of the biographical genre. Two *lives* were written by Monk Nestor of the Kyivan Cave Monastery in the eleventh century. *Chtenie* (Reading) described the lives of Saints Borys and Hlib and is an extended account of their tragic death in a biography written for Christians. *Skazanie* (Narrative) is about the life of the first abbot of the Kyivan Cave Monastery, St. Feodosii, and his spiritual development.

Tales were another prominent Eastern Slavic literary genre. Many tales depicted the construction of churches and the miracles performed by saints. One of the larger tales is about the conversion of the pagan ruler of Kyiv, Prince Volodymyr the Great, to Christianity in 988, and the murder of his sons Borys and Hlib by their brother Sviatopolk in 1015.

The Primary Chronicle, also known as *The Tale of Bygone Years,* compiled in Kyiv around 1113, is the earliest written testimony of the history of Eastern

Slavs and presumably one of the most intensively studied texts in history. *The Tale of Bygone Years* served as the foundation for later *Kyiv* and *Galician-Volhynian Chronicles*. *The Tale* was traditionally ascribed to Nestor, but he was probably the author of only one of its versions. The original version of the chronicle is lost. The oldest extant manuscripts are the *Laurentian Codex* from 1377 and the *Hypatian Codex* from the fifteenth century. The language of *The Tale* is a combination of Old Church Slavonic and the vernacular of the time.

The chronicle is a literary form based on historical materials taken from multiple sources: western and southern Slavonic literary works, Byzantine annals of John Malalas and George Hamartolus, Norse sagas, Greek religious texts, Russo-Byzantine treaties, and narratives of military leaders. Part of the *Laurentian Codex* is *Pouchenie ditiam* (Instruction for My Children) by Grand Prince Volodymyr Monomakh (1053–1125), a collection of philosophical comments and advice to his children on private, stately, and military matters. Monomakh presents himself as the embodiment of a unitary state, a wise ruler and a brave warrior; his writings suggest that he kept a diary of his 83 military campaigns.

While Kyiv was the primary literary center, the disintegration of the Kyivan realm in the twelfth century led to the appearance of new literary centers in Chernihiv, Turiv, Pereiaslav, and western Ukrainian lands. The most important preacher of the period was Cyril, Bishop of Turiv (ca. 1130–1140), author of sermons and symbolic tales of a moral and didactic nature.

The Patericon of the Kyivan Cave Monastery is a collection of tales that originated from correspondence between the monks Simeon and Polycarp of the Kyivan Cave Monastery. The *Patericon* is one of the most important works in old Eastern Slavic literature. The tales, ascetic and antisecular in spirit, paint a vivid picture of monastic and secular life of the time. They describe the judicial system, libraries and books, icon painting, and the cultural influence of the Vikings.

Slovo o Polku Ihorevi (The Tale of Ihor's War), although deemed by some scholars to be a falsification, is the greatest literary achievement of Kyivan Rus' and the last expression of its unity. It tells the story of Prince Ihor Sviatoslavych of Novhorod-Siversky, who, ignoring the bad omen of a solar eclipse in 1185, wages a war against the marauding Polovtsians. In spite of initial success, Ihor fails to unite with other powerful princes and suffers a defeat. Attempts to identify the author have failed, although it is presumed that he was a Galician boyar, a fervent patriot, and a Christian, who, in spite of his religion, used many pagan elements in his writing. Reality in the poem is virtually hidden behind symbolism. Symbols replace events and names and serve as good or bad omens. A battle is a harvest, the Rusychi are falcons, and the princes are suns. Bloody dawns, dark clouds, and the groan of the earth forebode evil. The four princes are portrayed as cosmic forces: they are strong enough to dry up swamps, hurl weights behind the clouds, and trample abysses. The poem is rhythmically metered, but not versed.

Political developments of the fourteenth century brought almost all of Ukraine into the Lithuanian-Polish Commonwealth, and literary activities became limited to monasteries. The old tradition continued in the reworking of old writings. New influences included the translations of new Christian writers Isaac the Syrian, Simeon "the New Theologian," Gregory of Sinai, Palamas, Kavasilas, and Maxim the Confessor. Some of these translations were done by the school of the Bulgarian Patriarch Euthymios of Trnovo, whose mystical religious beliefs and linguistic reforms had a certain influence on Ukrainian culture.

THE RENAISSANCE AND THE REFORMATION

Ukrainian literature of the sixteenth century shifted from Byzantine to Western European genres and standards. Since the Renaissance and the Reformation came to Ukraine more or less simultaneously, they became intermingled and modified. The Ukrainian Renaissance was not very influential because the bearers of the scholarly tradition at that time were primarily clergymen; universities as secular centers of scholarship emerged only later. The Reformation strengthened the role of religion, and church authorities emphasized the Bible as the Word of God speaking to people in their own language. A split within the Orthodox Church gave rise to the Uniate Church. Many translations of tales and the Holy Scriptures were made into vernacular in this period, with the greatest scholarly achievement being the Ostroh Bible of 1581. The common stylistic feature of all the scholarly and theological works of the period was rhetoric, that is, the use of epistles, dialogues, and orations. The most brilliant polemicist of the time was monk Ivan Vyshensky, who called for genuine Christianity in everyday social life and opposed modern trends. Other prominent polemicists were Herasym Smotrytsky, Vasyl Ostrozsky, and Adam Ipatii Potii. Unlike other literary epochs, the Renaissance and the Reformation in Ukrainian literature lasted only for a short time and did not produce other noteworthy literary figures.

BAROQUE

The Baroque period in Ukrainian literature spans the seventeenth and eighteenth centuries. Baroque aesthetics emphasized form in literary works, rejected simplicity, and sought to excite the reader. In Ukraine, the decline of statehood resulted in linguistic divergences, and literary works were published in Ukrainian, Polish, and Latin languages. The lack of scientific centers and the dominance of churchmen among the carriers of the literary tradition boosted the development of the sermon and the theological treatise. The outstanding theological treatise of the sixteenth century is Zacharias Kopystensky's *Palinodiia,* a brilliant example of Baroque humor and rhetoric..Baroque sermons differed from others in their abundant use of artistic devices that aimed to evoke a listener's interest. They included fables, tales, adages, anecdotes, references to historical events, and even some bold comparisons: Noah was portrayed as an admiral, and Moses was portrayed as a hetman. The most exceptional preachers of the day were Cyril Tranquillion Stavrovetsky, Petro Mohyla, Meletius Smotrytsky, Antin Radyvylovsky, Lazar Baranovych, and Ioannikii Galiatovsky.

The Baroque era was the golden age of Ukrainian verse. Its content became extraordinarily rich. Secular verses centered on sentimental, political, and national themes. Spiritual verses focused on Christ, the Mother of God, saints, icons, or feasts and were oftentimes sung. Versified quips came into fashion. In alphabet verses, each word or line began with the next letter of the alphabet. In acrostics, the first letter of each line or strophe formed a name. Figured verses had peculiar shapes and some verses could be read in both directions. Ivan Velychkovsky, Priest Clement, St. Dymytrii Tuptalo, Stephen Iavorsky, and, later, Hryhory Skovoroda were masters of versified quips.

Poet and philosopher Hryhory Skovoroda was intrigued by the idea of happiness, and his works were rich with symbolism. In addition to letters written in Latin and translations of antique philosophers, Skovoroda left behind a collection of 30 verses, *Sad Bozhestvennykh Pisen* (Garden of Divine Songs), and a collection of 30 fables, *Basni Kharkovskiia* (Kharkiv Fables). Some of Skovoroda's poems and songs became part of Ukrainian folklore, and his legacy played a significant role in the renaissance of Ukrainian culture in the twentieth century.

Ukrainian drama developed under the influence of Polish and Latin theaters. In its early works, the action took place behind the scenes and was reported by messengers. Modern drama developed in Ukraine in the late seventeenth century. Morality plays, with their abstract concepts and personified virtues, were the most original types of Baroque drama. Some of the best dramas of the time were written by St. Dymytrii Tuptalo, Feofan Prokopovych, Heorhy Konysky, and Metrofan Dovhalevsky.

The main historical work of the baroque period is *Cossack Chronicles* by Samovydets (The Eyewitness) and Samiilo Velychko. Given the political developments of the time, historical literature acquired great national importance and significantly influenced nineteenth-century writers, especially Taras Shevchenko (1814–1861) and Panteleimon Kulish (1819–1897).

CLASSICISM

Classicism, with its high style and return to the principles of ancient poetics, was rooted in Ukraine by the eighteenth century, at a time of national decline and political subjugation. For the first time, religious literature was reduced to a secondary position. Owing to the profound Polonization of the upper class of the population in then Polish territories, literary activity was concentrated to the left of the Dnipro, and in Transcarpathia. With the Cossack Hetmanate collapsing and the Ukrainian nobility Russified, even patriotic works were written in Russian.

Nevertheless, Classicism contributed to the development of Ukrainian literary language. High style did not become popular, and therefore the vernacular filled the vacuum. The authors of burlesque parodies and travesties were, for the most part, wandering cantors or teachers, and their works mixed the elements of high and low styles.

Poet and playwright Ivan Kotliarevsky (1769–1838) was the founder of modern Ukrainian literature in the vernacular. His greatest literary achievement is *Eneïda,* a travesty and the first literary work in the modern Ukrainian language. Taking material traditional for travesties, Kotliarevsky transformed Virgil's *Aeneid* to index Ukrainian Cossacks. This social satire, written at the height of national decline and tsarist oppression, became highly popular in Ukraine. Filled with the jargon of seminarians, wandering cantors, thieves, and drunkards, *Eneïda* is a brilliant example of the era's colloquial speech. It helped develop the Ukrainian vernacular as a literary language.

The successful theatrical works of this time continued the tradition of comedy interludes with well-developed caricatures and social themes. These included Kotliarevsky's operetta *Natalka-Poltavka* (The Girl from Poltava) and vaudeville *Moskal-Charivnyk* (The Muscovite-Sorcerer), and Vasyl Hohol's *Roman ta Paraska* (Roman and Paraska) and *Sobaka-vivtsia* (Dog or Sheep).

Hryhory Kvitka-Osnovianenko (1778–1843) was the most prominent Ukrainian classicist prose writer of the time. He was among the few writers who depicted peasant life without romantic overload. His stories, novelettes, anecdotes, travesties, and comedies were simple in composition, emphasized the goodness of human nature, and were philosophically close to the works of Jean-Jacques Rousseau. Kvitka-Osnovianenko has since earned the title of "father of Ukrainian prose."

ROMANTICISM

The Romantic era in Ukrainian literature marks the development of a modern Ukrainian literary language and literature. Ukrainian romanticists found inspiration in the ethnography and history of rural ethnic Ukrainians. The first manifestation of the Romantic movement in Ukrainian literature was the publication of ethnographic collections in the 1820s and 1830s and scholarly studies of Ukrainian history. The political situation in the mid-nineteenth century made manifestations of national identity virtually impossible. These gained strength in the late 1850s, following the death of Tsar Nikolai I. Nationalist feelings associated with the Romantic movement and popularized by the greatest Ukrainian poet, Taras Shevchenko, had a profound influence on Ukrainian culture and politics.

The first centers of Ukrainian Romanticism were Kharkiv, Galicia, and Kyiv. The Kharkiv Group of Romanticists, led by Izmail Sreznevsky (1812–1880), united Levko Borovykovsky (1806–1889), Amvrosii Metlynsky (1814–1870), Mykola Kostomarov (1817–1885), and others. For these intellectuals, who saw their country in gloomy colors and longed for its past, Romanticism gave voice to the national spirit and soul.

Kyivan Romanticism culminated in Ukraine's Romantic movement. Mykhailo Maksymovych (1804–1873), the first rector of Kyivan University, reached prominence as a literary historian and ethnographer. The writers

Taras Shevchenko monument in Kharkiv. Photo by Adriana Helbig.

Mykola Kostomarov (1817–1885), Panteleimon Kulish (1819–1897), and Taras Shevchenko (1814–1861), together with university students, created the secret Slavophile Brotherhood of Sts. Cyril and Methodius. Unlike the Kharkiv Romanticists and the *Ruska Triitsia* (Ruthenian Trinity), who focused on the past, the Kyivan circle of Romanticists looked to the future. *Knyhy bytiia ukrains'koho narodu* (The Books of the Genesis of the Ukrainian People) by Kostomarov pictured Ukraine's revival as a nation destined to be the keystone of a pan-Slavic federation. The brotherhood was arrested in 1847.

Taras Shevchenko (1814–1861) is the most revered Ukrainian poet and a symbol of Ukrainian national consciousness. An orphaned serf, he spent his early years in misery. His artistic talent, however, was noticed by his owner, Pavel Engelhardt. Engelhardt taught him to read and brought him to St. Petersburg, where Shevchenko entered the circles of top Russian artists, who later raised the funds necessary to free Shevchenko from serfdom.

Shevchenko's contribution to the development of the Ukrainian language is unsurpassed. His verses, extraordinarily expressive and musical, follow the rhythms of Ukrainian Christmas carols and dance tunes and are noted for a broad range of rhythmical variations and approximate rhymes. In his collection of poems *Kobzar* (The Bard) as well as in the poems "Haidamaky,"[3] "Rozryta Mohyla" (The Ransacked Mound), and "Poslanie" (The Epistle), he shared his concept of historical and social unity among all ethnic Ukrainians and called on Ukrainians to fight for freedom from foreign rule. Shevchenko evaluated present and past events through three main concepts: glory, or national tradition; word, or national culture; and truth, or universal human demands. He believed in the ultimate victory of these concepts and encouraged people to fight for them:

> Why can't the rich, grey-haired, and stout sleep?
> Why can't the poor, orphan, and elder sleep?
> One thinks how to build his palace.
> Another thinks how to earn for his funeral.
> One will be buried in a fancy grave,
> Another will rest in a ditch.
> And both rest without thought,
> And do not mention the poor one,
> And curse him at that. (Excerpt from *Vidma,* "The Witch," 1847)[4]

Shevchenko's rejection of the prevalent political attitudes and his belief in Ukraine's glorious future had a profound effect on his contemporaries. His literary, social, and political influence is still vibrant, and more than 600 monuments to Shevchenko have been erected throughout the world, including in Washington, D.C.; Paris; New York; Winnipeg, Canada; Tashkent, Uzbekistan; Tbilisi, Georgia; Budapest; Rome; Vilnius, Lithuania; Bucharest; Buenos Aires; and Curitiba, Brazil.[5]

Panteleimon Kulish (1819–1897) is second only to Shevchenko in his influence on Ukrainian thought. Kulish believed that mysterious higher powers ruled national destiny. He developed a philosophical theory of history and the nations, which differed greatly from the positivist populism of the day. This rejection of the prevailing ideology as well as his choice of genres—ballad, poem, and *duma*—diminished the popularity of Kulish during his lifetime.

Kulish initially imitated Shevchenko in his writings but soon found his own style. His poetic collections—*Dosvitky* (Glimmers of Dawn), *Khutorna Poeziia* (Poetry of the Manor), and *Dzvin* (The Bell)—are riddled with folkloric elements and complex romantic symbolism, the heart being the key symbol of cultural, moral, and psychological values. He mastered the art of the aphorism and introduced new strophic meters. Kulish's most outstanding work is *Chorna Rada* (The Black Council). The novel describes the events that took place before the Hetmanate of Briukhovetsky and describes a nation that consists of different groups with diverse interests and ideals. The social conflicts of *Chorna Rada* place this novel apart from other romantic works with their idyllic image of Ukraine. The short stories written by Kulish—"Sichovi hosti" (Guests from Sich), "Martyn Hak," and others—are among his best works. Trying to bring complex psychological conflicts to the short story, Kulish paved the way for the Ukrainian psychological novel.

REALISM

Realism fully replaced romanticism in Ukrainian literature in the second half of the nineteenth century, after several decades of coexistence. The repressive language policy of the tsarist government obstructed the development of realistic prose in eastern Ukraine. Some Ukrainian-language works had to be printed abroad and appeared in Ukraine after becoming part of literary history.

Early representatives of Ukrainian realism were Marko Vovchok (Maria Vilinska-Markovych, 1834–1907) and Oleksander Konysky (1836–1900). Vovchok's first work, *Narodni opovidannia* (Folk Stories), had great success among fellow writers. Her other important works include the stories "Ledashchytsia" (An Idle Young Woman), "Instytutka" (A Young Woman from Boarding School), and "Karmeliuk", based along Vovchok's major thematic lines: the lives of women and the lives of serfs, drawing on ethnographic material. Oleksander Konysky wrote about the trials and tribulations of serfdom, the peasants' struggle for their rights, and the life of the populist intelligentsia. His works had considerable influence at that time because of their attitude toward the tsarist regime and their emphasis on social obligations.

Ivan Nechui-Levytsky (1838–1918) was the first Ukrainian writer to address the life of the wage-earning class in his novels *Mykola Dzheria* and *Burlachka.* Other topics included the clergy, the gentry, and petty nobility. His novel *Khmary* (The Clouds) depicts the new Ukrainian intelligentsia and hails as the first large-scale social novel in Ukrainian literary history. Nechui-Levytsky emphasized the folk spirit and encouraged Ukrainian writers to reveal every aspect of Ukrainian life "from the Caucasus and the Volga to the estuary of the Danube itself, to the Carpathians and beyond."[6]

Panas Myrnyi (Athanasius Rudchenko, 1849–1920) is widely considered to be one of the most prominent Ukrainian prose writers of his day. Together with his brother Ivan Bilyk, Myrnyi wrote the most important social novel of the day—*Khiba revut' voly, yak yasla povni* (When One Has Enough, One Does Not Complain), also titled *Propashcha syla* (Wasted Strength). It tells the story of a talented peasant in a postreform village ruled by the new rich; embittered, the protagonist joins a band of robbers. Similar to his novels *Lykho davnie i s'ohochasne* (The Old Evil and the New) and *Za vodoiu* (With the Current), Myrnyi emphasizes the importance of psychological motivations.

Ivan Franko (1856–1916) is Ukraine's literary patriarch. The wealth of his subject matter is reflected in a wide range of genres: novels, stories, narratives, social and psychological studies, sketches, satires, and poems. A romantic at first, he turned to naturalism and ethnographic realism and later showed a tendency toward impressionism and modernism in his interest in psychology and in unusual states of mind caused by tough experiences. His romantic novel *Petrii and Dovbushchuky* features Carpathian brigands. The stories "Lisy i pasovys'ka" (The Forests and Pasturelands), "Dobryi Zarobok" (Good Earnings), "Slymak" (The Snail), and "Muliar" (The Mason) analyze the everyday struggles of freed serfs. In *Boa Constrictor* and in *Boryslav smiiet'sia,* Franko imitated Emile Zola in his naturalistic depiction of capitalism. A vivid depiction of prison life is given in the works *Na dni* (In the Depths) and *Do Svitla* (Toward the Light). Complex social and personal conflicts in the life of the new intelligentsia and large landowners were depicted in *Osnovy suspil'nosti* (The Foundations of a Society), *Dlia domashn'oho ohnyshcha* (For the Family Hearth), *Hryts'I panych* (Hryts and the Lordling), *Perekhresni stezhky* (The Crossroads), *Bat'kivshchyna* (The Fatherland), *Soichyne krylo* (The Jay's Wing), and *Velykyi shum* (The Big Noise).

Franko's poetry contains an extraordinary variety of strophes, rhythms, and rhymes. His most famous collections are the lyric *Mii Izmaragd* (My Emerald) and *Iz dniv zhurby* (From the Days of Sorrow), the naturalistic *Z vershyn i nyzyn* (From Heights and Depths), and the philosophical *Na stari temy* (On Old Themes). The monumental poem "Moisei" (Moses) summarizes his ideological beliefs.

MODERNISM

The birth of modernism was marked by the publication of Franko's collection of lyric poems *Ziviale lystia* (Withered Leaves), Lesia Ukrainka's psychological drama *Blakytna trojanda* (Blue Rose), and Olha Kobylianska's feminist novel *Tsarivna* (Princess) in 1896.

The modernist manifesto was published five years later:

Putting aside many worn-out tendencies and compelling morals that again and again have forced our young writers onto the path of cliché and narrow-mindedness and also avoiding works that are blatantly naturalistic and brutal, one would like instead to have works with a small dose of originality, with a free, independent outlook, and with contemporary content. One would like to have works with some philosophy, in which there would shine even a small piece of that distant blue sky, which for centuries has beckoned to us with its unreachable beauty, with its unfathomable mystery. The closest attention should be paid to the aesthetic aspect of the works.[7]

The arrival of modernism coincided with the legalization of the Ukrainian press in 1905, boosting the development of Ukrainian literature through publication and dissemination. Modernist trends in literature were concurrently evident in western Ukrainian lands under Austro-Hungarian rule. Many distinct literary groups emerged, mostly concentrated around the publications *Literaturno-naukovyi vistnyk* (Literary Scientific Herald), *Z-nad khmar i z dolyn* (From above the Clouds and from the Valleys), *Svit* (The World), and *Ukrainska khata* (Ukrainian Home).

Mykhailo Kotsiubynsky (1864–1913) was a renowned Ukrainian impressionist. He began as a realist with *Andrii Soloveiko* and *Dlia zahalnoho dobra* (For the Common Good) but gradually moved toward impressionism. In his works, events are presented through the eyes of the characters, and descriptions are replaced by impressions. Kotsiubynsky's greatest works are the novels *Tini zabytykh predkiv* (Shadows of Forgotten Ancestors) and *Fata Morgana*. In *Fata Morgana,* he depicts the traditional theme of social conflicts in the village through the confrontation between two kinds of dreams. Kotsiubynsky explored the conscious and the subconscious in his impressionist psychological sketches *Na kameni* (On the Rock) and *Tsvit iabluni* (The Apple Blossom), his lyrical monologue *Intermezzo,* and his stories "Vin ide" (He Comes), "Smikh" (Laughter), and "Podarunok na imenyny" (A Birthday Present).

Ahatanhel Krymsky (1871–1942) was a decadent scholar of the Orient, prose writer, and poet who, according to his own words, wrote "not for people who are physically healthy, but for those who are a little sick, with frayed nerves and lacking vigor."[8] His works *Pal'move hillia: Ekzotychni poezii* (Palm Branches: Exotic Poems; three books of lyrical poetry on Oriental themes published in 1901, 1908, and 1922), the novella *Andrii Lahovs'ky* (1905), the poetry collections *Povistky ta eskizy z ukrainskoho zhyttia* (Tales and Sketches from Ukrainian Life, 1895) and *Beirutski opovidannia* (Beirut Short Stories, 1906) are a quintessence of narcissism, loneliness, introspection, and mysticism.

Oleksander Oles (Oleksander Kandyba, 1878–1944) was a symbolist poet who considered prose commonplace. His works *Z zhurboiu radist obnialas* (Joy and Sorrow Embraced), *Dramatychny tvory* (Dramatic Works), and *Nad Dniprom* (On the Dnipro), among others, were very popular, and many of his poems were set to music. His later works, such as the dramatic etude *Po dorozi v kazku* (A Journey into the Dream), are noted for nostalgia and melancholy.

Lesia Ukrainka (Larysa Kosach, 1871–1913) is widely regarded as Ukraine's greatest female poet and dramatist. She is also the third cult figure in Ukrainian literature after Taras Shevchenko and Ivan Franko. Larysa began to write when she was nine. At 13, she was published under the literary name Lesia Ukrainka, suggested by her mother Olena Pchilka, a well-known feminist writer and the sister of Mykhailo Drahomanov, a prominent historian, literary critic, and promoter of Ukrainian democratic socialism. Drahomanov, a political émigré who settled in Switzerland, strongly influenced Lesia's Europeanism. From early on, Larysa was encouraged to learn foreign languages and read world literature in its original language of publication. In addition to Ukrainian, she learned Russian, Polish, Bulgarian, Greek, Latin, French, Italian, German, and English. Severe tuberculosis, from which she suffered for many years, forced her to seek medical treatment in Europe and live for extended periods in countries with a dry climate. Long stints in Germany, Austria, Italy, Bulgaria, Crimea, Egypt, and the Caucasus shaped Larysa's cosmopolitan outlook and made her call for the Europeanization of Ukrainian culture.

Ukrainka left behind a rich literary legacy. Despite physical suffering, she wrote inspiring revolutionary works centered on freedom, dignity, and personal integrity. She often borrowed subjects from world history and culture. Her first poetic collections, *Na krylakh pisen* (On Wings of Song) and *Nevilnychi pisni* (The Songs of the Slaves), were followed by the great dramatic poems "Kassandra," "Orhiia" (Orgy), "Na ruinakh" (On the Ruins), "Vavylonsky polon" (The Babylonian Captivity), "Na poli krovy" (On the Field of Blood), and "Oderzhyma" (A Possessed Woman), which she wrote in one night at the deathbed of her soul mate Serhii Merzhynsky. She also wrote several plays: *Blakytna troianda* (The Azure Rose), *Rufin i Pristsilla* (Rufinus and Priscilla), *Boiarynia* (The Boyar's Wife), *Lisova pisnia* (Song of the Forest), and *Kaminny hospodar* (The Stone Host). As a poet, she considered both the content and the form equally important. Her most outstanding poems are "Slovo, chomu ty ne tverdaia krytsia" (Word, Why Are You Not Like Tempered Steel?), "Zavzhdy ternovyi vinets" (Always a Wreath of Thorns), and "Contra spem spero" and are among the finest examples of Ukrainian poetry. In addition to poetry and drama, Lesia Ukrainka wrote prose, sociopolitical essays, literary criticism, and translated German, Russian, and Polish authors.

Olha Kobylianska (1865–1942) was the most prominent female prose writer of the modernist period. She was born and raised in Bukovyna, which at the time was part of the Austro-Hungarian Empire. The family made sure that their five sons received a higher education, but the education of Olha and her sister was limited to four years of elementary school. German was the official language in Bukovyna at the time, and Olha grew up under the strong influence of German culture. Her first works were written in German, and she was particularly inspired by Nietzsche. All critics but Lesia Ukrainka reproached Kobylianska for her dependence on German culture, to which she answered, "Preserve me, O Lord, from being a Galician-Ruthenian author!"[9] Her controversial *Valse mélancolique,* among other works, caused heated polemics. Her early novels *Liudyna* (A Human Being) and *Tsarivna* (Princess) were feminist in spirit. *Tsarivna* reflected a first attempt by an author in Ukraine to write a psychological novel. The diary form helped present the events through the prismatic consciousness of an intelligent, sophisticated young woman. Like many of Kobylianska's protagonists, the heroine resembles the author in her philosophy, aesthetic tastes, and contempt for the vulgarity and materialism of contemporary society. Two of Kobylianska's novels have a village setting: *V nediliu rano zillia kopala* (On Sunday Morning She Gathered Herbs) and *Zemlia* (The Earth), viewed by Ivan Franko as Kobylianska's best work.

Vasyl Stefanyk (1871–1936), a son of a peasant, wrote in his local dialect and distinguished himself through a total departure from the populist idealization of village life. His stories were human tragedies depicting extreme loneliness, misery, death, or expectation of death. Among his collections are *Synia knyzhechka* (Little Blue Book), *Kaminny khrest* (The Stone Cross), *Doroha* (The Road), and *Zemlia* (The Earth).

Volodymyr Vynnychenko (1880–1951) joins the ranks of Ukrainian writers of the prerevolutionary period. A statesman and a politician, he began to write as a student at Kyiv University, from which he was later expelled for his revolutionary activities. Vynnychenko is a modernist above all in his choice of themes: his stories are centered on psychological, social, and physical degradation; low instincts; and passions. His first story, "Krasa i syla" (Beauty and Strength), depicting the working class and the bourgeois milieu, was a sensation that brought his name instant recognition. Vynnychenko was accused of total amorality and individualism for a concept that he developed in his later works, such as the novel *Chesnist' z soboiu* (Honesty with Oneself), which holds that the immoral becomes moral if one is honest with oneself. This idea first appeared in his play and later in his novel with the same name: *Dyzharmoniia* (Disharmony). His other plays are *Velyky Molokh* (The Great Moloch), *Bazar* (The Marketplace), *Brekhnia* (A Lie), and *Chorna pantera i bily medvid* (Black Panther and White Bear). Vynnychenko's novel *Zapysky kyrpatoho Mefystofelia* (Notes of a Pug-nosed Mephistopheles) is noted for its irony toward the main character. His novel *Soniashna mashyna* (The Sun Machine) is a depiction of a future where machines would perform most operations currently performed by humans.

Unlike their Western European counterparts, modernists in Ukraine used social themes and folklore in their works. The search for new forms and ideas as well as the Europeanization of Ukrainian literature continued for several decades, until the onset of Stalinism in the 1930s.

THE SOVIET ERA

After the 1917 Socialist Revolution, the Bolsheviks usurped literature as a tool of proletarian propaganda. They set up a network of proletarian cultural organizations called *proletcults,* which later served as a basis for the organization of Soviet proletarian writers. Prevailing subject matter included themes of new life, revolution, civil war, collectivization, industrialization, and the conflict between national identity and social duty.

A short-lived liberation took place in the 1920s, when Ukrainian became the language of educational institutions and the authorities. The cultural renaissance that followed resulted in fine literary achievements, mostly in experimental literary forms. The young generation of writers emphasized technique and synthesized poetry, painting, sculpture, and architecture. Pavlo Tychyna (1891–1967) was the greatest representative of Ukrainian symbolism at the time. A lyric poet and a dreamer, he published several collections of poetry noted for their vibrant imagery and dynamic rhythms. The collection *Soniashni kliarnety* (Sunny Clarinets) was his first and best. Tychyna changed his style several times during his career and in the end praised communism. Mykhailo Semenko (1892–1938) represented the futurist movement. Semenko dreamed of revitalizing Ukrainian culture and found himself at the center of heated polemics following his attacks on the cult of Taras Shevchenko, viewing this cult as detrimental to Ukrainian culture.

The neoclassicists of the 1920s united in their opposition to all things mass and revolutionary. They were committed to world culture and were unwilling to accept the existing state of affairs. The outstanding representatives of this movement were Mykola Zerov (1890–1937), Maksym Rylsky (1895–1964), Pavlo Fylypovych (1891–1937), and Mykhailo Drai-Khmara (1889–1939).

At the center of the literary discussion was the brilliant polemicist Mykola Khvylovy (Fitilov, 1893–1933). A member of the Communist Party, he believed in a Soviet Ukraine independent of Russian influence. Stalin condemned his ideas as bourgeois nationalist. Khvylovy called on fellow writers to turn to Western Europe as the source of culture. Continuously harassed by Party officials, he committed suicide in protest to Communist ideology.

Mykola Kulish (1892–1942) explored concepts of truth through the prism of human emotions. From ethnographic realism, he went on to write highly original expressionistic plays using the elements of *vertep,* or Ukrainian puppet theater. His most famous works are *97, Komuna v stepakh* (A Commune in the Steppes), *Proshchai, selo* (Farewell, Village), *Otak zahynuv Huska* (That's How Huska Perished), *Khulii Khuryna, Narodnii Malakhii* (The People's Malakhii), *Patetychna sonata* (Sonata pathétique), and *Vichnyi bunt* (Eternal Rebellion). Less than half of his plays were published during his lifetime; two were irreversibly lost.

The period of pluralism ended by the late 1920s, and a sharp decline of literary activity began in the early 1930s. Some writers emigrated to the West. Some rewrote their works in the spirit of socialist realism. These rewritten works were void of an independent outlook and used a restricted range of themes: a happy life, the achievements of socialist labor, and friendship among the peoples of the Soviet Union. Many writers were expelled from the party, exiled, and deported, and their works were confiscated from libraries and banned. A study by G. N. Luckyj[10] shows that "two hundred fifty-four writers perished in the thirties as a result of police repression. This literary bloodbath was accompanied by purges of Ukrainian scholars, teachers, and clergymen." The details of the purges remain unclear—some devout Communists were also killed. Very few returned from the gulags, and most never continued writing prior to the repressions. Several other writers committed protest suicides before their expected arrests.

The years 1932–1953 were the zenith of socialist realism and did not bring any valuable literary works. The writings were focused on praising Stalin and the party, urban development, collectivization, revolution, the civil war, and the struggle against bourgeois nationalists.

During World War II, about 80 Ukrainian writers joined the army, and the rest worked in the hinterland. The years 1943–1946 saw a lessening in Russification activities; the Soviet authorities brought some leaders of Ukrainian culture back from exile. The postwar wave of persecution began in the summer of 1946. Particularly between 1945 and 1949, almost all literary activity outside the sphere of Soviet influence was produced by émigrés: Dokia Humenna (1904–1996), Ivan Bahrianyi (1907–1963), Yuri Kosach (1909–1990), Ihor Kostetsky (1913–1983), Yuri Klen (1901–1947), Vasyl Barka (1908–2003), Vadym Lesych (1909–1982), and others.

Nikita Khrushchev's speech to the Twentieth Party Congress in 1956 marked the beginning of the thaw. Some writers who had perished in the purges were rehabilitated, and many who were still alive were allowed to return home. However, this rehabilitation was selective and incomplete.

Most writers, with the exception of Tychyna, returned to their usual themes. Oles Honchar (1918–1995) was most prominent among those who turned to historical themes. His prose depicts the horrors of war and the effect of war on the human psyche. Yuri Yanovsky's novel *Zhivaya voda* (Living Water) deals with war and the postwar reality in Ukraine. The imagery of Yanovsky, when compared with other Soviet writers, has an intimate feel, but censors accused him of giving a "distorted picture of life and reality of the Soviet people" and exaggerating "the role of biological instincts."[11]

A regeneration of literature took place in the 1960s. A new generation of writers appeared: Vasyl Symonenko (1935–1963), Ivan Drach (b. 1936), Vitalii Korotych (b. 1936), Lina Kostenko (b. 1930), Yevhen Hutsalo (b. 1937), and Mykola Vinhranovsky (b. 1936). These so-called *Shestydesiatnyky,* or the Sixtiers, were mostly young poets who protested against socialist realism. They wrote in different styles but were all noted for a language full of vibrant images and free of clichés that broke with the idealized picture of Soviet life. They reintroduced human suffering as a key theme. At the same time, the dissident movement, fuelled by *samvydav* (self-publishing), emerged in 1964 after a fire destroyed part of the library of the Ukrainian Academy of Sciences. A letter of protest appeared in *samvydav,* accusing the Komitet Gosudarstvennoi Bezopasnosti (KGB), the Soviet State Security Committee, of arson, demanding freedom of speech, and criticizing the authorities for national discrimination. Two major waves of arrests followed. An eight-volume history of Ukrainian literature published in the late 1960s and early 1970s included some of the purged writers.

Although the general features of socialist realism persisted, literary works became more diverse and reflective of daily life. Vasyl Zemliak (1923–1977), Hryhir Tiutiunnyk (1931–1980), Yuri Shcherbak (b. 1934), Valerii Shevchuk

(b. 1939), and Pavlo Zahrebelny (b. 1924) were the most prominent writers of this time.

INDEPENDENCE

In 1987 the policy of glasnost, or openness, was proclaimed by the Soviet leader Mikhail Gorbachev. In his breakthrough speech, Gorbachev also talked about literature: "there should be no forgotten names or blank spots in either history or literature. Otherwise, what we have is not history or literature but artificial, opportunistic constructs."[12] Following these political changes, almost all writers who suffered under the Soviet regime were rehabilitated and their works were republished or published for the first time. Dissident writers who lived abroad were published in Ukraine. Authors such as Lina Kostenko, who chose not to be published rather than conform to socialist realism, were given complete freedom of creation. Writers worked to modernize the Ukrainian language; shrug off Soviet or traditionalist taboos; and provoke social, political, and cultural debate through their published works. Ukrainian literature followed popular cultural trends as well, turning to the West for inspiration. In the late 1980s and early 1990s, literature experienced a shift "from the search for mass identity to individual identity."[13] With the existence of an independent Ukrainian state, nationality was no longer the guiding force for artistic creation,[14] liberating contemporary Ukrainian authors to address a vast variety of themes.

The poets Yuri Andrukhovych (b. 1960), Viktor Neborak (b. 1961), and Oleksander Irvanets (b. 1961) have significantly transformed Ukrainian literary culture. Their literary performance group Bu-Ba-Bu, a Ukrainian acronym for "burlesque, farce, and buffoonery," offered an invigorating new perspective on poetry. The trio's anthology *Bu-Ba-Bu: T.v.o./ . . . /ry* (Bu-Ba-Bu: W.o.r./ . . . /ks) is a celebration of onomatopoeia, irony, and satire. Bu-Ba-Bu's performances, bustling with creative energy, gained enormous popularity among young intellectuals longing for change. By mixing poetry readings, theater, and rock music, the group's carnivalesque performances helped reach broad audiences. Bu-Ba-Bu had a lasting influence on Ukrainian literary culture and spawned numerous followers, the most notable of which are the groups Propala Hramota (The Lost Letter) and LuHoSad (A Meadow Garden), both bearing resemblance to the Beat Generation in the United States.[15]

The most acclaimed of the three Bu-Ba-Bu authors is the poet, prose writer, and essayist Yuri Andrukhovych. His books of essays *Nebo i ploschi* (The Sky and Squares), *Seredmistia* (Downtown), *Ekzotychni ptakhy i roslyny* (Exotic Birds and Plants), and *Dysorientatsiia na mistsevosti* (Disorientation on Location) as well as his novels *Rekreatsii* (Recreations), *Moskoviada*

(The Moscoviad), *Perversiia* (Perversion), and *Dvanadtsiat Obruchiv* (12 Rings) offer a subtle portrayal of Ukrainian society and explore the question of identity. Recent works by Andrukhovych have become increasingly more political.[16] Regarded as a highly controversial author, Andrukhovych is one of the most popular and widely translated contemporary Ukrainian writers.

The two other Bu-Ba-Bu authors, Viktor Neborak and Oleksander Irvanets, are also prominent on the Ukrainian literary scene. Neborak, a renowned poet, prose writer, and essayist, is noted for performing many of his poems as rock songs with the band called Neborok. Oleksandr Irvanets is well known for his poetry, novels, and dramas. His most famous prose work is the novel *Rivne/Rovno*, about the author's hometown and the wall that divides it into east and west, an allusion to the Berlin Wall that divided Germany.

Oksana Zabuzhko (b. 1960) is a versatile author deemed the enfant terrible and femme fatale of Ukrainian literature[17] due to her exploration of sexuality, particularly in her bestselling quasi-autobiography *Polovi doslidzhennia z ukrainskoho seksu* (Field Research of Ukrainian Sex). Among her other renowned works are poetry collections *Avtostop* (Hitchhiking) and *Dyryhent ostannoi svichky* (The Conductor of the Last Candle) as well as an essay collection *Khroniky vid Fortinbrasa* (The Fortinbras Chronicles). Along with Yuri Andrukhovych, Oksana Zabuzhko is one of the two most translated contemporary Ukrainian authors.

Oleh Lysheha (b. 1949) is a former dissident who was forbidden to publish for 16 years during the Soviet era. During his army service in Siberia, he developed a lasting interest in Asian philosophy and culture, which came to define his identity and lifestyle. The young Ukrainian poet Andriy Bondar describes Lysheha as someone who "exists in a parallel universe—he likes to walk barefoot in the city, to swim in the ice-cold river in winter, he catches fish with his teeth, knows how to make paper from mushrooms, never uses public transport, and does not have a job."[18] Lysheha's works are transcendentalist and metaphysical in nature. The miracle play *Friend Li Po, Brother Tu Fu*, about ancient Chinese poets, is a highlight of contemporary Ukrainian literature. His other publications are his poetry books *Velykyi Mist* (A High Bridge) and *Snihovi i vohniu* (To Snow and Fire).

Yuri Vynnychuk (b. 1952) is a versatile writer whose works range from philosophical stories to dark humor and from psychological fiction to pulp erotica.[19] Among his best works are *Spalakh* (The Pulsing Beacon), *Hy-hy-y* (Max and Me), *Ostriv Zyz* (The Island of Ziz), *Litopys vid ravlyka* (The Snail Chronicles), *Laskavo prosymo v Shchurohrad* (Welcome to Ratburg), *Vyshyvanyi svit* (An Embroidered World), *Prybluda* (The Vagrant), *Kit Abel'* (A Cat Named Abel), and *Son pro tramvai* (A Dream about a Tramcar). This array of themes has allowed Vynnychuk to reach broad audiences.

Volodymyr Dibrova's (b. 1951) short novels *Peltse* and *Pentameron* offer an ironic portrayal of people trapped by the limitations imposed by the Soviet system; this suffering is sustained due to their indecisiveness and lack of courage.

Solomea Pavlychko (1958–1999) was an outstanding writer, critic, and scholar whose works revitalized modernism and the feminist consciousness in Ukrainian literature. Her most prominent works are *Letters from Kyiv* and *Dyskurs modernizmu v ukrainsku literaturi* (Modernist Discourse in Ukrainian Literature). Pavlychko has published provoking analyses of works by Lesia Ukrainka and Olha Kobylianska.

Other important contemporary Ukrainian poets and writers include Natalka Bilotserkovets, Vasyl Herasymiuk, Vasyl Holoborodko, Yuri Izdryk, Yevhenia Kononenko, Andrii Kurkov, Vasyl Makhno, Ivan Malkovych, Gennadii Moroz, Kostiantyn Moskalets, Yevhen Pashkovsky, Iaroslav Pavliuk, Les Poderviansky, Yuri Pokalchuk, Taras Prokhasko, Mykola Riabchuk, Vasyl Ruban, Ihor Rymaruk, Vasyl Shkliar, Natalka Sniadanko, Liudmyla Taran, Mykola Vorobiov, Serhiy Zhadan, and Bohdan Zholdak. Some of these writers and poets work and live outside of Ukraine.

According to Ukrainian writer and intellectual Mykola Riabchuk, "the Nobel Prize remains an obsession for many Ukrainians—a stateless nation had few chances to be noticed, and even less to attract anybody's attention to its literature; nonetheless, it was the only chance for them to be heard and cared about in the world."[20] Ivan Franko was nominated for the Nobel Prize in 1916, but he died right after the nomination. Volodymyr Vynnychenko was withdrawn from the nomination after the outbreak of World War II. The processing of the Nobel Prize nomination for the dissident intellectual Vasyl Stus (1938–1985) was stopped after his death in a labor camp in 1985.[21]

With independence and the subsequent reduction of censorship, Ukrainian literature has been able to flourish. Freedom and diversity on the Ukrainian literary scene have helped foster remarkable achievements. Although Ukrainian authors do not yet enjoy global recognition per se, more Ukrainian works were translated during the 1990s than during the previous 100 years.[22] In the aftermath of the Orange Revolution, which brought Ukraine into the global spotlight, these positive trends continue to spawn a rich literary culture.

NOTES

1. Volodymyr Kubijovyc, ed., *Ukraine: A Concise Encyclopedia* (Toronto: University of Toronto Press, 1963), 963.

2. Ibid., 980.

3. Haidamaky were paramilitary bands fighting against the Polish nobility in Right Bank Ukraine.

4. Translated by Adriana Helbig, Oksana Kruhlij, and Helen Sanko. For a complete translation, see Adriana Helbig, " 'Play for Me, Old Gypsy': Music as Political Resource in the Roma Rights Movement in Ukraine" (PhD dissertation, Columbia University, 2005), 220–230.

5. Taras Shevenko Museum, in the Americas, http://www.infoukes.com/shevchenkomuseum/monuments.htm.

6. Kubijovyc, *Ukraine,* 1024.

7. "Khronika: ukrainsky almanakh," *Literaturno-naukovy vistnyk,* 16 (1901): 14

8. George Luckyj, *Ukrainian Literature in the Twentieth Century: A Reader's Guide* (Toronto: University of Toronto Press, 1992), 10.

9. Solomea Pavlychko, "Modernism vs. Populism in Fin de Siècle Ukrainian Literature: A Case of Gender Conflict," in *Engendering Slavic Literatures,* ed. Pamela Chester and Sibelan Forrester (Bloomington: Indiana University Press, 1966), 5.

10. George Luckyj, *Keeping a Record: Literary Purges in Soviet Ukraine (1930s): A Bio-Bibliography* (Edmonton: Canadian Institute of Ukrainian Studies, 1987).

11. Kubijovyc, *Ukraine,* 1071.

12. Luckyj, *Ukrainian Literature,* 104.

13. Michael M. Naydan, "Ukrainian Literary Identity Today: The Legacy of the Bu-Ba-Bu Generation after the Orange Revolution," *World Literature Today* 79 (2005): 24(4).

14. Ibid.

15. Ibid.

16. Barbara Burckhardt, *Das Stück.* In *Theater Heute,* Issue 1, 2006. Available at http://theaterheute.partituren.org/de/archiv/2006/Ausgabe_01_06/index.html?inhalt=20070611123454.

17. Vitaly Chernetsky, "Ukrainian Literature at the End of the Millennium: The Ten Best Works of the 1990s," *World Literature Today* 76 (2002): 98–101.

18. Andriy Bondar on Oleh Lysheha, http://ukraine.poetryinternationalweb.org/piw_cms/cms/cms_module/index.php?obj_id=5525&x=1, para. 2.

19. Tatiana Nazarenko, "Yuri Vynnychuk: The Windows of Time Frozen and Other Stories," *World Literature Today* 76 (2002).

20. Mykola Ryabchuk, "Minor Literature of a Major Country, or Between the Dniper River and D. H. Thoreau's Pond," Poetry International Web, http://international.poetryinternationalweb.org/piw_cms/cms/cms_module/index.php?o%20bj_id=5505.

21. Ibid.

22. Ibid.

9

Music

THIS CHAPTER EXPLORES developments in Ukrainian classical, folk, and popular music under the rule of the Russian and Austrian Empires and the Soviet regime. It also takes a closer look at the changes in musical production, consumption, and dissemination since Ukrainian independence in 1991 and the 2004 antigovernment movement known as the Orange Revolution. Many times in Ukraine's history, ruling authorities have attempted to draw the curtain on ethnic Ukrainian musical traditions. Taken as a whole, Ukrainian music, and especially Ukrainian-language music, has played a crucial role in supporting, forming, and legitimizing Ukrainian national identity, particularly when foreign occupiers attempted to suppress cultural expressions of Ukrainian ethnicity.

UKRAINIAN CLASSICAL MUSIC OF THE NINETEENTH CENTURY

One of the key figures in Ukrainian music is nineteenth-century Ukrainian composer, musical folklorist, pianist, and conductor Mykola Lysenko (1842–1912). Lysenko is largely credited by Ukrainian musicologists with establishing a Ukrainian classical music tradition that legitimized itself as a national school of music by infusing classical forms with Ukrainian folk music.[1] This development was influenced by nation-building initiatives promoted in the late nineteenth century by ethnically conscious Ukrainian intelligentsia in opposition to Russian rule, which relegated the majority of ethnic Ukrainians to the impoverished, illiterate rural peasant class. Mykola Lysenko's analyses of Ukrainian folklore as a unique artistic system played an instrumental role in legitimizing Ukrainian ethnic identity as separate and different from the Russian. Utilizing music as a political tool, Lysenko challenged Russian colonial authority and its cultural, economic, and sociopolitical oppression of the *Malorosy* (Little Russians, as Ukrainians were referred to in the Russian Empire). His work heightened awareness of Ukrainian musical folklore and played a key role in stirring national consciousness among Ukrainian intellectuals in Russified urban centers.

Lysenko's work in musical folklore resounds today in the context of the highly politicized debates regarding the use of Ukrainian vis-à-vis Russian in the public domain in contemporary Ukraine (discussed in earlier parts of this book and in the latter half of this chapter). The debate on language choice is rooted in the harsh Russification policies that curtailed and oftentimes prohibited publication in the Ukrainian language under tsarist rule. Ukrainian literary culture suffered the same fate under Soviet rule. Nevertheless, Mykola Lysenko worked to publish Ukrainian-language *dumy,* epic ballads, an important source of oral history. They depicted heroic exploits of the Cossacks as memorialized events of the past.[2] He also organized concerts by village folk musicians in Russified urban settings for ethnic Ukrainian audiences and set to music the Ukrainian-language poetry of revolutionary bard Taras Shevchenko (1814–1861). Among his most famous works are folk operas such as *Rizdvianna nich* (Christmas Night, 1872–1873), *Natalka-Poltavka* (1889), and *Taras Bulba* (1880–1890); children's operas such as *Koza-Dereza* (The Goat, 1883) and *Pan Kotsky* (1891); cantatas such as *Biut' porohy* (Raging Rapids, 1878), with words by Taras Shevchenko; and numerous orchestral, chamber, piano, and sacred works.[3]

Folk operas such as *Natalka-Poltavka* have been very important in the development of Ukrainian musical dramaturgy.[4] For one, they helped bridge the cultural differences between rural and urban Ukrainians. Folk music motifs served as signposts of ethnic Ukrainian identity in Russified Ukrainian cities and offered ethnic Ukrainian intelligentsia connections to cultural traditions practiced among the Ukrainian-speaking peasantry. The musical staging of idealized Ukrainian rural life was very threatening to Russian tsarist authorities, and Lysenko's folk operas and vocal works were often censored.

Many composers took an overt political stance against the ruling elite or were considered political through their musical activities. For instance, during the 1905 Russian Revolution, Kyrylo Stetsenko (1882–1922) published the Ukrainian national anthem, composed in 1863 by Father Mykhailo Verbytsky (1815–1870), a Catholic priest. Stetsenko was exiled from Kyiv in 1907. When the Ukrainian National Republic was declared in 1917, he was appointed head of the Music Section in the Ministry of Education. Two national choirs were created. One choir, led by composer Oleksander Koshyts (1875–1944), toured Europe and North America to promote Ukraine as an independent nation. This choir popularized "Shchedryk," a winter song of well-wishing, *shchedrivka,* arranged by Mykola Leontovych (1877–1921) in 1916, and from which "Carol of the Bells" was later adapted. The other state choir, led by Stetsenko, toured at home to promote national unity. With the Bolshevik takeover of Ukraine in 1920, the Koshyts choir was stranded abroad while the Communists disbanded Stetsenko's choir.

UKRAINIAN CLASSICAL MUSIC OF THE TWENTIETH CENTURY

One of Ukraine's most prominent contemporary composers is Yevhen Stankovych (b. 1942). A student of Myroslav Skoryk (b. 1938) and Borys Liatoshynsky (1895–1968), Stankovych has served as chairman of the Ukrainian Composers Union and has been working as a professor of composition at the National Music Academy of Ukraine in Kyiv since 1998. His oratorio "Slovo pro Pokhid Ihoriv, Syna Sviatoslava, Vnuka Oleha" (The Tale of Ihor's War, the Son of Sviatoslav, Grandson of Oleh) is based on the twelfth-century epic poem "Slovo o Polku Ihorevim" (The Tale of Ihor's War), a literary masterpiece from Kyivan Rus'. It tells the story of Prince Ihor of Chernihiv, who unsuccessfully fought the Polovtsians in 1185, and documents the warfare among the princes. In highlighting the disintegration of Kyivan unity, "Slovo" draws parallels between contemporary and historical processes and lessons that have influenced the development of an independent Ukrainian state.

Kyiv native Valentin Silvestrov (b. 1937), a student of Borys Liatoshynsky and Lev Revutsky (1889–1977), is one of the most prominent composers of avant-garde music. Once threatened with expulsion from the Composers Union in 1974 for his modernist style, Silvestrov has developed innovative approaches to modern musical expression. His "Silent Songs," composed in the mid-1970s, are a cycle of 24 songs for piano and voice that are performed without interval and create their powerful effect through the emotional intensity of dynamics. His "Metamusik" (1992) and "Postludium" (1982) reflect Silvestrov's interest in the role of echo, overtones, and sustainable notes and serve as an exploration in atonal sonorities.

Together with Silvestrov, composer Leonid Hrabovsky (b. 1935) belongs to the so-called Kyiv Avant-Garde and was one of the first Soviet composers to write music in the minimalist style. With the fall of the Soviet Union, Hrabovsky moved to the United States to assume the position of composer-in-residence at the Ukrainian Institute of America. He has since lectured at the Julliard School and at other prestigious universities, fostering new sensibilities of musical modernism in the postsocialist era.

CONTEMPORARY REVIVALS OF PRE-SOVIET MUSICAL GENRES

Authorities destroyed many Ukrainian folk music traditions during the era of Soviet rule in Ukraine, particularly collective village singing associated with religious feasts and kinship-based rituals such as weddings and funerals. Processes of forced collectivization and modernization also contributed to the loss of work-related singing traditions and seasonal and agricultural celebrations. A growing number of saved village traditions recorded by ethnomusicologists in the field have become available in Ukraine's growing music market. Recordings such as *As It Was from Ancient Times: Traditional Songs from the Right Bank of Kyiv Region* (ArtVeles, 2004) and *The Songs of Horyn River Region: Ethno-Cultural Heritage of Rivne Region's Polissya* (Etnodysk, 2004) feature performances by elderly village musicians who remember particular musical traditions that are no longer practiced by the younger generations. Multimedia discs such as *Project "My Ukraine": Bervy* (ArtVeles, 2003) and *The Green Murmur of Polissya: Traditional Culture of Polissya Region, Ukraine* (ArtVeles, 2003) feature elderly village musicians recorded during ethnographic expeditions as well as photos, illustrations, and articles written by leading folk music researchers in Ukraine. A growing number of young performers are re-learning the musical traditions of old from such recordings. Many perform the songs a cappella in *bilyi holos,* white voice (rural) style as recorded on the discs. Others splice these ethnographic recordings into hip-hop tracks, or use *bilyi holos* in rock and ethnopop music.

Holosinnia is one of the most important traditional genres featured on these compilations. *Holosinnia,* ritual wailing, was performed by female family members or by hired wailers, who lamented the deceased through song. Such lamentations are depicted in Sergei Parajanov's 1964 film *Shadows of Forgotten Ancestors,* the tragic love story of Ivanko and Marichka, similar to Romeo and Juliet, set among the Hutsuls in the Carpathian Mountains. The main protagonist is mourned through repetitive evocative cries such as "Ivanko has died, Ivanko is no longer with us." Traditionally, a wife, sister, mother, or child communicated with the deceased in a weeping voice, vocalizing what those who have been left behind will do without the deceased among them. Though many Ukrainians still mourn the deceased in the home rather than in funeral homes, *holosinnia* is no longer practiced, except in some rural contexts.

The mountain-dwelling Hutsuls use the *trembita,* a long horn from pine or spruce measuring approximately ten feet in length, to announce deaths, funerals, weddings, and other events. The melodic motifs are coded and functioned historically as a mountain cell phone to communicate between isolated villages. The sounds of the *trembita,* played by men who elevate the instrument into the air, echo throughout the mountains and can be heard from a great distance. Ethno-pop singer Ruslana Lyzhychko incorporates the sounds of the *trembita* into her songs, which draw on traditional Hutsul rhythms.

A rising contemporary interest in recordings of traditional music among consumers and government support for folk music collecting and dissemination signal a reaction against folk-based musical traditions that were enveloped for political gain by the Soviet regime. In line with Soviet cultural policy, traditional folk repertoires were manipulated in ways that consciously and inadvertently changed the meanings and functions of various musical genres and traditions. For instance, Soviet officials forbade Ukrainian scholars to document and analyze the *dumy* (epic songs) performed by wandering blind minstrels, *kobzari.* Ostap Veresai (1803–1900) is perhaps the most often referenced *kobzar* in scholarship. *Kobzari* were viewed as one of the greatest threats to the Soviet regime's political stability. They traveled from village to village, spreading news and singing about historical and contemporary events among the rural population. As blind minstrels, they lived from alms and were closely associated with the Orthodox Church. They accompanied themselves on the *kobza,* a plucked lute similar to the *bandura,* which has since been modernized as a concert instrument. *Lirnyky,* similar to *kobzari,* sang psalms, *psalmy,* and chants, *kanty.* They performed in market squares accompanying themselves on the *lira,* hurdy-gurdy, an instrument more audible in public contexts than the plucked *kobza.* The Soviet regime feared that these traveling musicians could spread anti-Communist, religious, and ethnic propaganda and that their village performances could not be controlled from above. Sometime in the 1930s (the exact date differs in various accounts), Ukrainian *kobzari* were invited to Kharkiv, the former capital of the Ukrainian Soviet Socialist Republic (SSR), under the pretense of an ethnographic conference, where they were told their songs and stories would be collected and recorded for posterity. Instead, the *kobzari* were brutally executed by the Soviet secret police (NKVD).[5] To ensure that *kobzar* lore would not be preserved and passed on to future generations, the NKVD also persecuted the scholars who researched *kobzar* traditions.[6] Between 1919 and 1930, a significant number of studies on *kobzari* and the musical traditions of blind minstrels were published by scholars, among them Klyment Kvitka (1880–1953), Hnat Khotkevych (1877–1938), and Kateryna Hrushevska (1900–1943), to name just a few. Many of these scholars perished in labor camps, in prisons, or in exile at the time of the greatest Stalinist repressions in the 1930s. Kateryna Hrushevska was arrested in 1934. She was imprisoned

Kobza player in Kharkiv honors the memory of kobzari persecuted by the Soviet regime in the 1930s. Photo by Adriana Helbig.

in 1937 and died in a labor camp in 1943. Hnat Khotkevych was shot in 1938. Klyment Kvitka was arrested repeatedly in the 1930s but survived his internment in a labor camp. He was forced into exile and lived in Moscow until his death in 1953.

Despite this turbulent history, many researchers in Ukraine and abroad perform, revive, and publish musical and textual analyses regarding this vocal and instrumental repertoire. Annual competitions, such as Mazepa Fest in Poltava, are held to encourage young musicians to learn the art of the *kobza, bandura, psalmy, kanty,* and *dumy.* Though repressed in Ukraine for their nationalist ideology in the 1930s, modernized *bandura* playing was allowed in the Soviet era. It became commonly associated with young women in particular, diffusing the more nationalist and religious association with the old, blind, saintly bard. Today it is being revived as a predominantly male musical tradition.

Numerous Ukrainian classical composers fought against the attempted silencing of Ukrainian musical expression by infusing Ukrainian folk music into classical forms. Filaret Kolessa (1871–1947), a contemporary of Mykola Lysenko and literary figures such as Lesia Ukrainka and Ivan Franko, published a series of monographs on *dumy* epic poems (1910 and 1913) collected in the eastern Ukrainian regions of Poltava and Kharkiv.[7] Kolessa also studied the rhythms of western Ukrainian folk songs from Halychyna, Volhynia,

Ukrainian students participate in a May Day parade, Lviv, 1975. The Russian-language banner reads "Lift higher the flag of socialist internationalism." Courtesy of Natalia Zaborska.

and Lemkivshchyna and was respected for the precision of his notations. His son Mykola Kolessa (1903–2006), similarly to composers such as Kolomyia-native Anatolii Kos-Anatolsky (1909–1983), combined folk idioms of the Carpathian Hutsul people with twentieth-century trends. Kolessa introduced additional musical instruments into the orchestra to achieve the sounding of folk Hutsul instruments and ensembles. He also influenced and developed regional studies of Ukrainian folk songs by drawing attention to the particulars of language, timbre, and performance style.

The Soviet regime only approved aesthetics devoid of nationalist, religious, and revolutionary ideology. Ethnic expression through staged musical practices severed the functions of music and dance from their roles in the everyday lives of citizens. Celebratory processions in ethnic costumes under the heading "Friendship of the Peoples" were mandatory for university students and were intended to contribute to the Soviet myth of ethnic equality. In reality, the Soviet government aimed to assimilate the various ethnic groups and nationalities into a collective Soviet whole. Regional ethnic idioms were modified and enveloped into a more collective national style that emphasized unity within diversity, as exemplified, for instance, by the Pavlo Virsky State Folk Dance Ensemble of Ukraine.

Pavlo Virsky established the Ukrainian State Folk Dance Company in Kyiv in 1951. Virsky modeled his company on the already prominent State Academic Ensemble of Folk Dances of the Peoples of the Soviet Union, established in Moscow by Igor Moiseyev in 1937. The State Ensemble, known also as the Moiseyev Dance Company, served as the prototype for state dance companies in all Soviet republics by the early 1950s. The choreography popularized by Virsky was rooted in rural dance traditions. As a stylized genre, it became a dance tradition parallel to everyday and ritual dance. Pavlo Virsky, like Moiseyev, further disassociated folk dance from the village by fusing folk idioms into a ballet framework. Dancers were accompanied by live music consisting of arranged folk melodies played on Western, rather than regional, instruments. Regional folk costumes were stylized for dance. Choreographies emphasized dancing in unison and blending into the dance collective. These stylized folk-ballet dances, popularized through tours throughout the Soviet Union and the West, became indexical of a progressive, modernized Ukrainian Soviet society. Virsky's choreographies helped essentialize and homogenize Ukrainian identity through movement; Moiseyev's company helped perform pan-Soviet unity into being.[8]

Through its manipulation of traditional cultural expressions, the Soviet culture-manufacturing machine created a collective Soviet identity by suppressing ideological difference. Contradicting its own slogan of "equality for all peoples," the Soviet system functioned on an ethnically based hierarchical division among groups, who were forced to struggle against each other for control of power and resources. Soviet censoring committees and the Union of Soviet Composers, established in 1932 to promote aesthetics of socialist realism, strictly controlled the publication and performance of certain musical repertoires in Ukraine, to various degrees, until independence in 1991.

UKRAINIAN RELIGIOUS MUSIC

Independence from the Soviet Union brought with it a cultural renaissance in Ukraine. With the celebration of Ukraine's 1,000 years of Christianity (988–1988) and the renewed expression of faith after the collapse of the atheist policies of the Communist regime, Ukrainian Christian choral music in particular began to enjoy unprecedented public performance. On Sundays and holidays, in the renovated and rebuilt churches of Kyiv, for instance, it is possible to hear Ukraine's most highly trained singers performing the religious compositions written during the eighteenth century, when Ukrainian church music enjoyed its greatest height. Among such compositions are those of Maksym Berezovsky (1745–1777), who greatly influenced the development of musical art not only in Ukraine, but abroad. Born in the small

Ukrainian town of Hlukhiv, Berezovsky gained his early musical education at the famous School of Vocal and Instrument Music in Hlukhiv, from which talented singers were recruited to the Tsar's Court Chapel Choir in St. Petersburg.[9] In 1766 Berezovsky was sent to Italy to study and, in 1771, was elected a member of the Academia Filarmonica at Bologna. He came to be best known for his sacred concertos. Dmytro Bortniansky (1751–1825) was also born in Hlukhiv, Ukraine, where he studied at the aforementioned music school. He continued his studies in Italy at the academies in Bologna, Rome, and Naples and, in 1796, became director of the Tsar's Court Chapel Choir in St. Petersburg, a position he held until his death. His greatest contributions were to sacred polyphonic music, namely, sacred choral concertos.[10] Artemii Vedel (1767–1808), born in Kyiv, was conductor of the Kyiv Academy Choir and later the Kharkiv State School Choir.[11] In 1799, by order of Tsar Paul, he was put in a prison/insane asylum for the rest of his life. The works of Berezovsky, Bortniansky, and Vedel, among others, are available on a growing number of recordings by choirs in Ukraine and are increasingly incorporated into religious repertoires performed by choirs abroad.

The religious revival in Ukraine has also spilled into the realm of opera. The religious opera *Moses* (2001), by composer Myroslav Skoryk, is the first opera on a biblical subject in Ukraine composed in nearly 100 years. The opera is in Ukrainian and is based on a poem written in 1905 by Ivan Franko, the renowned Ukrainian poet (1856–1916). Franko's "Moses" focuses on the final moments of Moses's life, when he struggles to lead his people into the Promised Land. The beginning invocation, "My people, tortured utterly and crippled/Like a poor beggar at the cross-roads," draws parallels between the Israelites who wandered in the desert for 40 years and the experiences of Ukrainians following independence from the Soviet Union. The opera had its premier during Pope John Paul II's first visit to Ukraine in 2001 and was subsidized and supported by the Vatican.[12]

FAMOUS CLASSICAL MUSIC PERFORMERS FROM UKRAINE

Johann Gottfried von Herder, the renowned German philosopher, historian, and literary critic, once stated of Ukraine, "In this country, the land is rich and the people are blessed with a great musical talent."[13] Vladimir Horowitz (1903–1989), considered one of the most brilliant pianists of the twentieth century, was born in Kyiv. At 15, he entered Kyiv's music conservatory and gave his performance debut in Kharkiv two years later. He went on to perform in Moscow, Leningrad, Berlin, Hamburg, and Paris. In Paris an American concert manager signed him for a tour of the United States in 1928. Of Jewish descent, Horowitz used this opportunity to escape political upheaval and immigrated to the West. He continued to triumph on the international stage, performing with the New York Philharmonic and Arturo Toscanini, whose daughter he married in 1942. In 1986 Horowitz performed concerts in Moscow and St. Petersburg at the age of 83. The Glier Kyiv Music Institute has sponsored the biannual International Competition for Young Pianists in Memory of Vladimir Horowitz since 1995; 738 young musicians from 32 different countries have participated to date.[14]

Numerous Ukrainian singers have also enjoyed careers on the international stage. Among them are Ivan Kozlovsky (1900–1993), a lyric tenor, one of the greatest stars of Soviet opera, and the numerous Ukrainian singers who have performed at the Metropolitan Opera, New York City Opera, La Scala, Bolshoi Opera, and Covent Garden, such as Igor Borko, Misha Didyk, Andrii Dobriansky, Oksana Dyka, Oksana Krovytska, Mykhailo Hryshko, Pavlo Hunka, Viktoria Lukyanets, Ivanka Myhal', Paul Plishka, and Stephan Pyatnychko.

The history of Ukrainian opera, in particular, is synonymous with the voice of Solomiya Krushelnytska (1872–1952). Krushelnytska graduated from the L'viv Conservatory in 1893 with distinction and appeared as Lenora in the L'viv Opera production of Gaetano Donizetti's *Favorita.* In 1904 she gained critical acclaim for Giacomo Puccini's *Madame Butterfly*—the opera that, at its premiere in Milan's La Scala, was harshly booed by the audience. Three months later, Khrushelnytska sang the role to highest acclaim. In August 1939, after the death of her husband, Italian attorney Cesare Ricchoni, Krushelnytska left Italy and came to L'viv, only to be prevented by Soviet forces from ever returning to Italy. In 1951 she was named honored artist of the Ukrainian SSR and, in 1952, was promoted to full professor at the L'viv Conservatory. The L'viv Opera House carries her name, as do an international opera competition and an international opera festival in L'viv.

There has been a concerted effort to fill the historical gaps in Ukrainian music history and to correct misinformation about Ukrainian musical figures and events propagated in the past. Source material that has only recently become available from once-closed Soviet archives has allowed much information regarding music personas, artistic works, and historic publications to be featured in print for the first time. Enjoying her due recognition in Ukraine today is the legendary pianist Lubka Kolessa (1902–1997), one of the most renowned Ukrainian classical music stars on the international stage in the 1920s–1930s. Kolessa moved to Canada in 1940, where she became one of Canada's most respected piano professors. She performed throughout North America and gave concerts with reputable orchestras such as the New York Philharmonic. Her uncle, the aforementioned Filaret Kolessa, was devoted to the research of Ukrainian folk music. Her cousin Mykola Kolessa was a prominent Ukrainian composer and conductor. Lubka Kolessa's name, however, was consciously silenced in Ukraine for most of her career because she lived and worked in the West.

BETWEEN UKRAINIAN AND RUSSIAN: LANGUAGE CHOICE IN POPULAR MUSIC

Volodymyr Ivasiuk (1949–1979) composed one of the most popular Ukrainian songs, "Chervona Ruta" (Red Rue), in 1970. "Chervona Ruta" became a megahit and won the Soviet Union's Best Song of the Year award in 1971. Ivasiuk's "Vodohrai" (Waterfall) was named best song of 1972. His unwavering popularity as a Ukrainian-language singer won Ivasiuk no favors with the Soviet authorities. He died in 1979 under mysterious circumstances. His body was found in a forest, and it is widely believed that he was murdered by the Komitet Gosudarstvennoi Bezopasnosti (KGB), the Soviet State Security Committee.

In the eyes of ethnic Ukrainians, Ivasiuk is a martyr who died for his love of Ukrainian song. Using him as a symbol of Ukrainian national identity during the movement for Ukrainian independence, members of Rukh, the People's Movement for Restructuring in Ukraine, launched the Chervona Ruta Festival in 1989 in Chernivtsi, Ivasiuk's hometown, in western Ukraine.[15] The festival featured Ukrainian-language music performers from Ukraine and the diaspora in North America. Many songs performed at the festival addressed the lower status of the Ukrainian language in the Ukrainian SSR and openly criticized the Communist Party and its policies of Russification. Eduard Drach's song "Viddaite movu" (Give Us Back Our Language) was one of the most evident songs that addressed this issue. Another was "My Zabuly Vse" (We Have Forgotten Everything), by singer Taras Kurchyk.[16]

Singers from the 1970s, such as Taras Petrynenko, Ihor Bilozir, and Viktor Morozov's satirical theater Ne Zhurys (Don't Worry, 1970s), led the way for a rebirth of Ukrainian-language consciousness during the independence movement. Prominent Ukrainian-language rock groups from the late 1980s included Braty Hadiukiny (Snake Brothers), Komu Vnyz (Going Down), Slid (Step), singer Vika Vradii, Vopli Vidopliasova, Zymovyi Sad (Winter Garden), Mertvyi Piven (Dead Rooster), and Plach Jaremii (Wails of Jeremiah).[17] Language choice in popular music has continued to be associated with political ideology. In 2001 Ihor Bilozir was beaten to death by two Russian youths for singing Ukrainian songs in a public café in L'viv, Ukraine.[18] The large public funeral procession in L'viv was comparable to that of Volodymyr Ivasiuk's and fueled people's anger against the government of President Leonid Kuchma (1994–2004), not considered by the electorate, particularly in western Ukraine, to act in the interests of ethnic Ukrainian citizens. In the 2004 presidential election campaign between Kuchma-anointed Viktor Yanukovych and opposition leader Viktor Yushchenko, politicians consciously used Russian and Ukrainian-language popular music to gain support from particular segments of the population. Presidential candidates garnered support from Ukrainian musicians, who divided along linguistic lines, with 38 Russian-language popular singers supporting the Kuchma-appointed pro-Russia government candidate Viktor Yanukovych and 22 Ukrainian-language rock singers supporting the Western-leaning reformist Viktor Yushchenko. Among those who sang in support of Viktor Yanukovych were the group Skryabin and singers Taisia Povaliy, Victor Pavlik, Ani Lorak, Ian Tabachnik, and Natalia Mohylevska.

MUSIC AND THE 2004 ORANGE REVOLUTION

Ukrainian-language rock and hip-hop played an undeniably important role during the Orange Revolution, when the electorate contested the outcome of the elections rigged in favor of the government. On November 21, 2004, more than 1 million citizens poured onto the streets of Kyiv to contest the results of the rigged presidential elections. The song "Nas bahato, nas ne podolaty" (Together We Are Many, We Can't Be Defeated) became Ukraine's version of "El pueblo unido jamás será vencido" (The People United Will Never Be Defeated), Che Guevara's statement made famous through song during Pinochet's September 1973 coup in Chile. In the first days of the protests, the Carpathian music group Gryndzholy (a Hutsul word meaning "wooden sleigh"), who would later change their name to the anglicized GreenJolly after being chosen to represent Ukraine at the Eurovision contest that took place in Kyiv in May 2005, rapped the following words in Ukrainian to a hip-hop beat and uploaded their song to a Web site sponsored by the opposition. Downloaded more than 100,000 times after only two days of becoming available online, "Razom Nas Bahato" quickly became the anthem of the Orange Revolution:

Razom Nas Bahato (Together We Are Many)

Together we are many,
We will not be defeated . . .

Falsifications, no!
Machinations, no!
Understandings, no! no!
No to lies!

Yushchenko, yes!
Is our President, yes!
Yushchenko, yes! yes! yes!

Together we are many,
We will not be defeated . . .

We aren't goats
We are Ukraine's
Sons and daughters.
It's now or never,
Enough waiting!
Together we are many
We will not be defeated.

Together we are many,
We will not be defeated . . .

Sviatoslav Vakarchuk, Oleh Skrypka, Taras Chubai, Maria Burmaka, Ruslana Lyzhychko, and Oleksandr Ponomariov as well as groups such as Haidamaky, Tartak, Tanok Na Maidani Kongo, Mandry, Okean Elzy, Vopli Vidopliasova, and Plach Jaremii took center stage and performed daily for protestors in Kyiv during the Orange Revolution.[19] The physical presence of musicians performing live during the election campaign and on the Maidan stage greatly contributed to the political strength of the music itself.

Following the Orange Revolution, Russian-language singer Ani Lorak's support for Yanukovych resulted in an overturn of her attempt to represent Ukraine at Eurovision 2005. Lorak lost the vote to GreenJolly, who composed the Orange Revolution's anthem "Razom Nas Bahato." The Eurovision committee initially rejected GreenJolly's entry, until they changed the overtly political text of "Razom Nas Bahato." Politics prevailed, however, and GreenJolly placed 20th out of 26 bands, receiving two and zero points from the Russian and Belarusian judges, respectively. Ani Lorak has since represented Ukraine in the 2008 Eurovision contest, coming in second to Russia's Dima Bilan. Verka Serdiuchka, the 2007 representative and perhaps the most unusual of Ukraine's Eurovision entries to date, reminds listeners that things are not all they seem to be. Verka Serdiuchka, played by a cross-dressing male comedian who performs in the Ukrainian-Russian language mix known as *surzhyk,* has enjoyed relative popularity by challenging ethnic, linguistic, and gender ideologies.

After almost two decades of independence, Ukrainian music and musicians have begun their ascent onto the international stage. The post-Soviet Ukrainian music industry is experiencing a boom in production. The government and entrepreneurs have sponsored numerous festivals of ethnic, choral, and contemporary music, enabling young musicians to share their talent. Opera houses, which suffered a tremendous blow during the economic downfall in the initial years of Ukrainian independence, are filling once empty seats with concertgoers. The proliferation of Internet technology has made globalized music markets more accessible. Ukrainian singer Ruslana Lyzhychko won the Eurovision contest in 2004 with her song "Wild Dances." Kyiv hosted the event the following year, marking Ukraine's prominent place in contemporary world music. Kyiv has since hosted a growing number of popular music concerts featuring well-known musicians from the West. Among the most widely attended have been the free concerts on Independence Square performed by Elton John in 2007 and Paul McCartney in 2008.

NOTES

1. Taras Filenko and Tamara Bulat, *The World of Mykola Lysenko: Ethnic Identity, Music, and Politics in Nineteenth-century Ukraine* (Toronto: Ukraine Millennium Foundation, 2001).

2. A rising interest in the *bandura* and the *duma* genre in the nineteenth century by scholars and composers in Ukraine coincided with the rise of Ukrainian nationalism.

3. Ihor Sonevyts'kyi and Nataliia Palidvor-Sonevyts'ka, *Dictionary of Ukrainian Composers* (L'viv, Ukraine: Union of Ukrainian Composers, 1997), 173–74.

4. The first such opera, *Zaporozhets za Dunayem* (Kozak beyond the Danube, 1863), was composed by Semen Hulak-Artemovskyi (1813–1873), who lived and worked in imperial Russia and was a close friend of poet Taras Shevchenko (1814–1861).

5. Natalie Kononenko, *Ukrainian Minstrels . . . and the Blind Shall Sing* (New York: M. E. Sharpe, 1998), 4.

6. William Noll, "Selecting Partners: Questions of Personal Choice and Problems of History in Fieldwork and Its Interpretation," in *Shadows in the Field: New Perspectives for Fieldwork in Ethnomusicology,* ed. Gregory Barz and Timothy Cooley (New York: Oxford University Press, 1997), 182–83.

7. David Clegg, "Philaret Kolessa's Classification of the Ukrainian Recitative Songs," *Studia Musicologica Academiae Scientiarum Hungaricae* 7 (1965): 247–51.

8. Anthony Shay, *Choreographic Politics: State Folk Dance Companies, Representation and Power* (Middletown, CT: Wesleyan University Press, 2002).

9. Vladimir Morosan, *Choral Performance in Pre-Revolutionary Russia* (San Diego, CA: Musica Russia, 1994).

10. Marika Kuzma, "Bortniansky à la Bortniansky: An Examination of the Sources of Dmitry Bortniansky's Choral Concertos," *Journal of Musicology* 14 (1996): 183–212.

11. Lidia Kornij, *History of Ukrainian Music,* vol. 2, *Second Half of the XVIII Century* (Kyiv: Naukove Tovarystvo Shevchenka, 1998).

12. Joe McLellan, *"Moses . . .* A New Opera for a Nation in Search of Itself," ArtUkraine, http://www.artukraine.com/music/moses4.htm.

13. Olga Bench, "Ukrainian Folk Music," http://www.cck.kiev.ua/en/cd/d18ukr_nar_muz2/text.htm, para. 4.

14. International Competition for Young Pianists in Memory of Vladimir Horowitz, http://www.horowitzv.org.

15. Catherine Wanner, "Nationalism on Stage: Music and Change in Soviet Ukraine," in *Retuning Culture: Musical Changes in Central and Eastern Europe,* ed. Mark Slobin (Durham, NC: Duke University Press, 1996), 136–56.

16. Romana Bahry, "Rock Culture and Rock Music in Ukraine," in *Rocking the State: Rock Music and Politics in Eastern Europe and Russia,* ed. Sabrina Petra Ramet (Boulder, CO: Westview Press, 1994), 243–96.

17. Ibid.

18. Maria Sochan, "Thousands Attend Funeral of Composer Ihor Bilozir," *Ukrainian Weekly,* July 2, 2000, http://www.ukrweekly.com/old/archive/2000/270010.shtml.

19. Many of these musicians had played prominent roles during the Ukrainian independence movement in the late 1980s.

10

Theater and Cinema
in the Twentieth Century

THEATER AND CINEMA are powerful artistic media that blend the senses and draw on allegory, symbolism, stylization, and character development to parlay meaning and emotion. Expression is gleamed from representation that embodies and signifies historical layers of experience, shared memory, and feeling. To show the role of these media in Ukraine, this chapter charts the developments of theatrical and cinematic forms in the twentieth century. The utter destruction of Ukrainian theater and its main proponents during the Stalinist purges of the 1930s is still a deeply felt wound. A discussion of Ukrainian film encompasses the development of a film industry in Soviet Ukraine and the present status of Ukrainian-language films, focusing on people who have played instrumental roles in using the cinematic medium to chart new directions in the poetics and politics of Ukrainian cinematography.

HERITAGE OF *VERTEP*, THE PUPPET THEATER

The *vertep,* or puppet theater, first appeared in Ukraine in the late sixteenth century. Literally meaning "cave" (where Christ was born), it was originally a big wooden box in which puppeteers performed plays with sacred and profane puppet figures. The first half of the show featured the sacred and presented the Nativity narrative. The second half featured satire of local situations, happenings, and characters. Traditionally, a *vertep* had up to 40 different characters, including a priest, angels, shepherds, Herod, the three kings,

Satan, Death, Russian soldiers, Gypsies, a Polish couple, a Jewish man, a Ukrainian peasant couple, and various animals. The action was controlled by one puppeteer and was accompanied by singing.

The *vertep* had a fluid form as regarded secular characters. These were adjusted to local situations to better appeal to commoners. Thus the secular characters within the *vertep* reflected the historical context in which they were added. For instance, the Cossack figure was introduced during the reign of Catherine the Great, who ordered the destruction of the Cossack stronghold, the Zaporozhian Sich, on the Dnipro River.[1]

Ukrainian-born Nikolai Gogol (1809–1852), Mylcola Hohol in Ukrainian, heavily relied on Ukrainian folklore and on aspects of the Ukrainian *vertep* to develop characters and motifs in his compilation of tales *Evenings in a Village near Dikanka* (1831–1832). Each character within the *vertep* signified a particular trait, whether cunning, pride, or vanity.[2] In his discussion of Gogol's appropriation of *vertep,* literary scholar Victor Erlich points out, "What passes for comedy in *Evenings* . . . rests more often than not on unabashedly farcical, slap-stick effects drawn from the traditional repertory of the Ukrainian puppet theater . . . for example, the shrewish wife, the cunning gypsy, the gullible peasant, the 'dashing' Cossack."[3] The *vertep* reached the height of its popularity in the second half of the eighteenth century and was popularized by itinerant precentors, *diaky,* lay people within the Orthodox Church who assisted with church services and taught reading and writing. The *vertep* began to decline in the mid-nineteenth century, but it was common for Christmas carolers to dress up as characters from the traditional puppet theater.

The expressionist theater director Les Kurbas, in his attempts to develop new, sharper, modern roles for the actors in his Molodyi Theater (Young Theater) in Kharkiv, staged a "Christmas *Vertep*" in 1918–1919. He transformed the *vertep* from puppet theater to live theater, and the actors, dressed in costumes similar to those of *vertep* puppets, mimicked the angular motions of puppets. The affected, stylized movements of the actors served as one of Kurbas's experiments in how to communicate with and create new connections with the audience.

The *vertep* embodies a keen sense of ethnic Ukrainian identity, particularly as fused by historical folk elements and religion. The period of Kurbas's experimentation with traditional forms such as *vertep* was marked by cultural revival and a movement for Ukrainianization based on initial Soviet policies that supported national awareness and progress. The cultural purges of the 1930s contributed to the virtual destruction of the *vertep* tradition in all of its expressive forms. The revival of such forms played an integral role during Ukraine's independence movement in the 1980s. For instance, Ne Zhurys' (Don't Worry), a L'viv based cabaret-style musical group known for their Ukrainian-language political satire, issued a cassette in 1989 with the title *Vertep* that incorporated Christmas carols as well as patriotic songs (Kobza, KOB C010).

NEW THEATER TRENDS AND STALINIST PURGES: LES KURBAS AND MYKOLA KULISH

Les (Oleksander) Kurbas (1887–1937) was one of the most influential and groundbreaking figures in Ukrainian theater of the early twentieth century. Born in Galicia, then a part of the Austro-Hungarian Empire, he traveled with his parents' acting troupe and lived in Vienna from 1907 to 1908. Founding the Molodyi Theater in Kyiv during World War I, he drew from the theater's cadres to establish the avant-garde Berezil Artistic Association (1922–1933). Berezil was located in Kyiv (1922–1926) and was later moved to Kharkiv (1926–1933). In his theater, Kurbas put on plays written by Mykola Kulish, who wrote expressionistic plays that drew on elements of *vertep*. Kurbas also staged avant-garde interpretations of Shakespeare's plays such as *Macbeth* (1924) and *King Lear* (1935). Scholar Irene Makaryk notes that *Macbeth* received no reviews in the Soviet press of the time due to an "alleged paper shortage." This silence indicated official disapproval of his bold artistic experimentations.[4] Kurbas developed his technique of transformative gesture (*peretvorennia*), in opposition to the Stanislavski method (developed by Constantin Stanislavski (1863–1938), a Russian actor and theater director) and imposed on theatrical performance by Soviet authorities. Kurbas also worked against the dulling of the senses that Stalin's cultural policies promoted. Rather than feeding ideology to the audience, Kurbas wanted to challenge his viewers to look beyond representation and to understand the meanings embodied in the nuances of each action. Kurbas argued, "When there is perfect harmony between the theatre and the audience, then it's time to close the theatres. Revolutionary theatre must be revolutionary."[5] In 1933 Kurbas was arrested for not adhering to the principles of socialist realism. He was executed in 1937 by Stalin's order, and his body was thrown into an unmarked grave. His date of death was falsified to 1942 to hide his target execution and to position him as a casualty of war.[6] Kurbas was not rehabilitated until the late 1980s, in the glasnost period. It was not until 1991, with Ukrainian independence, that basic truths regarding Kurbas were made public. Avant-garde theater director Andriy Zholdak (b. 1962) and Kharkiv's Arabesque Theater-Studio are among the growing number of troupes and individuals who work to advance Ukrainian avant-garde theater in Ukraine and abroad.

Stalinist purges of cultural figures in the 1930s curtailed all modernist and ethnically influenced cultural expression. Ukrainian theaters were subjected to state censorship and control. The All-Ukrainian Theater Committee institutionalized workers' and collective-farm theaters. Many figures in theater were forced to put on plays that propagated Communist ideology and a movement away from individualized, personalized theatrical expression. Intellectuals and artistic figures who did not promote socialist realism in their work and ideas were either executed or exiled to labor camps, gulags, in Siberia.

As already noted, Kurbas staged the plays of Mykola Kulish (1892–1937) at the Berezil theater. In the plays *Narodnii Malakhii* (The People's Malakhii, 1927), *Patetychna sonata* (Sonata pathétique, 1930), and *Vichnyi bunt* (Eternal Rebellion, 1932), Kulish exposed the dualities of personal aspiration and social conformity, looking at the ironies between Ukrainian expectations and Soviet reality. His numerous works were either banned or heavily censored, among them his first play *97* (1924), *Myna Mazailo* (1929), and *Proshchai, selo* (Farewell, Village, 1933). He was forced to rename the latter *Povorot Marka* (Marko's Return, 1934) so as not to expose the reality regarding Soviet destruction of village life.[7] Like Kurbas, Kulish was arrested in 1934 and sentenced to 10 years in prison in the Soviet Arctic. He was murdered during the mass executions of political prisoners in 1937.

With the mass emigration of Ukrainian intellectuals during World War II from Ukraine, many artists continued their work abroad. Most Ukrainians lived in displaced persons camps in West Germany before traveling across the Atlantic Ocean. Among active troupes in the camps were the Ensemble of Ukrainian Actors, which later became the Ukrainian Theater in Philadelphia, and the Theater-Studio of actor, director Iosip Hirniak and his wife, actress Olimpiia Dobrovolska. Amateur theaters were very active in North American Ukrainian diaspora communities and offered Ukrainians opportunities to stage classical and new Ukrainian-language productions. The Toronto Zahrava Theater (est. 1953), the Avant-Garde Ukrainian Theater (est. 1983), the Ukrainian Theatrical Society in Detroit (est. 1960), the Ukrainian Theater Ensemble in New York (est. 1965), headed by Lidiia Krushelnytska, and the Yara Arts Group directed by Virlana Tkacz, have been among the most prominent in Ukrainian diaspora theater circles.[8]

UKRAINIAN CINEMA: BETWEEN CREATIVE EXPRESSION AND PROPAGANDA IN THE SOVIET ERA, AND POST-SOVIET DEVELOPMENTS

Soviet ideology of modernizing the peasant did not escape its hold on cinema. Joseph Stalin himself recognized cinema as an effective tool of propaganda. Soviet directives changed so often, however, that filmmakers such as Alexander Dovzhenko (1894–1956) constantly fell in and out of favor with the Party leadership.[9] As social historian George Liber explains, "Over the course of [a film's] long-term production the party changed direction and left Dovzhenko, who could not transform his films as quickly as the Politburo could issue decrees, open to attack."[10] Significant, however, is the fact that Dovzhenko, unlike Kurbas and Kulish, conformed and/or tried to conform to party ideology. He often reached out to Stalin himself to gain support for his projects. In 1940 the All-Union Committee on Cinematography appointed him artistic director of the Kyiv Film Studio. In March 1941 he received the Stalin Prize, First Class, for his film *Shchors,* a cinematic biography of the Red Army leader Mykola Shchors.

Born in Viunyshche, a district in the small town of Sosnytsia in the Chernihiv Province of Ukraine, Dovzhenko was one of 14 children, only 2 of whom survived into middle age. His social background, combined with fear of arrest and death, the fate of so many artists throughout the 1930s, propelled him to support the Stalinist order. Dovzhenko was able to use education to pull himself up from his rural roots and sought to use film to promote the ideals of modernization and progress from which he benefited. As states Liber, "His filmmaking became a war against ignorance by other means."[11] His film *Earth* (1930) explores the transition toward modernization and collectivization through the story of a dying peasant grandfather and his grandson, who is in favor of new machinery that will make life easier for toiling peasants. Dovzhenko lyrically represents the life cycle of man, which he portrays as being intimately tied to the land. *Earth* is the third of Dovzhenko's silent film trilogy, which includes *Zvenyhora* (1928) and *Arsenal* (1929). Party officials condemned *Earth* for being too abstract and for displaying elements of Ukrainian nationalism. Similarly, Stalin strongly denounced his screenplay for *Ukraine in Flames* (1944). Dovzhenko was also forced to repeatedly reshoot and reedit *Michurin* (1948).

Despite such restrictions, Dovzhenko's poetics inspired a new generation of cinematographers, among them the Armenian director Sergei Paradzhanov (1924–1990). His Ukrainian-themed *Tini Zabutykh Predkiv* (Shadows of Forgotten Ancestors, 1964) features the lovers Ivanko and Marichka, whose feuding families oppose their match. This poetic film draws heavily on essentalized folk elements of the Hutsuls in the Carpathian Mountains. The sound track incorporates folk and folk-inspired classical music composed by Myroslav Skoryk. Ivan Mykolaichuk (1940–1987), an actor who dominated the Ukrainian cinematic scene after his appearance in *Shadows,* embodies the psychological drama the protagonist endures in the film. Each scene is rich with emotion, symbolism, and artistic interpretation, inspired in no small part by Dovzhenko's groundbreaking explorations in cinematic drama.

Ivan Mykolaichuk and Larisa Kadochnikova in *Shadows of Forgotten Ancestors* (1964). Courtesy of Photofest.

Yuri Ilyenko (b. 1936) did the camera work on *Shadows,* which propelled his career at the Dovzhenko Studios in Kyiv, named after Dovzhenko in 1957. Of particular note is Ilyenko's 1971 film *Bilyi ptakh z chornoiu oznakoiu* (The White Bird with a Black Spot). It is set in World War II Bukovyna and depicts Soviet annexation of the region from Romania. Like *Shadows,* it draws heavily on local folklore. Throughout the 1970s Ukrainian cinema experienced bouts of disapproval from the Soviet regime, which tried to control the power of the ethnic revivals that had gained strength in Khrushchev's thaw in the 1960s.

The Soviet film industry collapsed with the fall of the Soviet Union, and the 1990s in Ukraine were marred with such great economic difficulty that an independent film industry could not be sustained. Yuri Ilyenko's 2002 epic film *Prayer for Hetman Mazepa* is one of the few that has been released in Ukraine since the fall of the Soviet Union and was long anticipated because of its distinctly Ukrainian theme. Acclaimed actor Bohdan Stupka is featured in the title role of Hetman Ivan Mazepa, the seventeenth-century Cossack general under whose leadership Ukraine experienced a degree of revival and self-rule.

The film uses allegory, lyrical imagery, and symbolism to relay the tragedy of Mazepa's failed war of insurrection against Tsar Peter I. Peter the Great is represented as a homosexual, which attests to only one of the many reasons why the film is banned in Russia. The film sparked controversy among audiences in Ukraine as well, particularly as regards the scene toward the end of the film in which the character Mazepa makes love in an Orthodox church to a woman who symbolizes Ukraine.

Films such as *Prayer for Hetman Mazepa* and the recently released *Bohdan Zynovii Khmel'nyts'kyi* (2008) by Mykola Mashchenko represent a trend toward depicting a more recent history of Soviet-time oppression and unveiling the Ukrainian resistance and nationalistic movements of the time. This principle guides the films of award-winning director Oles Yanchuk (b. 1956), who lives and works in Kyiv and runs his own production studio, Oles-Film, at the Dovzhenko Film Studios. The film *Holod 33* (1991) relays the tragedy of Holodomor, the death by famine experienced in 1932–1933 by 7–10 million villagers in eastern Ukraine. The famine was orchestrated by Stalin to break the will of the *kurkuls,* land-owning peasants, as a way of forcing them to comply with collectivization. *Holod 33* relays the tragedy from the point of view of one family. The film won the Grand Prize at the National Film Festival held in Kyiv, Ukraine, in 1991. Between 1992 and 1993, the film was screened at the Film Forum in New York and at the AFI International Film Festival in Los Angeles and Washington, D.C. Yanchuk's 1995 film *Atentat* (Assassination: An Autumn Murder in Munich) is based on the life of Stepan Bandera, the leader of the Organization of Ukrainian Nationalists during World War II. The Ukrainian Insurgent Army, Ukrainska Povstanska Armia (UPA), fought guerilla-style insurgence well into the 1950s, following the annexation of western Ukrainian lands into the Union of Soviet Socialist Republics. This film was screened at the Gdansk International Film Festival (Poland), the Karlovyj Var Film Festival (Czech Republic), and the Freedom Film Festival in Washington, D.C., as well as at the International Film Festival in Los Angeles in 1998. Themes relating to the fight for freedom against Soviet forces are explored again in his 2004 film *Zalizna Sotnia* (The Company of Heroes), a film coproduced by companies in Ukraine and Australia and features the struggle of the UPA in Polish territories. It is based on the recollections of Yuri Borec, an UPA veteran who survived a joint Soviet-Polish deportation campaign in western Ukraine.

Yanchuk's film *Neskorennyi* (The Undefeated) focuses on the life of Roman Shukhevych, also known by his pseudonym Taras Chuprynka, commander in chief of the UPA. Like *Atentat, Neskorennyi* was financed by the Ukrainian Congress Committee of America, a Ukrainian-American diaspora organization based in New York City.[12] This collaboration continues with a forthcoming film titled *Vladyka Andrey*, which explores the life of Metropolitan Andrey Sheptytsky, head of the Ukrainian Catholic Church until his death in 1946, the same year that the Church was formally dissolved by Soviet occupiers and forced into hiding.[13] These films focus on publicly disseminating awareness of historical events that took place in western Ukraine and shaped the lives of generations in the twentieth century.

Oles Sanin (b. 1972) is among other important contemporary filmmakers in Ukraine. His *Mamay* (2003) is the first Ukrainian film to be nominated for an Oscar and reinterprets historical Cossack-Tatar relations, commonly known from the point of view only of the Cossacks. The story is built in a ballad that interweaves both cultures and reflects on three brothers who escape from Turkish prison but have only two horses. They leave the youngest brother behind and promise to return for him. The brother stays in the steppes and falls in love with a Tatar woman, Omai. The word *mamay* translates in Turkic as "no one," though in Persian languages it means "spirit of the steppes."

Films such as *Mamay* and Yanchuk's movies, however, are not often seen on the screens of Ukrainian cinema houses because there is very little infrastructure for both the production and distribution of Ukrainian-language films. Many films, even when imported from abroad, particularly Hollywood blockbusters (and many B films), have to date been dubbed only in Russian. Early Ukrainian translations included one person's voice relaying all characters, though translations have increasingly improved. Most videos available for purchase in Ukraine are, however, American films dubbed in Russian and imported from the Russian market, and/or Russian-made movies. Recently, however, Hollywood blockbusters such as *Indiana Jones and the Kingdom of the Crystal Skull* (2008) have appeared in movie theaters dubbed only in Ukrainian. Among the Ukrainian diaspora in North America, the Ukrainian Film Club at Columbia University, led by Ukrainian cinema scholar Yuri Shevchuk, has played a key role in disseminating Ukrainian-language films in North America and has presented many premiers of art films made by filmmakers in Ukraine.[14] Such films, however, are passed hand-to-hand from the film directors in Ukraine to Shevchuk, who premiers them in the West. Much financing is needed on the part of the Ukrainian government to ensure that the Ukrainian film industry becomes a viable, self-sustaining industry in the postsocialist context. To date, it battles issues of piracy, black market sales, and the lack of a national infrastructure to produce and disseminate art and popular films.

NEW TRANSNATIONAL NETWORKS

Many artists rely on community networks and individual collaborations to help disseminate their work. Teater v Koshyku (Theater in a Basket), led and directed by Iryna Volytska, is among many Ukrainian theater groups that have traveled to the West since independence to perform for American and Ukrainian diaspora audiences. Similarly, the New York–based Yara Arts Group led by Virlana Tkacz, a Ukrainian-American theater director, has worked extensively in Ukraine. Tkacz creates English-language works based on Ukrainian drama, poetry, and documentary material. In 2007 she received the title of Honored Artist of Ukraine from the Ukrainian government.[15] Though it is still difficult for Ukrainian citizens to obtain visas to travel abroad, there is no government opposition against it on the part of Ukraine, as there was in the Soviet era. As it is well known, citizens of the Soviet Union could only travel within the borders of the Soviet Union. During the Soviet era, one had to schedule ahead of time to to make a phone call abroad. Thus direct cultural contact was minimal and not accessible to the majority of people until well after independence in 1991.

Since independence, many Ukrainians have travelled abroad in search of work and new opportunity. This movement across borders has brought Ukrainians into direct physical and cultural contact with the West. Goods from abroad, such as movies, CDs, books, clothes, food, and technology are now commonly accessible in Ukraine, though for a much higher price that one might expect to pay in the West. Exchanges among artists, students, and politicians have greatly contributed to a change in customs. This dynamic movement in all aspects of life, particularly following the suppression and usurpation by the Soviet state throughout the twentieth century, continues to open doors unimaginable only a few years ago. Ukraine is truly a society on the move and, for the first time in history, has the opportunity to choose the directions it was to take.

NOTES

1. Valerian Revutsky, "Vertep," Encyclopedia of Ukraine, http://www.encyclopediaofukraine.com/pages/V/E/VertepIT.htm.

2. Madhu Malik, "*Vertep* and the Sacred/Profane Dichotomy in Gogol's Dikan'ka Stories," *Slavic and East European Journal* 34 (1990): 332–47.

3. Victor Erlich, *Gogol* (New Haven, CT: Yale University Press, 1969), 29.

4. Irene Makaryk, *Shakespeare in the Undiscovered Bourn: Les Kurbas, Ukrainian Modernism, and Early Soviet Cultural Politics* (Toronto: University of Toronto Press, 2004), 53.

5. Ibid., 182.

6. Spencer Golub, "Book Review of *Shakespeare in the Undiscovered Bourn: Les Kurbas, Ukrainian Modernism, and Early Soviet Cultural Politics,* by Irene Makaryk," *Theatre Journal* 57 (2005): 546–47.

7. Valerian Revutsky, Roman Senkus, and Marko Robert Stech, "Kulish, Mykola," Encyclopedia of Ukraine, http://www.encyclopediaofukraine.com/pages/K/U/KulishMykola.htm.

8. Valerian Revutsky "Theater" in *Encyclopedia of Ukraine,* Vol. 5 (1993), paragraph 14, 15 http://www.encyclopediaofukraine.com/pages/T/H/Theater.htm.

9. George Liber, "Adapting to the Stalinist Order: Alexander Dovzhenko's Psychological Journey, 1933–1953," *Europe-Asia Studies* 53 (2001): 1097–116.

10. Ibid., 1104.

11. George Liber, "Death, Birth Order and Alexander Dovzhenko's Cinematic Visions," Kinema, http://www.kinema.uwaterloo.ca/liber001.htm, para. 37.

12. Ukrainian Congress Committee of America, http://www.ucca.org/home/.

13. Khristina Lew, "Yanchuk Continues to Explore Ukraine's History with Sheptytsky Film," *Ukrainian Weekly* No. 34, Vol. 74, August 20, 2006, http://www.ukrweekly.com/old/archive/2006/340613.shtml.

14. Ukrainian Film Club of Columbia University, Forum for Ukrainian Cinema in North America, http://www.columbia.edu/cu/ufc/.

15. Valentyn Labunsky, "Ukraine Grants Awards to Ukrainian Americans," http://www.brama.com/yara/zvannia.html.

Glossary

Avtonomna Respublika Krym   The Autonomous Republic of Crimea.

Babtsia   Grandmother.

Bandura   A plucked string lute considered to be the national instrument of Ukraine.

Berehynia   A nurturing, protecting female spirit in Slavic mythology.

Bilyi holos   Literally, white voice. A style of singing in rural Ukraine characterized by a specific vocal timbre.

Borsch   Beet soup that is part of everyday cuisine and traditional religious meals.

Bylina, also *staryna*   An old epic narrative about heroic events of the past, sorcerers, and heroes.

Dacha   Country home or summer cottage.

Dazhboh   The sun god in Slavic mythology.

Diak   A lay person within the Orthodox Church who assisted with church services and taught reading and writing.

Didukh   Sheaf of grain placed in the corner of the room as part of Christmas Eve tradition.

Duma   A literary genre; also a sung epic.

Glasnost   A policy of openness proclaimed by Mikhail Gorbachev in the late 1980s.

Gulag   A Soviet labor camp; comes from GULAG, an acronym for State Administration of Camps.

Hahilky　Spring dances rooted in pre-Christian traditions performed by young girls at Easter time.

Haidamaky　Paramilitary bands that fought against the Polish nobility in Right Bank Ukraine.

Halushky　Boiled dumplings.

Hetman　Cossack leader.

Hetmanate　Autonomous region under Cossack system of government.

Holosinnia　Ritual weeping; crying performed by women at rural funerals.

Holubtsi　Stuffed cabbage rolls.

Horilka　Ukrainian vodka.

Hryvnia　Ukrainian currency introduced in 1996; the name of currency used in Kyivan Rus'.

Hutsuls　An ethnic group that lives in the Carpathian Mountains.

Khanate　Crimean Tatar state from 1441 to 1783.

Kobza　A plucked lute played by blind, wandering minstrels.

Kolach　Traditional braided Christmas Eve bread.

Koliada　Winter solstice; coincides with Christmas festivities.

Korovai　Elaborate ceremonial wedding bread.

Kurkul **(kulak in Russian)**　Name attributed to landowning peasants in eastern Ukraine prior to Soviet collectivization.

Kutia　Ancient ceremonial dish made with boiled wheat kernels, honey, and poppy seeds.

Kvas　Popular drink made from fermented rye bread.

Lavra　In Orthodox Christianity, a network of caves for hermits that often includes a church.

Lira　Hurdy-gurdy played by blind, wandering minstrels.

Malorosy **(Little Russians)**　Name for Ukrainians in the Russian Empire.

Mejlis　Parliament of Crimean Tatars founded in 1991.

Nomenklatura　Privileged class of senior bureaucrats in the Soviet system.

Oblast　An administrative region in countries of the Soviet Union; Ukraine has 24.

Oligarch　A person who wields a relative amount of social, economic, or political power and has a significantly conspicuous amount of wealth.

Perestroika　A policy of restructuring proclaimed by Mikhail Gorbachev.

Politburo (political bureau)　Executive organization in the Communist regime.

Polovtsians (Cumans)　A Turkic nomadic tribe.

Proletcults　Proletarian cultural organizations.

Pysanka (pl. *pysanky*)   Traditional Easter eggs decorated with dyes using a stylus and beeswax.

Ridna mova   Native language.

Robitfaky   Educational departments for workers.

Rukh   People's Movement for Restructuring in Ukraine, founded in 1989.

Rushnyk   Embroidered ceremonial towel.

Samvydav   Self-publishing.

Shchedrivka   Winter well-wishing song.

Shestydesiatnyky (the Sixtiers)   A literary movement in the 1960s that opposed Russification.

Shtetls   Small Jewish towns within the Pale of Settlement.

Skazanie   A narrative.

Sloboda Ukraine/Slobozhanshchyna   Settlers in the southwestern frontier of the Russian Empire (today, eastern Ukraine), who were exempt from taxes. *Sloboda* means "free."

Staryna   *See* **Bylina.**

Surzhyk   A combination of the Ukrainian and Russian languages.

Sviata Vechera   Traditional Christmas Eve dinner.

Szlachta   The noble class in the Kingdom of Poland, the Grand Duchy of Lithuania, and in territories under Polish rule until the early twentieth century.

Temnyky   Secret instructions sent to media personnel regarding which topics to cover and how; a form of government media censorship prior to the Orange Revolution.

Trembita   A wooden alpine horn used by Hutsuls in the Carpathian Mountains.

UAOC   Ukrainian Autocephalous Orthodox Church.

UOC–KP   Ukrainian Orthodox Church, Kyiv Patriarchate.

UOC–MP   Ukrainian Orthodox Church, Moscow Patriarchate.

Varenyky   Dumplings traditionally stuffed with potatoes or cabbage.

Verkhovna Rada   Ukrainian parliament.

Vyshyvanka   Traditional embroidery; designs have symbolic meaning.

Zemstvo   Local self-rule committee under Russian imperial rule.

Selected Bibliography

CHAPTER 1: CONTEXT

Batt, Judy, and Kataryna Wolczuk, eds. *Region, State and Identity in Central and Eastern Europe.* Portland, OR: Frank Cass, 2002.

Duncan, Peter J. S. "Ukraine and the Ukrainians." In *The Nationalities Question in the Post-Soviet States,* ed. Graham Smith. New York: Longman, 1996.

Kubijovyc, Volodymyr, ed. *Ukraine: A Concise Encyclopedia.* Prepared by Shevchenko Scientific Society. Toronto: University of Toronto Press, 1963.

Kuzio, Taras, Robert Kravchuk, and Paul D'Anieri, eds. *State and Institution Building in Ukraine.* New York: St. Martin's Press, 1999.

Magocsi, Paul Robert. *A History of Ukraine.* Seattle: University of Washington Press, 1998.

———. *Ukraine: A Historical Atlas.* Toronto: University of Toronto Press, 1985.

National Cancer Institute. "The Chornobyl Accident: 20 Years of Study Leukemia and Thyroid Cancer Research." National Cancer Institute. http://chornobyl.cancer.gov/accident.php?lev=0&page=1.

Staff Administration of the President of Ukraine. *Ukraine: 5 Years of Independence.* Preshov, Slovakia: ARC-Ukraine, 1996.

State Statistics Committee of Ukraine. "All-Ukrainian Population Census 2001." State Statistics Committee of Ukraine. http://www.ukrcensus.gov.ua/eng.

Stebelsky, Ihor. "National Identity of Ukraine." In *Geography and National Identity,* ed. David Hooson. Oxford: Blackwell, 1994.

Subtleny, Orest. *Ukraine: A History.* Toronto: University of Toronto Press, 2000.

Taras, Ray. "Redefining National Identity after Communism: A Preliminary Comparison of Ukraine and Poland." In *National Identities and Ethnic Minorities in Eastern Europe,* ed. Ray Taras. New York: St. Martin's Press, 1998.

Wilson, Andrew. *The Ukrainians: An Unexpected Nation.* New Haven, CT: Yale University Press, 2002.

Chapter 2: Religion

Hanover, Nathan. *The Abyss of Despair,* trans. Abraham Mesch. With a foreword by William Helmreich. New Brunswick, NJ: Transaction, 1983.

Himka, John-Paul. "The Greek Catholic Church in Galicia, 1848–1914." *Harvard Ukrainian Studies* 26 (2002–2003): 245–60.

Kononenko, Natalie. *Ukrainian Minstrels . . . and the Blind Shall Sing.* New York: M. E. Sharpe, 1998.

Kuzio, Taras. "The Struggle to Establish the World's Largest Orthodox Church." *Radio Free Europe/Radio Liberty Newsline, Part I* 4 (2000). www.rferl.org/content/Article/1142232.html.

Lesiv, Mariya. "Glory to Dazhbog: Neopaganism in Ukraine and the Ukrainian Diaspora." Paper presented at the 39th national convention of the American Association for the Advancement of Slavic Studies, New Orleans, LA, November 15–18, 2007.

Makhnonos, Maryna. "Ukraine Marks Solemn 60th Anniversary of Babyn Yar Massacre." *Ukrainian Weekly,* October 7, 2001.

Rosman, Moshe. *Founder of Hasidism: A Quest for the Historical Ba'al Shem Tov.* Berkeley: University of California Press, 1996.

Subtelny, Orest. *Ukraine: A History.* 3rd ed. Toronto: University of Toronto Press, 2000.

Uehling, Greta Lynn. *Beyond Memory: The Crimean Tatars' Deportation and Return.* New York: Palgrave Macmillan, 2004.

Wanner, Catherine. *Communities of the Converted: Ukrainians and Global Evangelism.* Ithaca, NY: Cornell University Press, 2007.

Wolff, Larry. "The Uniate Church and the Partitions of Poland: Religious Survival in the Age of Enlightened Absolutism." *Harvard Ukrainian Studies* 26 (2002–2003): 153–244.

Zenkovsky, Serge. *Medieval Russia's Epics, Chronicles, and Tales.* New York: E. P. Dutton, 1963.

Chapter 3: Language

Abdelal, Rawi. "Memories of Nations and States: Institutional History and National Identity in Post-Soviet Eurasia." *Nationalities Papers* 30 (2002): 459–84.

Arel, Dominique. "Interpreting 'Nationality' and 'Language' in the 2001 Ukrainian Census." *Post-Soviet Affairs* 18 (2002): 213–49.

Arel, Dominique, and Valeri Khmel'ko. "The Russian Factor and Territorial Polarization in Ukraine." *Harriman Review* 9 (1996): 81–91.

Barrington, Lowell. "Region, Language and Nationality: Rethinking Support in Ukraine for Maintaining Distance from Russia." In *Dilemmas of State-Led Nation Building in Ukraine,* ed. Taras Kuzio and Paul D'Anieri. Westport, CT: Praeger, 2002.

Barrington, Lowell, and Erik Herron. "One Ukraine or Many?: Regionalism in Ukraine and Its Political Consequences." *Nationalities Papers* 32 (2004): 53–86.

Bernhand, Niklas. "Surzhyk and National Identity in Ukrainian Nationalist Language Ideology." *Berlin Osteuropa Info* 17 (2001): 38–41.

Bilaniuk, Laada. *Contested Tongues: Language Politics and Cultural Correction in Ukraine.* Ithaca, NY: Cornell University Press, 2006.

Constant, Amelie, Martin Kahanec, and Klaus F. Zimmerman. "The Russian-Ukrainian Earnings Divide." IZA Discussion Paper No. 2330, Bonn, Germany, September 2006.

Constitution of Ukraine. http://www.rada.kiev.ua/const/conengl.htm.

Council of Europe. *National Report on Ukraine.* Strasbourg, France: Council of Europe, May 2004.

D'Anieri, Paul, Robert Kravchuk, and Taras Kuzio. *Politics and Society in Ukraine.* Boulder, CO: Westview Press, 1999.

Encyclopædia Britannica. "Ukrainian Language." Encyclopædia Britannica. http://www.britannica.com/eb/article-9074133/Ukrainian-language.

Encyclopedia of Ukraine. "Ukrainian Language." Encyclopedia of Ukraine. http://www.encyclopediaofukraine.com/display.asp?AddButton=pages\U\K\Ukrainianlanguage.htm.

Fishman, Joshua A. *In Praise of the Beloved Language: A Comparative View of Positive Ethnolinguistic Consciousness.* Berlin: Mouton de Gruyter, 1997.

Harlig, Jeffrey, and Csaba Pleh, eds. *When East Met West: Sociolinguistics in the Former Socialist Bloc.* Berlin: Mouton de Gruyter, 1995.

Hrytsak, Yaroslav. "National Identities in Post-Soviet Ukraine: The Case of L'viv and Donetsk." In *Cultures and Nations of Central and Eastern Europe: Essays in Honor of Roman Szporluk,* ed. Zvi Gitelman, Hajda Lubomyr, John-Paul Himka, and Roman Solchanyk. Cambridge, MA: Harvard Ukrainian Research Institute, 2000; *Harvard Ukrainian Studies* 22 (1998): 263–83.

Hrytsenko, Oleksandr. *Svoya mudrist': Natsional'ni mifolohiyi ta hromadyans'ka reli-hiya v Ukrayini.* Kyiv: Instytut kul'turnoyi poliyky, 1998.

Kertzer, David I., and Dominique Arel. "Censuses, Identity Formation, and the Struggle for Political Power." In *Census and Identity: The Politics of Race, Ethnicity and Language in National Censuses,* ed. D. Kertzer and D. Arel. Cambridge: Cambridge University Press, 2002.

Kubijovyc, Volodymyr, ed. *Ukraine: A Concise Encyclopedia.* Prepared by Shevchenko Scientific Society. Toronto: University of Toronto Press, 1963.

Kuzio, Taras. *Ukraine: State and Nation Building.* London: Routledge, 1998.

Lewytzkyj, Borys. *Politics and Society in Soviet Ukraine 1953–1980.* Edmonton: Canadian Institute of Ukrainian Studies, University of Alberta, 1984.

Magocsi, Paul Robert. *A History of Ukraine.* Seattle: University of Washington Press, 1998.

Protsyk, Oleh. "Majority-Minority Relations in Ukraine," *Journal on Ethnopolitics and Minority Issues in Europe* (JEMIE), Vol. 7, issue 1 (2008) .

Rodgers, Peter. "Rewriting History in Post-Soviet Ukraine: Contestation and Negotiation in Ukraine's Eastern Borderlands." Paper presented at the International Graduate Student Symposium "New Perspectives on Contemporary Ukraine: Politics, History, and Culture," Toronto, March 17–19, 2006.

Schieffelin, Bambi, Kathryn Woolard, and Paul Kroskrity. *Language Ideologies: Theory and Practice.* New York: Cambridge University Press, 1998.

Shimahara, Nobuo, Ivan Z. Holowinsky, and Saundra Tomlinson-Clarke, eds. *Ethnicity, Race, and Nationality in Education: A Global Perspective.* Rutgers International Symposium on Education Issues. Mahwah, NJ: Lawrence Erlbaum Associates, 2001.

State Statistics Committee of Ukraine. "All-Ukrainian Population Census 2001." State Statistics Committee of Ukraine. http://www.ukrcensus.gov.ua/eng.

Stepanenko, Viktor. "Identities and Language Politics in Ukraine: The Challenges of Nation-State Building." In *Nation-building, Ethnicity and Language Politics in Transition Countries,* ed. François Grin and Farimah Daftary. Flensburg, Germany: European Center for Minority Issues, 2003.

Trier, Tom. *Interethnic Relations in Transcarpathian Ukraine.* Flensburg, Germany: European Center for Minority Issues, 2003.

Wilson, Andrew. *The Ukrainians: Unexpected Nation.* New Haven, CT: Yale University Press, 2000.

Zawada, Zenon, and Maria Shevchuk. "Ukrainian Representative at Eurovision 2007 Is Pop Icon Verka Serduchka." *Ukrainian Weekly,* May 13, 2007.

CHAPTER 4: GENDER

"Abortion." *Encyclopedia of Ukraine.* http://www.encyclopediaofukraine.com/display.asp?AddButton=pages\A\B\Abortion.htm.

Belser, Patrick. *Forced Labour and Human Trafficking: Estimating the Profits.* Geneva, Switzerland: International Labor Organization, 2005.

Bohachevsky-Chomiak, Martha. *Feminists Despite Themselves: Women in Ukrainian Community Life, 1884–1939.* Edmonton: University of Alberta, 1988.

Constitution of Ukraine. http://www.rada.kiev.ua/const/conengl.htm.

Dudwick, Nora, Radhika Srinivasan, and Jeanine Braithwaite. *Ukraine: Gender Review.* Washington, DC: World Bank, 2002.

"Marriage." *Encyclopedia of Ukraine.* http://www.encyclopediaofukraine.com/display.asp?AddButton=pages\M\A\Marriage.htm.

Govorun, Tamara, and Borys M. Vornyk. "Ukraine (Ukrayina)." Humboldt University of Berlin Magnus Hirschfeld Archive for Sexology. http://www2.hu-berlin.de/sexology/GESUND/ARCHIV/IES/UKRAINE.HTM.

Hrycak, Alexandra. "The Dilemmas of Civic Revival: Ukrainian Women since Independence." *Journal of Ukrainian Studies* 26 (2001): 135–58.

———. "Foundation Feminism and the Articulation of Hybrid Feminisms in Post-Socialist Ukraine." *East European Politics and Societies* 20 (2006): 69–100.

Malarek, Victor. *The Natashas: Inside the New Global Sex Trade.* New York: Arcade, 2005.

Marsh, Rosalind, ed. *Women in Russia and Ukraine.* New York: Cambridge University Press, 1996.

State Statistics Committee of Ukraine. "All-Ukrainian Population Census 2001." State Statistics Committee of Ukraine. http://www.ukrcensus.gov.ua/eng.

United Nations Development Programme. *Gender Issues in Ukraine: Challenges and Opportunities.* Kyiv: United Nations Development Programme, 2003.

Wolowyna, Oleh. "Abortion in Ukraine: A Health Crisis." *Ukrainian Weekly,* September 3, 2000.

Yakushko, Oksana. "Ambivalent Sexism and Relationship Patterns among Women and Men in Ukraine." *Sex Roles* 52 (2005): 589–96.

Chapter 5: Education

European Education Directory. http://www.euroeducation.net/prof/ukrco.htm.

Gorodnichenko, Yuriy, and Klara Sabirianova Peter. "Returns to Schooling in Russia and Ukraine: A Semiparametric Approach to Cross-Country Comparative Analysis." *Journal of Comparative Economics* 33 (2005): 324–50.

Kubijovyc, Volodymyr, ed. *Ukraine: A Concise Encyclopaedia.* Prepared by Shevchenko Scientific Society. Toronto: University of Toronto Press, 1963.

Kuropas, M. B. "Education in Ukraine: Dilemmas and Concerns." *Ukrainian Weekly,* July 21, 2001.

Ministry of Education and Science of Ukraine. http://www.education.gov.ua/pls/edu/educ.home.eng.

Ministry of Education and Science of Ukraine. *Reform Strategy for Education in Ukraine: Educational Policy Recommendations.* Kyiv: KIS, 2003.

Shimahara, Nobuo, Ivan Z. Holowinsky, and Saundra Tomlinson-Clarke, eds. *Ethnicity, Race, and Nationality in Education: A Global Perspective.* Mahwah, NJ: Lawrence Erlbaum Associates, 2001.

State Statistics Committee of Ukraine. "All-Ukrainian Population Census 2001." State Statistics Committee of Ukraine. http://www.ukrcensus.gov.ua/eng.

Ukrainian State Centre of International Education. "System of Education in Ukraine." Ministry of Education and Science of Ukraine. http://intered.gov.ua/site/home/ukraine/system/.

Ukrainian Weekly. http://www.ukrweekly.com/.

CHAPTER 6: CUSTOMS, HOLIDAYS, AND CUISINE

Aslund, Anders. "Revolution, Red Directors and Oligarchs in Ukraine." *Ukrainian Quarterly* 60, Vol. 60, No.1–2 (Spring-Summer 2004): 5–18.

Biloukha, O. O., and V. Utermohlen. "Healthy Eating in Ukraine: Attitudes, Barriers and Information Sources." *Public Health Nutrition* 4 (2001): 207–15.

Center for International Development and Conflict Management. "Minorities at Risk." University of Maryland. http://www.cidcm.umd.edu/mar/.

Deychakiwsky, Orest. "National Minorities in Ukraine." *Ukrainian Quarterly* 50 (1994): 371–89.

Govorun, Tamara, and Borys M. Vornyk. "Ukraine." In *The International Encyclopedia of Sexuality,* ed. Robert T. Francoeur. 4 vols. New York: Continuum, 1997–2001. http://www2.hu-berlin.de/sexology/IES/index.html.

International Foundation for Electoral Systems and U.S. AID. *Attitudes of Ukrainians prior to 2007 Rada Elections.* August–September 2007. http://www.ifes.org/publication/c02e80ae0eb56679827e3a5c38b27f15/Ukraine%20Exec%20Summary.pdf.

Kostenko, Natalia, Tatyana Androsenko, and Ludmila Males. "In Search of Holidays: The Case of Ukraine." In *National Days/National Ways: Historical, Political, and Religious Celebrations around the World,* ed. Linda K. Fuller. Westport, CT: Praeger, 2004.

Maksymiuk, Jan. *Ukraine: Leftists Commemorate Bolshevik Revolution with Antigovernment Rallies.* Radio Free Europe, Radio Liberty. November 8, 2005. http://www.rferl.org/featuresarticle/2005/11/fa0431a7-d7cb-43b5-8164-6c23455f2976.html.

Naydan, Micheal M. "Ukrainian Prose of the 1990s as It Reflects Contemporary Social Structures." *Ukrainian Quarterly* 51 (1995): 45–61.

Pisetska Farely, Marta. *Festive Ukrainian Cooking.* Pittsburgh, PA: University of Pittsburgh Press, 1990.

Rudnytzky Leonid. "The Undiscovered Realm: Notes on the Nature of Ukrainian Literature." In *Ukraine at the Crossroads,* ed. Nicolas Hayoz and Andrej N. Lushnycky. Bern: Peter Lang, 2005.

Snowyd, D. *Spirit of Ukraine: Ukrainian Contributions to World's Culture.* New York: United Ukrainian Organizations of the United States, 1935.

State Statistics Committee of Ukraine. "All-Ukrainian Population Census 2001." State Statistics Committee of Ukraine. http://www.ukrcensus.gov.ua/eng.

Suwyn, Barbara J. *The Magic Egg and Other Tales from Ukraine.* Englewood, CO: Libraries Unlimited, 1997.

Transparency International. *Report on the Transparency International Global Corruption Barometer 2007.* Berlin: Transparency International, International Secretariat. http://www.transparency.org/policy_research/surveys_indices/gcb/2007.

Turkewicz-Sanko, Helene, ed. *Treasury of Ukrainian Love Poems, Quotations and Proverbs.* New York: Hippocrene Books, 1997.

Ukrainian Folklore Center. "Ukrainian Traditional Folklore." University of Alberta. http://www.arts.ualberta.ca/ukisite/Index.htm.

World Health Organization. "Ukraine." World Health Organization. http://www. who.int/countries/ukr/en/.

Chapter 7: Media

BBC News Europe. "The Press in Ukraine." BBC News Europe. http://news.bbc. co.uk/2/hi/europe/4073375.stm.

Committee to Protect Journalists. *Ukraine Report 1999.* Committee to Protect Journalists. http://www.cpj.org/attacks99/europe99/Ukraine.html.

Constitution of Ukraine, "Chapter II: Human and Citizens' Rights, Freedoms and Duties." http://www.rada.kiev.ua/const/conengl.htm#r2.

Dyczok, Marta. "The Politics of Media in Ukraine: Election 2002." In *Ukraine at the Crossroads,* ed. Nicolas Hayoz and Andrej N. Lushnycky. Bern: Peter Lang, 2005.

———. "Was Kuchma's Censorship Effective? Mass Media in Ukraine before 2004." *Europe Asia Studies* 58 (2006): 215–38.

Freedom House. "Ukraine: 2007." Freedom House. http://www.freedomhouse.org/ template.cfm?page=251&country=7295&year=2007.

Hollander, Gayle Durham. "Recent Developments in Soviet Radio and Television News Reporting." *Public Opinion Quarterly* 31 (1967): 359–65.

Human Rights Watch Report. "Negotiating the News: Informal State Censorship of Ukrainian Television." *Human Rights Watch* 15, no. 2(D) (2003). http:// www.hrw.org/reports/2003/ukraine0303/Ukraine0303.pdf.

International Foundation for Electoral Systems and U.S. AID. *Attitudes of Ukrainians prior to 2007 Rada Elections.* August–September 2007. http://www.ifes.org/publica tion/c02e80ae0eb56679827e3a5c38b27f15/Ukraine%20Exec%20Summary. pdf.

Library of Congress. "A Country Study: Soviet Union (Former)." Library of Congress. http://lcweb2.loc.gov/frd/cs/sutoc.html.

McNair, Brian. *Glasnost, Perestroika and the Soviet Media.* London: Routledge, 1991.

Mickiewicz, Ellen. "Policy Issues in the Soviet Media System." *Proceedings of the Academy of Political Science* 35 (1984): 113–23.

Open Society Archives. "Records of Radio Free Europe/Radio Liberty Research Institute (RFE/RL RI), Samizdat Archives, 1968–1992." Open Society Archives. http://www.osa.ceu.hu/db/fa/300.htm.

Prytula, Olena. "The Ukrainian Media Rebellion." In *Revolution in Orange: The Origins of Ukraine's Democratic Breakthrough,* ed. Anders Aslund and Michael McFaul. Washington, DC: Carnegie Endowment for International Peace, 2006.

Sussman, Leonard R. "Mass Media: Opportunities and Threats." *Annals of the American Academy of Political and Social Science* 442 (1979): 77–83.

CHAPTER 8: LITERATURE

Andrukhovych, Yuri. *Recreations.* Edmonton, AB: CIUS, 1998.

Andryczyk, Mark. "Bu-Ba-Bu: Poetry and Performance." *Journal of Ukrainian Studies* 27 (2002): 257–72.

Chernetsky, Vitaly. "The New Ukrainian Literature: Between the Postmodern and the Postcolonial." *Soviet and Post-Soviet Review* 28 (2001): 29–45.

———. "The Trope of Displacement and Identity Construction in Post-colonial Ukrainian Fiction." *Journal of Ukrainian Studies* 27 (2002): 215–32.

———. "Ukrainian Literature at the End of the Millennium: The Ten Best Works of the 1990s." *World Literature Today* 76 (2002): 98–101.

Chyzhevsky, Dmytro. *A History of Ukrainian Literature from the 11th to the End of the 19th Centuries.* 2nd ed. New York: Ukrainian Academic Press, 1997.

Encyclopedia of Ukraine. "The Literature of Kyivan Rus': Chronicles, Lives of Saints, Epics." Encyclopedia of Ukraine. http://www.encyclopediaofukraine.com/literature.asp.

Hogan, Ed, et al., eds. *From Three Worlds: New Writing from Ukraine.* Boston: Zephyr Press, 1996.

Hundorova, Tamara. "The Canon Reversed: New Ukrainian Literature of the 1990s." *Journal of Ukrainian Studies* 26 (2001): 249–70.

Kubijovyc, Volodymyr, ed. *Ukraine: A Concise Encyclopedia.* Prepared by Shevchenko Scientific Society. Toronto: University of Toronto Press, 1963.

Kulyk, Volodymyr. "The Search for Post-Soviet Identity in Ukraine and Russia and Its Influence on the Relations between the Two States." *Harriman Review* 9 (1996): 16–27.

Kulyk-Keefer, Janice, and Solomea Pavlychko, eds. *Two Lands, New Visions: Stories from Canada and Ukraine.* Montreal: Coteau Books, 1998.

Kurkov, Andrey. *Death and the Penguin.* London: Harvill, 2001.

Luchuk, Olha, and Mykhailo M. Naydan, eds. *A Hundred Years of Youth: A Bilingual Anthology of 20th Century Ukrainian Poetry.* L'viv, Ukraine: Litopys, 2000.

Luckyj, George. *The Battle for Literature in the Soviet Ukraine; a Documentary Study of Vaplite, 1925–1928.* The Hague: Mouton, 1957.

———, ed. *Discordant Voices: The Non-Russian Soviet Literatures, 1953–1973.* Oakville, ON: Mosaic Press, 1975.

———. *Keeping a Record: Literary Purges in Soviet Ukraine* (1930s): *A Bio-Bibliography.* Edmonton: Canadian Institute of Ukrainian Studies, in association with Ukrainian Famine Research Centre, 1987.

———. *Literary Politics in the Soviet Ukraine, 1917–1934.* Durham, NC: Duke University Press, 1990.

———. *Panteleimon Kulish: A Sketch of His Life and Times.* Boulder, CO: East European Monographs, 1983.

———. *Shevchenko's Unforgotten Journey.* Toronto: Canadian Scholars' Press, 1996.

———. *Ukrainian Literature: The Last Twenty-five Years.* Norman: Oklahoma University Press, 1956.

———. *Ukrainian Literature in the Twentieth Century: A Reader's Guide.* Toronto: University of Toronto Press, 1992.

Naydan, Mykhailo M. "Translating a Novel's Novelty: Yuri Andrukhovych's Perverzion in English." *Yale Journal of Criticism* 16 (2003): 455–64.

———. "Ukrainian Literary Identity Today: The Legacy of the Bu-Ba-Bu Generation after the Orange Revolution." *World Literature Today* 79 (2005): 24–27.

———. "Ukrainian Prose of the 1990s as It Reflects Contemporary Social Structures." *Ukrainian Quarterly* 51 (1995): 45–61.

Nazarenko, Tatiana. "Yuri Vynnychuk: The Windows of Time Frozen and Other Stories." *World Literature Today* 76 (2002).

Pavlychko, Solomea. "Feminism in Post-communist Ukrainian Society." In *Women in Russia and Ukraine,* ed. Rosalind Marsh. New York: Cambridge University Press, 1996.

Pavlyshyn, Marko. "Postcolonial Features in Contemporary Ukrainian Culture." *Australian Slavonic and East European Studies* 6 (1992): 41–55.

———. "Ukrainian Literature and the Erotics of Postcolonialism: Some Modest Propositions." *Harvard Ukrainian Studies* 12 (1993): 110–26.

Ryabchuk, Mykola. "Minor Literature of a Major Country, or Between the Dniper River and D. H. Thoreau's Pond." Poetry International Web. http://international.poetryinternationalweb.org/piw_cms/cms/cms_module/index.php?o%20bj_id=5505.

Shkandrij, Myroslav. "Polarities in Contemporary Ukrainian Literature." *Dalhousie Review* 72 (1992): 235–50.

———. *Russia and Ukraine: Literature and the Discourse of Empire from Napoleonic to Postcolonial Times.* Montreal: McGill-Queen's University Press, 2001.

Ukraine: Poetry International Web. http://international.poetryinternationalweb.org/piw_cms/cms/cms_module/index.php?obj_name=international.

Ukrainian Literature: A Journal of Translations. http://www.ukrainianliterature.org.

CHAPTER 9: MUSIC

Bahry, Romana. "Rock Culture and Rock Music in Ukraine." In *Rocking the State: Rock Music and Politics in Eastern Europe and Russia,* ed. Sabrina Petra Ramet. Boulder, CO: Westview Press, 1994.

Bench, Olga. "Ukrainian Folk Music." http://www.cck.kiev.ua/en/cd/d18ukr_nar_muz2/text.htm.

Clegg, David. "Philaret Kolessa's Classification of the Ukrainian Recitative Songs." *Studia Musicologica Academiae Scientiarum Hungaricae* 7 (1965): 247–51.

Filenko, Taras, and Tamara Bulat. *The World of Mykola Lysenko: Ethnic Identity, Music, and Politics in Nineteenth-century Ukraine.* Toronto: Ukraine Millennium Foundation, 2001.

Kononenko, Natalie. *Ukrainian Minstrels . . . and the Blind Shall Sing.* New York: M. E. Sharpe, 1998.

Kornij, Lidia. *History of Ukrainian Music.* Vol. 2, *Second Half of the XVIII Century.* Kyiv: Naukove Tovarystvo Shevchenka, 1998.

Kuzma, Marika. "Bortniansky à la Bortniansky: An Examination of the Sources of Dmitry Bortniansky's Choral Concerts." *Journal of Musicology* 14 (1996): 183–212.

McLellan, Joe. "*Moses . . .* A New Opera for a Nation in Search of Itself." ArtUkraine. http://www.artukraine.com/music/moses4.htm.

Morosan, Vladimir. *Choral Performance in Pre-Revolutionary Russia.* San Diego, CA: Musica Russica, 1994.

Noll, William. "Selecting Partners: Questions of Personal Choice and Problems of History in Fieldwork and Its Interpretation." In *Shadows in the Field: New Perspectives for Fieldwork in Ethnomusicology,* ed. Gregory Barz and Timothy Cooley. New York: Oxford University Press, 1997.

Sochan, Maria. "Thousands Attend Funeral of Composer Ihor Bilozir." *Ukrainian Weekly,* July 2, 2000.

Sonevyts'kyi, Ihor, and Nataliia Palidvor-Sonevyts'ka. *Dictionary of Ukrainian Composers.* L'viv, Ukraine: Union of Ukrainian Composers, 1997.

Wanner, Catherine. "Nationalism on Stage: Music and Change in Soviet Ukraine." In *Retuning Culture: Musical Changes in Central and Eastern Europe,* ed. Mark Slobin. Durham, NC: Duke University Press, 1996.

CHAPTER 10: THEATER AND CINEMA IN THE TWENTIETH CENTURY

Erlich, Victor. *Gogol.* New Haven, CT: Yale University Press, 1969.

Liber, George. "Adapting to the Stalinist Order: Alexander Dovzhenko's Psychological Journey, 1933–1953." *Europe-Asia Studies* 53 (2001): 1097–116.

———. *Alexander Dovzhenko: A Life in Soviet Film.* London: British Film Institute, 2002.

———. "Death, Birth Order and Alexander Dovzhenko's Cinematic Visions." Kinema. http://www.kinema.uwaterloo.ca/liber001.htm.

Makaryk, Irene. *Shakespeare in the Undiscovered Bourn: Les Kurbas, Ukrainian Modernism, and Early Soviet Cultural Politics.* Toronto: University of Toronto Press, 2004.

Malik, Madhu. "*Vertep* and the Sacred/Profane Dichotomy in Gogol's Dikan'ka Stories." *Slavic and East European Journal* 34 (1990): 332–47.

Revutsky, Valerian. "Vertep." Encyclopedia of Ukraine. http://www.encyclopediaofukraine.com/pages/V/E/VertepIT.htm.

Revutsky, Valerian, Roman Senkus, and Marko Robert Stech. "Kulish, Mykola." Encyclopedia of Ukraine. http://www.encyclopediaofukraine.com/pages/K/U/KulishMykola.htm.

Index

About the Authors

ADRIANA HELBIG is Assistant Professor of Music and Affiliated Faculty with the Center for Russian and East European Studies at the University of Pittsburgh. She holds a Ph.D. in Ethnomusicology from Columbia University (2005) where she has also taught in the Ukrainian Studies Program. Her articles on Romani (Gypsy) music, post-socialist cultural policy, and global hip-hop have appeared in edited collections and journals such as *Yearbook for Traditional Music, Current Musicology,* and *Anthropology of East Europe Review.*

OKSANA BURANBAEVA is co-author of the book *Cultures of the World: Dagestan* and has worked for international organizations in Eastern Europe and Central Asia. She is a graduate of Columbia University's Harriman Institute, a leading center for the advancement of knowledge in the field of Russian and Eurasian studies.

VANJA MLADINEO holds a Master's degree from Columbia University's School of International and Public Affairs and a Certificate from its East Central European Center. She has professional experience in the public and non-profit sectors and has done policy research in Eastern Europe and Central Asia. She is a co-recipient of the 2006 AAAS Title VIII Honorable Mention award for an outstanding policy paper on Eurasian Affairs.

Recent Titles in
Culture and Customs of Europe

Culture and Customs of Spain
Edward F. Stanton

Culture and Customs of Germany
Eckhard Bernstein

Culture and Customs of Italy
Charles Killinger

Culture and Customs of the Baltic States
Kevin O'Connor

Culture and Customs of Ireland
Margaret Scanlan

Culture and Customs of the Czech Republic and Slovakia
Craig Cravens

Culture and Customs of Ireland
W. Scott Haine